Reclaiming AUTHENTIC CHRISTIANITY

Exploring the Essentials of Christian Faith

What the Bible Teaches about
an Authentic Christian
and an Authentic Christian Church

CALVIN EUGENE DOLLAR, JR

Kevin Armstrong, Editorial Assistant
Alan Carlton, Editorial Assistant

WESTBOW
PRESS®
A DIVISION OF THOMAS NELSON
& ZONDERVAN

Unless otherwise noted, all Scripture quotations are taken from the Holman Christian Standard
Bible® Copyright ©1999, 2000, 2002, 2003 by Holman Bible Publishers. Used by permission.

Scripture taken from the New American Standard Bible© 1960, 1962,
1963, 1968, 1971, 1972, 1973, 1975, 1977, 1995 by The Lockman
Foundation are indicated by NASB and are used by permission.

Scripture taken from The Holy Bible New International Version
Copyright ©1973, 1978, International Bible Society, are indicated by
NIV and used by permission of Zondervan Bible Publishers.

Scriptures used from the New King James Version © 1988 by Thomas
Nelson Publishers are used by permission and indicated by NKJV.

Scriptures used from the King James Version are indicated by KJV.

WestBow Press books may be ordered through booksellers or by contacting:

WestBow Press
A Division of Thomas Nelson & Zondervan
1663 Liberty Drive
Bloomington, IN 47403
www.westbowpress.com
1 (866) 928-1240

ISBN: 978-1-9736-0511-9 (sc)
ISBN: 978-1-9736-0510-2 (hc)
ISBN: 978-1-9736-0512-6 (e)

Library of Congress Control Number: 2017915689

Print information available on the last page.

WestBow Press rev. date: 06/18/2018

Dedication

In loving memory of my father,
Calvin Eugene Dollar, Sr.
Soldier, Salesman & Servant of Christ

and

To my wife, Diana

The love of my life
and my partner in ministry

Christianity in America –
The Challenge We Face

Christianity in America is in serious trouble, and yet many Christians and Christian leaders are either unaware of this fact or seem to ignore what needs to be done to reverse the situation. The following statistics prove how serious it is. The statistics are taken from Dr. Edward H. Hammett, Southern Baptist seminary professor; from Dr. Thom Rainer, President of Lifeway, the resources division of the Southern Baptist Convention; and from *Battle Cry for a Generation,* by Ron Luce.

Over 4,000 churches in the United States of all denominations have closed each year for the five years leading up to 2010. Dr. Thom Rainer of the Southern Baptist Convention predicted that from 2000 to 2010, 50,000 churches will have closed. And an estimated 90-95% of all Southern Baptist churches (once one of the fastest growing denominations in the U.S.) have plateaued and are declining. Alarmingly, 70% of the U.S. population is unchurched and only 4% of all U.S. teenagers are attending a church of any kind.

And there arose another generation after them who did not know the Lord (Judges 2:10b NASB).

Analysis of the Beliefs of the Generations

Builders	Born 1927-1945	65% Bible-based believers
Boomers	Born 1946-1964	35% Bible-based believers
Busters	Born 1965-1983	16% Bible-based believers
Bridgers (Millennials)	Born 1984 or later	4% Bible-based believers

What is the dire diagnosis? Christianity is dying in America! Many of our churches are dying in the United States!

The decline of authentic Christianity in America has occurred for a number of reasons. First, because calculated attacks undermining the integrity of the Bible have eroded confidence in its inerrancy and authority. In addition, modern science has propagated the spurious theory of evolution resulting in loss of confidence in the biblical narrative of creation and in a creator. Evolution has established materialism and naturalism as the worldview in people's minds and has undermined belief in the supernatural, including God. Media and cultural influences have also promoted the philosophy of pluralism, existentialism, and relativism that define all religious beliefs as equally valid and equally true. This has lowered Christianity to the same level as other religions and made it only one viable choice out of many.

Add to all the foregoing attacks on faith the confusion that has been created by various denominations and cults spinning their version of Christianity. All of that has confused the public as to what authentic Christianity is. To put the final nail in the coffin, there is public distaste for dogmatism because of the prevailing spirit of rebellion against anything authoritative. Churches have compromised with that worldly spirit by avoiding teaching doctrine. And because doctrine is rarely taught, the doctrines or fundamental foundations of Christian faith are no longer known by the majority of people who profess to be Christian. People of faith and the public in general have become shallow in their beliefs and ignorant of Christian truth. Postmodernism has gutted our culture of absolutes. "For truth is fallen in the street." (Isaiah 59:14 NKJV)

In *Developing Your Secret Closet of Prayer*, Richard Burr explains what has happened to Christianity through the process of time and the influence of cultures. He states: "When the Gospel was exported to the Greeks they eventually turned it into a *philosophy*. Then it emerged in Rome where it became an *institution*. From there it surfaced in Europe where they turned it into a *culture*. Finally it was exported to

America where we, in this generation, have turned it into *entertainment*, *excitement* and *enterprise*" (emphasis added).

Contemporary Christianity in America has lost its authenticity for the most part. It no longer reflects Christianity as God intended it to be. This statement will be proven as we painstakingly examine the Scriptures to discover God's view of authentic Christianity. Every foundational truth, church practice, and discipleship principle will be thoroughly documented by the New Testament.

There is only one way to reverse the downward trend for Christianity in our nation—and that is a rigorous return to the teachings and practices of authentic Christianity. Rather than being defeated by the decline, our perspective should be a positive one focusing on the opportunity and challenge before us. Let us remember that the apostles in the first century faced an equally daunting challenge, and yet they prevailed to lay a strong and solid foundation for the Christian faith in a godless and hostile world.

Now is the hour to recognize that God is looking for men and women who will "stand in the gap and make up the hedge." If you sense that challenge in your heart, I ask you to join me now on an enlightening and exciting journey. Discover with clarity and conviction what authentic Christianity is. Become one of many who will commit to being an authentic disciple of Jesus Christ and who will strive to make your church authentic.

This book provides an indisputable definition and a poignant portrayal of authentic Christianity in its principles and practices. It unpacks a clear description of Christianity from the New Testament and persuasively demonstrates it with abundant biblical documentation. It charts a plain path for Christian disciples as they seek to follow Christ unfolding for them what it means to be an authentic Christian. In addition, *Reclaiming Authentic Christianity* presents a biblical pattern for pastors and churches to utilize in their pursuit of authentic Christianity.

The principles and practices of authentic Christianity are non-negotiable. No individual or church can be truly and thoroughly Christian without embracing them. The fervent desire of my heart in writing this book is that searchers will come to a firm faith in Jesus Christ as their Lord and Savior and that believers will be strengthened in their faith and commitment to live for their Lord.

I have experienced God's pleasure in fulfilling the responsibility He laid on me to write this. I hope that your life will be blessed by the truth of God's Word as we explore it together.

Soli Deo Gloria – to God alone be all glory!

Calvin Eugene Dollar, Jr.

Contents

Introduction

It was a beautiful, lazy spring day in South Georgia, a little hot and somewhat sultry. I was a senior at Bainbridge High School. In the last period of study hall, I was about to doze off from sheer boredom. A couple of guys in the same study hall happened to be friends from my church youth group. To stave off the doldrums, we began making some casual conversation. Our half-hearted efforts to kill time led to a discovery that instantly aroused our attention. Jerry Knight told Nolan Thompson and me that across the road from his home was a large and amazing cave. The cave was one of several that are called the Climax Caves near Climax, Georgia. Boredom was rapidly replaced by a sense of anticipation and adventure. Our excitement grew as we decided to grab some supplies and go cave exploring as soon as school let out.

We rounded up some flashlights and a huge roll of twine while the anticipation of our adventure grew inside each of us. The twine was to lead us back out of the cave. After arriving at Jerry's home and parking, we crossed the road and soon reached the mouth of the cave. Its opening was a sizable hole in the ground with a ladder protruding out of it. Climbing down the ladder, we came to the cool floor of the cave. After glancing above at the light flowing into the cave's opening, we walked through the short tunnel that was like a large hallway and then entered the first open cavern of the cave. Shining our flashlights in every direction into the deep and dark recesses, we chose what seemed to be the most promising path. Soon we found ourselves in an even larger cavern. The darkness was so deep that our flashlights seemed to barely illuminate the room. A spooky sense of foreboding quickly crept into us, but no one admitted his fears to the others. The still air was cool and dank. This definitely was not study hall! I was in charge of the important task of unwinding the twine that would provide a trail back to the mouth of the cave. We had secured it near the cave's opening. I put the stick it was wrapped around into my hands and just let it unwind as we walked deeper and deeper into the unknown interior. Jerry, Nolan and I were fascinated, but also a little frightened, as we got farther and farther from the cave's opening. That opening into our world was now long lost and far away in the dark distance.

An intense anticipation was building as we ventured farther into the cave and through several caverns. At the very moment when our tensions seemed to peak, we became aware of our flashlights growing dim. A sinking feeling began to creep into us as our courage was dying with our batteries. We immediately decided that we needed to quickly find our way back out to get some fresh batteries. At that point leaving the cave and heading for daylight was a welcome relief for all.

But then we made a discovery that was both shocking and disturbing! I had not realized that our security string had run out some distance back. Suddenly our sense of adventure was replaced by a feeling of being lost and hopeless. We were instantly at the point of panic.

Everything in the cave suddenly looked the same. The rocks and caverns all appeared so similar that discerning the right way to get out of the cave was impossible. There were several directions we could take, and each one of us thought a different direction was the correct one. Confusion and disagreement ensued and pandemonium was ready to erupt. The tension and blame was shifting quickly in my direction. To fend off the blame before it came, I suggested a plan. We left one flashlight shining where we were and fanned out in different directions to try to find the end of the twine. The idea was to stay close enough to see one another and to maintain contact. While still seized by anxiety, we began frantically looking for the end of the twine. It felt like time seemed suspended, it felt as if it stood still. I felt my heart pounding in my chest. Finally one of us discovered the end of the twine. With a huge sigh of relief, we were able to make our way out of the cave without a problem. As the light welcomed us at the top of the ladder and we set our feet above ground, a light-hearted happiness entered into us.

On the walk back to Jerry's home, we unanimously concluded that we didn't have enough time left in the day to get to the store for fresh batteries and return to the cave. So we decided to plan for another day.

The situation my friends and I faced in the cave illustrates Satan's overall strategy: confuse humanity by creating numerous religions, cults and heretical movements that all appear to be "the right way." Each religion or cult has just enough truth to make it seem plausible. People cannot discern which way is the right way out, and most end up choosing a wrong religious system, never finding the "string" of truth that God has given to lead us home. Satan is the mastermind behind all of the various, nefarious schemes to deceive mankind. Revelation 12:9 is the most sweeping statement of this.

> And the great dragon was thrown down, the serpent of old that is called the devil and Satan, who deceives the whole world (Revelation 12:9 NASB).

In commenting on this verse, Dr. Robert Thomas observes that "He (Satan) is the master of deception with an uncanny ability to mislead people. It is his chief aim and occupation."

Every day, thousands across the world are misled into false paths leading away from God. This fact makes the necessity and urgency of a book such as this patently apparent. Pointing people to the right way to God, they will be able to avoid wrong ways that lead them away from Him. Informing Christians regarding false teachings and religions will enable them to stand strong for truth in the face of the tidal wave of Satan's false teachings.

Chapter 1

The Declaration of Authentic Christianity
The Ten Truths of the Gospel Proclamation

What is the Gospel?

Peter's Preaching
The Five Facts of the Gospel
The Three Commands of the Gospel
The Two Promises of the Gospel

The Gospel according to Paul
The Nature of the Gospel – Grace Alone
The Implications of the Gospel

The Ten Truths of the Gospel Proclamation

According to Dave Harvey, "The gospel is the heart of the Bible. Everything in Scripture is either preparation for the gospel, presentation of the gospel, or participation in the gospel." And the apostle Paul calls the gospel "of first importance" (1 Corinthians 15:3). This is the reason we begin by examining what the Bible says about the gospel or good news.

The gospel is "good news." As news always does, the gospel contains specific contents. That is, its proclamation emphasizes certain specific and important truths. These truths must be believed in the heart and mind and embraced by the will as a life-choice in order for someone to have true, biblical, genuine faith in Jesus Christ.

God didn't waste any time in making the good news clear. The very first Christian sermons recorded in Scripture announced clearly the content of the gospel or good news.

The Preaching of Peter

The truths of the gospel were all expressed in Peter's first sermon on the Day of Pentecost when the Holy Spirit came and the Church was born. That sermon is recorded in Acts 2:14–40 and was the very first Christian sermon. On that day approximately three thousand Jews believed in Jesus as Savior, Lord and Messiah and were baptized. Later, Peter also preached the first Christian sermon ever preached to Gentiles. That sermon is recorded in Acts 10:34–43.

In carefully studying these sermons, I discovered that both sermons follow precisely the same outline, possess exactly and clearly the same specific truths, and unfold those truths in precisely the same order.

The following basic structure of the contents of each of Peter's two sermons is clear. As we will observe in detail:

- Peter presented the five truths of the gospel.
- He then declared the three commands of the gospel.
- Finally, he stated the two promises of the gospel.

We will now consider them with some measure of detail after seeing a simple but complete outline of the two sermons.

The Five Truths of the Gospel

1. The Name of Jesus
2. The Ministry of Jesus
3. The Death of Jesus
4. The Resurrection of Jesus
5. The Lordship of Jesus

The Three Commands of the Gospel

1. Repent
2. Believe
3. Be Baptized

The Two Promises of the Gospel

1. The Forgiveness of Sins
2. The Gift of the Holy Spirit

We will discover wonderful truths by unpacking both of Peter's sermons. Each subject will be developed in its context and compared with other scriptures in order to have an accurate understanding of the wonderful truths.

The Five Facts of the Gospel

1. The Name of Jesus

Peter's Sermon to the Jews	Peter's Sermon to the Gentiles
Acts 2:21	Acts 10:36

Then whoever calls on *the name* of the Lord will be saved (Acts 2:21; emphasis added).

He sent the message to the Israelites, proclaiming the good news of peace through *Jesus Christ*—He is Lord of all (Acts 10:36, emphasis added).

Of first and foremost importance in regard to His name are the truths given in Matthew 1:21 and Isaiah 43:11:

She will give birth to a son, and you are *to name Him Jesus*, because He will save His people from their sins (Matthew 1:21; emphasis added).

"I, even I, am the Lord, and there is no savior besides Me" (Isaiah 43:11 NASB).

It is in the nature of Yahweh or Jehovah to save His people. Of Jesus it is said, "You will call his name 'Jesus,' for He will save His people from their sins." Jesus means: "Yahweh or Jehovah is savior." He is called "Jehovah is savior" for *He* will save *His* people from their sins. And the prophet Isaiah makes it clear that besides Yahweh or Jehovah, there is no savior. The great and crucial truth that is being emphasized by His name, Jesus, is that salvation is exclusively provided by and through Him and Him alone.

Let it be known to all of you and to all the people of Israel, that by *the name of Jesus* Christ the Nazarene—whom you crucified and whom God raised from the dead—by Him this man is standing here before you healthy. This Jesus is "the stone despised by you builders, who has become the cornerstone. There is salvation in no one else, for there is *no other name* under heaven given to people *by which we must be saved*" (Acts 4:10–12; emphasis added; cf. John 14:6 and Acts 13:38–39).

Jesus Christ is the only name through whom anyone might be saved. There are no other true saviors or true ways of salvation. This was and is a unique and absolute claim. It distinguishes the gospel and Christianity from all other religions and philosophies.

> But as many as received Him, to them He gave the right to become the children of God, even to those who believe in *His name* (John 1:12 NASB; emphasis added).

> Anyone who believes in Him is not condemned, but anyone who does not believe is already condemned, because he has not believed in *the name* of the One and Only Son of God (John 3:18; emphasis added).

> But these (signs) have been written so that you may believe that Jesus is the Christ (Messiah), the Son of God; and that believing you may have life in *His name* (John 20:31 NASB; emphasis added).

These scriptures declare that "the name," that is, the person of Jesus, is absolutely essential to salvation from sin and sin's condemnation or judgment. As far as God is concerned, this is the central and core issue in relation to salvation. Faith in His Son is not an option. It is not one way among others to become right with God. It is the only way!

> "Repent," Peter said to them, "and be baptized, each of you, in *the name of Jesus* the Messiah for the forgiveness of your sins, and you will receive the gift of the Holy Spirit (Acts 2:38; emphasis added).

Forgiveness of sins and the gift of the Holy Spirit are both bestowed through the merits of Jesus Christ, that is, through His name.

> By faith in *His name, His name* has made this man strong, whom you see and know. So the faith that comes through Him has given him this perfect health in front of all of you (Acts 3:16; emphasis added).

> So they called for them and ordered them not to preach or teach at all in *the name of Jesus* (Acts 4:18; emphasis added).

The world and religious systems that reject Jesus Christ as the only way of salvation find offensive the proclamation of Jesus Christ as the sole means of salvation. They do not want to be confronted with the news of their lost condition and need of a savior. Because of human pride, they would rather trust in their religious beliefs and practices for their acceptance by their god, or they would rather be comfortable in the self-deception of being a good person and having no need of salvation.

A recent Pew Study revealed that 70 percent of Americans with a religious affiliation say that many religions – not just their own – can lead to eternal life (The Pew Forum on Religion and Public Life, "Summary of Key Findings" *U. S. Religions Landscape Survey* February 2008). And from the same source just referenced, a 2008 poll of thirty-five thousand Americans revealed that 57 percent of evangelical church attenders believe that many religions can lead to eternal life. This is the startling and dangerous result of politically correct propaganda. The last of the two results of the research reveal a paradigm shift in the beliefs of people in our churches. They have lost the most fundamental truth and principle of the gospel!

The world also rejects the message of Christ because unsaved humanity wants to retain sinful lifestyles. Change is difficult, especially when we enjoy what we are doing. The world is aware that to truly embrace Jesus Christ means that people will necessarily have to repudiate their sin and forsake their sinful ways. It also means that they will have to relinquish control of their lives to the lordship of Christ. The sinful nature tenaciously clings to self-autonomy and rebels against the idea of submitting one's life and choices to the Lord.

> But when they believed Philip, as he proclaimed the good news about the kingdom of God and *the name of Jesus Christ*, both men and women were baptized (Acts 8:12; emphasis added).

The good news or gospel and the name of Jesus Christ are inseparably bound together. You cannot have one without the other. There are other numerous references in the book of Acts to "the name" and its importance and significance: Acts 3:6; 4:10, 12, 13, 17, & 30; 5:28, 40, 41; 8:16; 9:15, 16, 21, 27, & 28; 10:43 & 48; 15:26; 19:5, 13, 17.

> For everyone who calls on *the name* of the Lord will be saved (Romans 10:13; emphasis added).

This statement is found in the context of one of the great declarations concerning Jesus Christ. Verse nine in this passage proclaims, "If you confess with your mouth, 'Jesus is Lord,' and believe in your heart that God raised Him from the dead, you will be saved." The quotation of Romans 10:13 comes from Joel 2:32 and is speaking about the Lord or Yahweh. In Romans 10 Paul is referring to calling on Jesus Christ the Lord for salvation!

> To God's church at Corinth, to those who are sanctified in Christ Jesus and called as saints, with all those in every place who call on *the name of Jesus Christ* our Lord— theirs and ours (1 Corinthians 1:2; emphasis added).

As indicated by the phrase "who call on," every true act of worship by Christians is confessing who Jesus Christ was and is. Furthermore, worship can only be acceptable to God as it is offered through Jesus Christ. This affirms and exalts the name and person of Jesus Christ because of the gospel – because of His saving power.

> For this reason God also highly exalted Him and gave Him *the name* that is above every name, so that at *the name of Jesus* every knee should bow—of those who are in heaven and on earth and under the earth—and every tongue should confess that Jesus Christ is Lord, to the glory of God the Father (Philippians 2:9–11; emphasis added).

7

Jesus Christ is the only name or being through whom anyone might be saved. There are no other true saviors or true ways of salvation. This unique and absolute claim is divisive in that it demands that each person must accept and embrace Him and His salvation or choose to refuse and reject Him as Savior and Lord.

Dr. Robert Jeffress states: "Almost 60 percent of those in American evangelical churches believe that many religions can lead to eternal life. But if Jesus is to be trusted when he says that no one comes to the Father except through him, the church is failing in its mission. And it's not hard to guess why. An exclusive Jesus just isn't popular in our inclusive world." (*Not All Roads Lead to Heaven – Sharing an Exclusive Jesus in an Inclusive World*)

In today's relativistic, pluralistic culture, many people revolt against the exclusive claims of Jesus Christ, but that reaction must not deter Christians from proclaiming the truth of the gospel. The world is becoming more antagonistic to the gospel and it's therefore tempting to soften the message in order to make it less offensive and more appealing. We must not dilute the message, but we must share the gospel with love and compassion for people. We must share it for people to know God, to experience His love, to have their lives redeemed from the ruin and emptiness of sin, and to be transformed by His wonderful grace and power.

The gospel must be proclaimed in all its truth and power if our Christianity is to be authentic and faithful to our Lord and Savior. There are cultures that will persecute Christians for their faith and for our proclaiming the gospel. This was true from the very beginning.

> After they called in the apostles and had them flogged, they ordered them not to speak in *the name of Jesus* and released them. Then they went out from the presence of the Sanhedrin, rejoicing that they were counted worthy to be dishonored (KJV "to suffer shame") for *the name* (Acts 5:40–41; emphasis added).

2. The Ministry of Jesus

<table>
<tr><td align="center">Peter's Sermon to the Jews
Acts 2:22</td><td align="center">Peter's Sermon to the Gentiles
Acts 10:38-39a</td></tr>
</table>

> Men of Israel, listen to these words: This Jesus the
> Nazarene was a man pointed out to you by God with
> miracles, wonders, and signs that God did among you
> through Him (Acts 2:22).

Jesus's ministry commenced immediately after His baptism and
temptation. Although it lasted only three years, it was an amazing,
astounding ministry. He packed most every day with preaching and
powerful works. There were two primary aspects of Jesus's ministry:
His words were oracles, and His works were miracles.

The Kinds of Miracles

There are four kinds of miracles that Jesus performed during His
ministry.

1. Miracles of Healing
2. Miracles of Nature
    - Changing water to wine at the marriage in Cana of Galilee
    - Large catch of fish to call four of His disciples who were
      fishermen
    - Fish with money in its mouth to pay taxes
    - Calming the winds and waves on the Sea of Galilee
    - Jesus walking on the water on Sea of Galilee
3. Miracles of Deliverance from Demonic Power
4. Miracles of Resurrection
    - Tabitha – the young woman who had just died
    - Son of widow of Nain – Jesus stopped funeral procession
    - Lazarus – Dead four days

Aspects of Miracles

Miracles

Jesus performed miracles of healing, transformed water into wine, walked on water, calmed the wind and sea by His command, and fed thousands with five small loaves of bread and two fish. Such miracles or displays of power were supernatural. That is, they required a power that transcended natural scientific laws. They were works that only God could do. They were miracles!

Wonders

Wonders are miracles that produce a sense of wonder, amazement, and astonishment. They are miracles that cause people to marvel. They create a sense of awe. The New Testament states numerous times that Jesus's words and works caused people to be amazed and to marvel at Him. He was not ordinary—He was extraordinary! The crowds said, "No man ever spoke like this man." On one occasion, His disciples said to one another: "What kind of man is this that even the winds and the waves obey him?" In these, and many other similar situations, a spirit of reverent fear filled people who witnessed His powerful acts.

Signs

The term "signs" as used in regard to Jesus's miracles expresses the significance or meaning of the miracles. His miracles demonstrated authoritatively and convincingly that Jesus was from God. More importantly, some of His miracles were signs that He Himself was God. The Gospel of John particularly points out this truth. John uses the Greek word for "signs" throughout his Gospel as proof of Jesus's deity or godhood.

In addition to demonstrating His deity, many of His miracles as "signs" had significance in other ways. His miracles as signs were often spiritual lessons to picture His power to heal people spiritually. When He raised the dead it demonstrated His power to raise people from spiritual death and to give them new life. When He healed the blind, He demonstrated that He could give spiritual sight to the spiritually blind. When He healed people with leprosy, an incurable disease that made them social outcasts, He demonstrated His power to heal the sinner of the incurable and destructive disease of sin and to make the sinner worthy of respect. When He healed the man with a withered hand that could not reach out physically to shake another's hand and could do no useful work with it, Jesus demonstrated that He could restore the spiritually withered hand to have fellowship with God and man and to do useful work. These are all like parables of the wonderful power of Christ to meet all the spiritual needs of sinners as pictured in the physical or material realm by the miraculous signs He performed.

The Purpose of Miracles

- To demonstrate the deity of Christ—one greater than men stood among them!
- To display God's power and grace as available for people's lives
- To attest to the authority of Christ in His preaching
- To attest to the authority of Christ to forgive sins
- To symbolically portray the spiritual healing of people's lives by Christ
- To declare that Christ is the resurrection and the life
- To encourage His disciples to trust Him and serve Him

While miracles can attest to authority, we must be cautious with that principle. Richard Trench explains this in his classic work, *Notes on the Miracles of Our Lord*:

> A miracle does not prove the truth of doctrine, or the divine mission of him that brings it to pass. That which alone it claims for him at the first is a right to be listened to: it puts him in the alternative of being from heaven or from hell. The doctrine must first commend itself to the conscience as being *good*, and only then can the miracle

seal it as *divine*. . . . The miracle shall be credentials for the bearer of that good word, a manifest sign that he has a special mission for the realization of the purposes of God with man.

What Trench stated certainly applies to the earthly ministry of the Lord Jesus Christ.

The Power of Miracles

How *God anointed Jesus* of Nazareth with the Holy Spirit and with power, and how He went about doing good and curing all who were under the tyranny of the Devil, because God was with Him (Acts 10:38; emphasis added).

Anointed

The fact that God anointed Him means that He set Him apart as the Messiah to perform special work in that capacity. God was with Him in all He did, demonstrating to those who witnessed Christ's activities that He was indeed from God and was truly the Messiah.

The word *Messiah* is the Hebrew word that means "anointed one," and the word *Christ* is the Greek word that means "anointed one." So the words "Messiah" and "Christ" are exact equivalents. They mean the same thing.

There were three offices in the Old Testament that required a man to be anointed with oil, symbolizing his special calling by God to that office. Those offices were prophet, priest, and king. Oil, a symbol of the Holy Spirit, was used for the purpose of these sacred acts of anointing.

Jesus Christ was the Messiah, the anointed one, and he was the only man who was anointed to all three offices: prophet, priest, and king! Some, like David, were anointed to two offices. In David's case, he was both a prophet and a king. Melchizedek was both a king and priest. Only Jesus Christ is prophet, priest and king.

He was anointed as a prophet (Deuteronomy 18:15–19). His literal anointing occurred at His baptism when the Holy Spirit descended upon Him (Matthew 3:13-17). His earthly ministry was the ministry of a prophet speaking with divine authority the Word of God to the people. One of Isaiah's messianic prophecies is the salient statement that describes Jesus's messianic ministry as a prophet:

> The Spirit of the Lord God is on Me, because *the Lord has anointed Me* to bring good news to the poor. He has sent Me to heal the brokenhearted, to proclaim liberty to the captives, and freedom to the prisoners; to proclaim the year of the LORD's favor, and the day of our God's vengeance; to comfort all who mourn, to provide for those who mourn in Zion; to give them a crown of beauty instead of ashes, festive oil instead of mourning, and splendid clothes instead of despair. And they will be called righteous trees, planted by the Lord, to glorify Him (Isaiah 61:1–3; emphasis added).

He was also anointed to become a priest. He was appointed by God to be a High Priest (Psalm 110:4; Hebrews 7:21–27). In His office of high priest He offered a once-for-all sacrifice for sin (Hebrews 7:26–27; 10:10–14). And He presently represents us to God as our great High Priest (Hebrews 4:14–16 & 7:24–25). As a priest He is also the one and only mediator between God and man (1 Timothy 2:5).

In regard to being anointed as a king, in view of His future kingship over the earth, He was anointed to become King of kings and Lord of lords (Genesis 49:10; 2 Samuel 7:8-17; Psalm 110:1; Isaiah 9:6 & 11:1-10; Daniel 7:9-14; Hebrews 1:8–9; Revelation 19:15–16).

These God-ordained offices or positions of leadership of Jesus as the Messiah were God's plan before He ever created the universe. So the significance of Jesus's anointing in the context of Peter's sermon in Acts 2 had to do with Him being anointed as the Messiah.

With the Holy Spirit

The act of anointing the kings and priests with oil seems to have been emblematic of the influences of the Holy Spirit. Oil is a symbol of the Holy Spirit. The significance of Jesus's anointing with the Holy Spirit is that God communicated to Jesus as the Messiah the ministry and power of the Holy Spirit to assist Him in His human capacity to fulfill His work as prophet, priest, and king. At His baptism, the Spirit descended upon Jesus in the form of a dove. Immediately after the baptism of Jesus (Luke 3:21–22), the Bible declares: "Then Jesus returned from the Jordan, full of the Holy Spirit" (Luke 4:1). Immediately after His baptism, He was led by the Spirit into the wilderness to be tested by the Devil.

After those forty days of testing, the Bible says: "Then Jesus returned to Galilee in the power of the Spirit" (Luke 4:14). He then began preaching and teaching. Early in His ministry He visited His hometown of Nazareth. While in Nazareth He went into the synagogue on the Sabbath. As a visiting rabbi, He was asked to read from the Scriptures. The passage He chose to read was Isaiah 61:1–2. It begins with "The Spirit of the Lord God is on Me because the Lord has anointed Me."

The essential truth Peter is pointing out in his sermon to the Gentiles in Acts 10 is that Jesus was anointed by God as the Messiah, and *that* is the reason His ministry was empowered by the Spirit and why it manifested mighty miracles.

And with Power

This phrase follows naturally as a result of Jesus being anointed by the Spirit. In both the Old and New Testaments, the anointing of the Spirit is always for the purpose of performing special works for God to fulfill His purposes and to display His power. Therefore, Peter also emphasizes that the anointing was with power. The power was special in that He was endued with power for healing the sick, raising the dead, for confronting demonic powers, and for all the various miracles He performed.

The Blessing of Miracles

Who Went about Doing Good

Jesus's ministry was to travel from place to place to do good to people. He blessed, healed, lifted up those who were hurting emotionally, and encouraged those who felt like they had failed in life. He did not travel for fame, wealth, comfort, or ease, but to give guidance and hope everywhere and to everyone He could touch with His life. This is the simple but sublime record of His life and ministry.

He traversed the dusty roads and pathways of Israel, over huge hills and through deep valleys. He often slept under the night skies in the wild. He prayed beneath the stars throughout the night into the damp, cool of early morning with dew fresh on the ground. He worked long hours preaching, teaching, and healing until He became bone-tired and weary. What a picture of the selfless, servant of the Lord! What a picture of one who loved people so much that He expended Himself to the very limits of human strength and endurance to bless and help them in their need!

The Testimony of Miracles

God Was with Him

God appointed Him, and by His miracles God furnished the highest evidence that He had sent Him. His miracles were of such character and quality that they could be accomplished only by God. In John 3:2, Nicodemus said, "Rabbi, we know that thou art a teacher come from God, for no man can do the miracles that thou doest, except God be with him" (KJV).

The supreme power and amazing compassion of His ministry powerfully proved that He was extraordinary even by the measure of all previous prophets who had worked miracles. The ministry of Jesus attested to all that He was in His divinely appointed office of prophet as well as in His compassion as mankind's priest. In addition, the number of miracles Jesus performed far exceeded those of any other prophet. The evidence of this is in the number of miracles recorded that He performed. This is expressed in hyperbole by the apostle John:

> Therefore many other signs (miracles) Jesus also performed in the presence of the disciples, which are not written in this book; but these have been written so that you may believe that Jesus is the Christ (Messiah), the Son of God; and that believing you may have life in His name (John 20:30-31 NASB).

> And there are also many other things which Jesus did, which if they were written in detail, I suppose that even the world itself would not contain the books that would be written (John 21:25 NASB – using hyperbole).

Peter emphasized the works or miracles of Jesus rather than Jesus's words or oracles. He was establishing the credentials of Jesus, that is, that He was sent from God and that He was the true Messiah and Son of God. While Jesus's teaching and preaching was amazing in its wisdom and power, His miracles would naturally convey evidence that He was Messiah and would thus authenticate His divine mission.

3. The Death of Jesus

Peter's Sermon to the Jews   Peter's Sermon to the Gentiles
        Acts 2:23   Acts 10:39b

> Though He was delivered up according to God's determined plan and foreknowledge, you used lawless people to nail Him to a cross and kill him (Acts 2:23).

The word "delivered" is commonly used to describe those who are surrendered or delivered into the hands of enemies or adversaries. It means that Jesus was surrendered or handed over to His enemies through a voluntary plan and act of God. As for man's part, we all murdered the Son of God. Jews and Gentiles, all other nations represented by the Romans, killed Him. Therefore all humanity was involved. "They killed him . . . with wicked hands . . . hanging him on a tree." He became a curse. It was the form of capital punishment in that day. It was a shameful death! Yet it was all planned by God because it was the only way He could provide justice for sin's guilt. It was the only way God could offer forgiveness and bring us back into a relationship with Him. And He planned it because it was His way of demonstrating His justice and His love, His indescribable love for us!

As the Scriptures show us, the death of Christ was sacrificial. His death was an offering for sin. And death was the penalty for sin that had to be paid. Jesus paid that penalty! His death was also substitutionary in nature. He died in the place of all sinners, in the place of all humanity.

> But He was pierced because of our transgression, crushed because of our iniquities; punishment for our peace was on Him, and we are healed by His wounds. We *all* went astray like sheep; we *all* have turned to our own way; and the LORD has punished Him for the iniquity of us *all* (Isaiah 53:5; emphasis added).

In the same chapter, Isaiah also states: "My righteous servant will justify many, and He will carry their iniquities" (v. 11b). Then in verse 12c it says, "Yet He bore the sin of many and interceded for the rebels."

Many other scriptures also state the substitutionary nature of Christ's death on our behalf, telling us that He died in the place of sinners:

> But God proves His own love for us in that while we were still sinners Christ died for us (Romans 5:8).

> Christ died for our sins according to the Scriptures (1 Corinthians 15:3).

He made the One who did not know sin to be sin for us, so that we might become the righteousness of God in Him (2 Corinthians 5:21).

He Himself bore our sins in His body on the tree (the cross) (1 Peter 2:24).

For Christ also suffered for sins once for all, the righteous for the unrighteous, that He might bring you to God (1 Peter 3:18).

So also the Messiah, having been offered once to bear the sins of many . . . (Hebrews 9:28).

What was behind the death of Christ on the cross? Wayne Grudem correctly observes there were two things behind it: "the love and justice of God." Let me explain what Grudem means. God's justice demanded a payment for sin. It would only be possible for God to forgive a person's guilt and offense when that person's sin was paid for. And only then could a person be qualified to have fellowship with God (Romans 3:25–26). However, God's love compelled God to provide the payment for our sin so that it could be possible for us to be made right with God and to enjoy fellowship with Him (John 3:16; 1 John 4:9–10). Isn't it amazing that God actually desires fellowship with humans? But in His infinite capacity to love, He yearns for friendship and fellowship with every human being!

Jesus Christ took the penalty for our sins and made the full and complete payment for them. The term "once for all" in 1 Peter 3:18 affirms that His sacrifice was a full payment for sin and the only sacrifice that would be needed. Again and again the book of Hebrews extols this "once for all" significance of Christ's sacrifice on the cross (Hebrews 7:27; 9:7, 12; 9:26, 28; 10:10, 12, 14).

The full payment for sin was announced by the Lord Jesus Christ Himself from the cross. "It is finished" (John 19:30). This cry, which was only one word in Greek (the language the New Testament was originally written in), was more than an announcement that He had finished His sufferings. Christ made the full and complete payment for our sins so that we would not have to suffer for them for eternity in hell (John 3:36; Romans 5:9). Jesus took our place as a substitute and paid the total penalty for us. He took God's holy and just wrath against our sins and suffered for them (Romans 3:25; Hebrews 2:17; 1 John 2:2 & 4:10).

On the cross Jesus was the propitiation for our sins. Propitiation means something that satisfies the justice of God's wrath against sin and therefore makes a provision for mercy. Wayne Grudem comments on the need for propitiation saying, "There is an eternal, unchangeable requirement in the holiness and justice of God that sin be paid for."

Grudem makes a very clear point of the need and results of Christ's atoning work on the cross. He gives us this clear and simple outline as follows:

- We deserve to die as the penalty for sin—thus Christ's sacrifice.
- We deserve to bear God's wrath against sin—thus Christ's propitiation.
- We are separated from God by our sins—thus Christ's reconciliation.
- We are in bondage to sin and to Satan's kingdom—thus Christ's redemption.

Allow me to explain further.

- Christ's death was a sacrifice that paid the penalty of death for our sin so that sin's penalty of temporal and eternal death could be absolved.
- Christ's death provided propitiation. It absorbed the wrath of God for our sin and therefore satisfied God's holy justice.
- Christ's death accomplished reconciliation. It made it possible for God to forgive and receive man, and it gave incentive for man to want to be restored to fellowship with God.
- Christ's death provided redemption. It paid the ransom price that enables a sinner to be set free, and at the same time, provides the purchase price making it possible for the sinner to belong to God.

All of these needs that we have are wonderfully met by Jesus's death on the cross! He is strong and mighty to save! With the songwriter, we all exclaim with joy and excitement, "Hallelujah, what a Savior!"

Man of Sorrows, What a Name!
By Paul Bliss

"Man of sorrows," what a name, for the Son of God who came –
Ruined sinners to reclaim, Hallelujah! What a Savior!
Lifted up was he to die. It is finished was his cry.
Now in heaven exalted high. Hallelujah! What a Savior!
Bearing shame and scoffing rude, In my place condemned He stood;
Sealed my pardon with His blood; Hallelujah! What a Savior!
Guilty, vile, and helpless, we, Spotless Lamb of God was He;
Full redemption—can it be? Hallelujah! What a Savior!
When He comes, our glorious King, To His kingdom us to bring,
Then anew this song we'll sing, Hallelujah! What a Savior!

4. The Resurrection of Jesus

Peter's Sermon to the Jews	Peter's Sermon to the Gentiles
Acts 2:24, 32	Acts 10:40–41

God raised Him up, ending the pains of death, because it was not possible for Him to be held by it . . . God has resurrected this Jesus. We are all witnesses of this (Acts 2:24, 32).

In *The Cross Is Not Enough: Living as Witnesses to the Resurrection*, Ross Clifford and Philip Johnson point out that every single proclamation of the gospel in the book of Acts includes and emphasizes the resurrection.

The realities resulting from the resurrection of Christ are all fundamental to the gospel. These are apparent in four major blessings of the believer's salvation secured by the resurrection:

1. Regeneration (1 Peter 1:3; Titus 3:5; cf. Ephesians 2:1, 5–6 & Romans 6:4)

   Regeneration means "new birth." It is a spiritual birth. New life, spiritual life, eternal life is a gift to believers because sin and death have been overcome. Because Jesus has conquered sin and death, and because He lives, we share in His resurrection life (cf. Romans 6:23).

2. Justification (Romans 4:25)

   Jesus was raised again thus proving our justification. Justification means that one has been judicially declared to be righteous. Our justification was due to the perfection of Jesus's life and the offering of Himself as the sacrifice for our sins. Jesus was raised from the dead because His sacrifice was found acceptable to God. He had overcome death, the result of sin. Therefore He had overcome sin by His sacrifice. For this reason His resurrection declares that He had overcome sin and therefore that the one believing in Christ can be declared righteous.

3. Sanctification (Romans 6:5–10 & 8:9–11)

   It is the power of His victory over sin and death by His resurrection that empowers us to live a righteous life. He lives and by the Holy Spirit He lives in us. While this provision and power for righteous living is provided by His resurrection, it is still necessary for us to yield to the leading of the Spirit each day. He will not force our obedience.

4. Glorification (Romans 8:34–39; 1 Cor. 6:14; 15:50–58; Philippians 3:20–21)

   His victory over death assures that we too will have victory over death by being raised and made immortal.

The apostle Paul says: "concerning His Son, Jesus Christ our Lord, who . . . was established as the powerful Son of God by the resurrection from the dead" (Romans 1:3–4).

The resurrection of Jesus was the powerful and persuasive proof of:

1. Who He was.
2. The effectiveness of His death as a sacrifice for sins.
3. His victory over sin and death strongly confirming the reality of eternal life and future resurrection for those who trust in Jesus.

The first of these statements, "proof of who He was" is evident on the surface by a casual reading of Romans 1:4 (NIV): "and who through the Spirit of holiness was *declared with power to be the Son of God* by his resurrection from the dead: Jesus Christ our Lord" (emphasis added).

The second statement that His resurrection was proof of the effectiveness of His death as a sacrifice for sins is only recognized with consideration of the facts. As Paul is careful to explain in Romans 5, sin brought death into the world. Death was the result of sin and demonstrated sin's victory. But now Christ has risen as the conqueror of death. The fact that He has conquered death means that He has overcome the cause of death–sin. So now sin is no longer the victor, but the victor is the Son of God! And the fact that His resurrection proves the effectiveness of His sacrifice for sin is patently stated by Romans 4:25–"He was raised again on account of our justification."

For the early apostles, the cross was not the most compelling argument for the Christian message, as vitally and profoundly important as that was to their faith. Nothing about the cross "appears" to be miraculous. It was the resurrection that was the unique and powerful demonstration of the Christian gospel. The resurrection calls and compels people to place their faith in Jesus Christ. The resurrection declares Him to be the Son of God (Romans 1:4). The resurrection is the basis and proof of his lordship (Romans 10:9).

The truth of this victory was at the very heart of gospel preaching: "If you confess with your mouth, 'Jesus is Lord,' and believe in your heart that God raised Him from the dead, you will be saved (Romans 10:9).

When preaching on Mars Hill in Athens to the erudite philosophers and intellectuals of that day, Paul made sure to proclaim the proof of the resurrection: "because He has set a day on which He is going to judge the world in righteousness by the Man He has appointed. He has provided *proof of this* to everyone by raising Him from the dead" (Acts 17:31; emphasis added). It is patently apparent that Paul and all other apostolic preachers preached the resurrection with regularity in their proclamation of the gospel.

The fact of a preeminent place for the resurrection in the preaching of the gospel is seen in one of the longest chapters of the New Testament, 1 Corinthians 15. Paul took pains in this entire chapter to defend the resurrection of Christ. During this defense, he makes an interesting statement that affirms that the resurrection of Christ was a vitally important part of the preaching of the gospel. In 1 Corinthians 15:11–13, he states:

> Therefore, whether it is I or they, so we *preach* and so you have believed. Now if Christ is *preached* as raised from the dead, how can some of you say, 'There is no resurrection of the dead?' But if there is no resurrection of the dead, then Christ has not been raised; and if Christ has not been raised, then our *preaching* is without foundation, and so is your faith (emphasis added).

Paul furthermore declares that the resurrection of Christ is attested to by credible historical witnesses. In 1 Corinthians 15:5–8, he cites that Christ appeared to Peter, to the twelve (the apostles), to over five hundred brothers at one time, most of whom were alive at the time of Paul's writing, to James the half-brother of Christ, to the apostles again, and then later to the apostle Paul himself. He does not mention Mary Magdalene or the two disciples on the road to Emmaus, but they also had personal encounters with the risen Lord as recorded in the Gospels.

The highest realization of the reality and relevance of the resurrection is found in the nature of the risen Savior and Lord. He is the immortal God-man who finished and finalized God's redemptive plan and provision. Because of this He is the very embodiment of our salvation. All saving power and merit reside in Him, in His risen person. This truth is symbolically demonstrated in John 20 when Jesus appeared to the apostles the second time after His resurrection and Thomas was present. Jesus presented Himself as risen and remarkably revealed the scars of His crucifixion to Thomas. This was proof to Thomas that He had indeed been raised from death. In addition, the scars symbolized that the merits of His redemptive, sacrificial death remain in the risen Savior. It brought the apostles and brings us face to face with the fact that all saving power and merit reside in the risen Son of God! The scars of His sacrifice in His risen body represent the merits of His sacrificial death on the cross.

One specific statement of the residing of saving power in the risen Christ is found in 1 John 2:2: "And He Himself *is* the propitiation for our sins" (NASB; emphasis added). Note in this verse that it specifically states "is." It does not say that He "was" the propitiation for our sins, but that He "is" the propitiation for our sins. Right now, in His risen existence, He is our propitiation or mercy seat. Jesus absorbed all God's holy wrath against our sins. And since God's wrath was expended on Him, mercy now resides in Him and is available through Him.

Remarkably the book of Revelation opens with the scene of a vision of the risen Son of God. Following John's description of this ineffable vision, he records the first words of the risen one: "Do not be afraid; I am the first and the last, and the living One; and I was dead, and behold, I am alive forevermore, and I have the keys of death and of Hades" (Revelation 1:17b-18 NASB). The remainder of the book hails Him as the risen, victorious Lamb twenty-four times! As the Lamb, He embodies the merit and power of His saving sacrifice.

The embodiment of saving merit and power means that the resurrection is as essential and necessary to our salvation as His saving death and sacrifice. In fact, it means that the resurrection is more than proof positive of who He was or even of the satisfactory nature of His sacrifice. It means that His resurrection is the climax and culmination of His saving work.

According to the author of Hebrews, Jesus entered the holiest part of the sanctuary – not the earthly one, but the perfect heavenly one—in order to present Himself as the savior and high priest who had provided the perfect sacrifice of His blood (Hebrews 9:6–14). To do this, He had to be risen! Furthermore, it is because He rose again that presently He is able to safe-guard and guarantee our salvation by His on-going mediational, high priestly work of intercession on our behalf!

> But He, because He continues forever, has an unchangeable priesthood. Therefore He is also able to save to the uttermost (completely) those who come to God through Him, since He always lives to make intercession for them (Hebrews 7:24–25 NKJV).

The two primary functions of the gospel are the cross and the resurrection.

> For what I received I passed on to you as of first importance: that Christ died for our sins according to the Scriptures, that he was buried, that he was raised on the third day according to the Scriptures (1 Corinthians 15:3–4).

It is time that we evaluate the content of the message we are proclaiming. Most gospel presentations today do well in emphasizing the cross, the sacrificial death of our Savior, but they fail to proclaim the powerful resurrection of our Lord. Whether in sermon, or tract, or book, too often we are giving a weakened presentation of the gospel. We are frequently failing to proclaim the good news in the fullness of its power and blessing. If the gospel is powerful, and it certainly is (Romans 1:16), then we should preach the whole gospel including its powerful climax! Only then will our proclamation be truly authentic and full of power.

Let us be firm in our faith in the resurrection of Christ, knowing that it was a historical event witnessed and passed down as rock-firm tradition. In *Paul–Apostle of the Heart Set Free*, F. F. Bruce quotes C. T. Craig in *The Beginning of Christianity*: "The early Christians did not believe in the resurrection of Christ because they could not find his dead body. They believed because they did find a living Christ" (F. F. Bruce

p. 93). Bruce then declares: "for Paul the gospel was more than a body of affirmations or factual data. The gospel was also for him . . . an ongoing entity in which one can be or stand (1 Corinthians 15:1) . . . Paul himself stood . . . in its saving dynamism he participated." It appears that nothing else impelled Paul like the resurrection and the living Lord. After all, his first encounter with Christianity was the appearance of the risen Lord to him on the road to Damascus (Acts 9). And so we too should be impelled by our living Lord!

5. The Lordship of Jesus

Peter's Sermon to the Jews	Peter's Sermon to the Gentiles
Acts 2:33	Acts 10:42

> Therefore, since He has been exalted to the right hand
> of God (Acts 2:33).

To be "exalted to the right hand of God" is an expression clearly indicating His lordship, according to Philippians 2:9–11. This passage proclaims that God exalted Him because of His obedient life and obedient death and that God gave Him a name above every name so that every knee would bow to Him and every tongue would confess that He (Jesus) is Lord! Furthermore, the truth of Christ being "at the right hand of God" is repeated numerous times in the New Testament (Matthew 22:44 & 26:64; Acts 2:33–34, 5:31 & 7:55; Romans 8:34; Ephesians 1:20; Colossians 3:1; Hebrews 1:3, 13 & 8:1 & 10:12 & 12:2; 1 Peter 3:22). The fact that He is at the right hand of God is an absolute announcement of His lordship!

The chapter, *The Doctrines of Authentic Christianity*, goes into greater detail about the lordship of Christ. In considering the preaching of His lordship and its implications, you may want to refer ahead to that chapter for a full explanation of Christ's lordship. It will be sufficient for now to be made aware that the lordship of Christ was the keystone of the early, apostolic church. It was therefore prominent in the gospel proclamation.

The exaltation and lordship of Christ is an element of true faith in

Christ. While a person believing in Christ may lack a clear understanding of the implications of Christ's lordship initially, the spirit of submission to Christ will be present in true repentance and faith. It often takes time and growth in spiritual knowledge for a new believer to begin to understand the fuller import of Christ's lordship and His claims on the believer's life. In fact, the recognition of his lordship over our lives is tested and confirmed again and again throughout a believer's life.

The lordship of Christ is the basis of all true discipleship. While Jesus Christ is called Savior twenty-four times in the New Testament, He is called Lord four hundred and thirty-three times! There can be no question as to the importance of the lordship of Jesus!

The Three Commands of the Gospel

1. Repent of Your Sin and Unbelief

Acts 2:38 (and implied in 10:42)

There are two Hebrew words in the Old Testament and two Greek words in the New Testament that are translated "repent or repentance." Summarizing their core meaning, repentance is genuine sorrow for your sins. This sorrow includes regret and remorse that are accompanied by a change of both mental perspective and change of choice by the individual's will. The result is a choice to turn away from sin and from a sinful way of life and to turn toward God for His forgiveness and salvation. It is a heart-felt decision to love Him, worship Him, and serve Him. Repentance is a response of a person's heart prompted by the Holy Spirit's work in their heart that convicts them of their sinfulness (John 16:8-11; Acts 2:37-40).

Unfortunately, many churches fail to preach this as a part of the authentic gospel. There is a deplorable absence of preaching that addresses sin and the need for repentance. Many pastors, preachers, and Christians refrain from speaking about God's wrath toward sin and that God's justice requires punishment for sin in hell. These are repugnant words and principles to a society that is soft on sin, that demands that there are no moral absolutes and that constantly pushes the politically correct propaganda that promotes toleration of all differing views and lifestyles. For this reason, many who preach the message of the gospel soft-pedal and water it down if they preach it at all.

Repentance must be preached knowing that sin is destructive to people's lives like cancer is to the body. It must be preached in order to help people come to the Savior by helping them to see their sin and need of a savior. By loving and compassionate preaching of the authentic gospel we are demonstrating genuine love for people and seeking to rescue them from eternal separation from God as well as from ruined and wasted lives.

> I testified to both Jews and Greeks about *repentance* toward God and faith in our Lord Jesus (Acts 20:21; emphasis added).

"Testified" is a formal term of gravity and responsibility. It carries the idea of sharing what you know to be true in a courtroom in front of a judge.

> For they themselves report about us what kind of reception we had from you: how you *turned to God from idols* to serve the living and true God, and to wait for His Son from heaven, whom He raised from the dead—Jesus, who rescues us from the coming wrath (1 Thessalonians 1:9–10; emphasis added).

2. Believe in Jesus Christ with Intellect, Emotion and Will

> If you confess with your mouth, "Jesus is Lord," and *believe* in your heart that God raised Him from the dead, you will be saved. With the heart one *believes*, resulting in righteousness, and with the mouth one confesses, resulting in salvation. Now the Scripture says, No one who *believes* on Him will be put to shame, for there is no distinction between Jew and Greek, since

28

the same Lord of all is rich to all who call on Him. For everyone who calls on the name of the Lord will be saved (Romans 10:9–13; emphasis added).

Repentance and faith are two sides of the same coin. Believing or faith is implied in Acts 2:37 and is specific in Acts 10:43. Faith as the primary response to the gospel will be dealt with extensively in the chapter *The Doctrines of Authentic Christianity* in the section titled: *One Faith: The Gospel* – the subheading: "The gospel in its appropriation or acceptance: *faith alone.*" Faith is not simply intellectual assent. It is a conviction regarding specific truth and a commitment of one's life in view of an eternal destiny.

Due to the audience being Jews in Acts 2, Peter emphasized repentance. But when preaching to the Gentiles in Acts 10, he emphasized faith. Both are essential and necessary responses to the gospel in order for a person to receive the gospel and become a Christian or disciple of Jesus Christ.

Has there been that moment in your life when you have realized that you are a sinner and guilty under the law of God, and when you chose to place your faith and trust in Jesus Christ to be your Savior and Lord? If not, would you this very moment ask the Lord to save you from the guilt of your sins, to forgive you, to accept you into His family, telling Him that you are committing your life and eternal destiny to Him? The Bible says, "Whoever calls on the name of the Lord (Jesus Christ) will be saved"(Romans 10:13). God has made you a promise, but you must decide and act in order to claim that promise. If you call on Him to save you, He has promised that He will save you!

3. Be Baptized as an Act of Obedience and Identification

Acts 2:38 & 10:47–48

The Holy Spirit came on Cornelius and the other Gentiles present who believed *before* they were baptized. This clearly indicates that baptism does not produce salvation. However, baptism as a testimony

of salvation is commanded by Christ (Matthew 28:19) and by Peter
(Acts 2:38 & 10:48) and is a very important and foundational step
of obedience. It acknowledges your faith in Christ and identifies you
as His disciple. Baptism as a subject of Scripture will be surveyed
thoroughly in the chapter on *The Doctrines of Authentic Christianity*.

The Two Promises of the Gospel

1. You Are Promised Forgiveness of Sins

    Acts 2:38 & 10:43

Forgiveness of sins is mentioned in both passages, Acts 2 and 10,
and is preeminently important! Both repentance and forgiveness focus
on the issue of sin that separates humanity from God. Forgiveness is
therefore mentioned frequently in regards to salvation. See the following
references as examples.

> Therefore, let it be known to you, brothers, that through
> this man (Jesus Christ) *forgiveness of sins* is being proclaimed
> to you, and everyone who believes in Him is justified from
> everything, which you could not be justified from through
> the law of Moses (Acts 13:38–39; emphasis added).

> To open their eyes that they may turn from darkness to
> light and from the power of Satan to God, that they may
> receive *forgiveness of sins* and a share among those who are
> sanctified by faith in Me (Acts 26:18; emphasis added).

> In Him we have redemption through His blood, the
> *forgiveness of our trespasses* (sins), according to the riches
> of His grace (Ephesians 1:7; emphasis added).

> In whom (Jesus Christ) we have redemption, *the*
> *forgiveness of sins* (Colossians 1:14; emphasis added).

> I am writing to you, little children, because *your sins have been forgiven* on account of His name (1 John 2:12; emphasis added).

Forgiveness means that the guilt of sin has been absolved. There is no more offense between you as a sinner and God who is holy. He has forgiven all your sin because of Christ's payment for your sin on the cross. The moment we repent and believe our sins are forgiven. To know our sins are forgiven is a wonderful blessing. A weight of guilt is lifted! Forgiveness affords a peace and comfort that defy understanding. Sometimes a sense of rapturous joy results from the comfort and peace experienced in our heart. What can compare to knowing that all is right between God and me?

2. You Are Promised the Holy Spirit

    Acts 2:38 & 10:44–45

    > In Him you also, when you heard the word of truth, the gospel of your salvation — in Him when you believed — were *sealed with* the promised Holy Spirit. He is *the down payment* of our inheritance, for the redemption of the possession, to the praise of His glory (Ephesians 1:13–14; emphasis added).

The Holy Spirit lives in the believer securing and preserving his eternal salvation. You are sealed with the Holy Spirit. A seal is an official mark of identification on a letter, contract, or other document. Four primary truths are signified by the seal:

Security	The contents are secured and safe-kept by the seal.
Authenticity	The seal validates who has secured the contents.
Ownership	The seal indicates ownership of the contents.
Authority	A seal expresses the authority of the one who placed the seal.

The Spirit is also the earnest or down-payment of our salvation. He is a pledge of the believer's future inheritance in eternity.

Comparing One Other Sermon by Peter

Acts 3:11–26

Peter preaches a third sermon in this passage –the second sermon he preached to Jews. Naturally we assume that it was similar to the one first preached to the Jews on the day of Pentecost. The details of this sermon are sketchy and incomplete compared to the sermons in Acts 2 and 10. Nevertheless, this sermon also follows exactly the same outline and lists some of the same truths. In addition, the order of the truths remains exactly the same as in the other two sermons. See this demonstrated below:

Truths of the Gospel

His Name (3:13) "glorified His servant Jesus"
His Death (3:15a)
His Resurrection (3:15b)

Commands of the Gospel

Repent (3:19)

Promises of the Gospel

Forgiveness of sins (3:19)

Response

Many believed (4:4)

The outline Peter gave us by inspiration of the Spirit is not given for us to follow to the letter. But it does emphasize the truths that must be proclaimed to give people a good understanding of the gospel. The gospel may be presented in different ways and using various methods depending on the culture and circumstances, but the truths of the gospel should be proclaimed in full as much as possible, because the gospel itself is the power of God for salvation!

In addition to Peter, the apostle Paul also unfolds the nature of the good news. He proclaims and defends the gospel as being the gospel of grace. He insists that a person is not saved by works of the law or by human merit of any kind, but as a free and gracious gift from God.

Are we proclaiming the gospel to the lost? Are we teaching members of our churches to proclaim the gospel? The authentic gospel should be woven into most of our preaching and teaching. Do some pastors and teachers unintentionally or intentionally leave out certain aspects of the gospel when preaching or teaching it?

> Go into all the world and preach the gospel to every person (Mark 16:15).

The Gospel According to Paul

In Romans Paul *declared* the gospel, while in Galatians he *defended* the gospel. The essential principles of the gospel as preached by Peter are also proclaimed by Paul. However, Paul enlarges on the gospel by explaining its nature and implications. For that reason, a succinct summary of Romans and Galatians will yield a more complete picture of the gospel.

Paul begins the book of Romans with his opening theme in Romans 1:16–17. Let us first consider this to see Paul's primary principle regarding the gospel.

> For I am not ashamed of the gospel, because it is God's power for salvation to everyone who believes, first to the Jew, and also to the Greek. For in it (the gospel) God's righteousness is revealed from faith to faith, just as it is written: "The righteous will live by faith" (Romans 1:16–17).

Paul saw three great dynamics in the gospel: power, pervasiveness, and provision.

The Power of the Gospel

The gospel is powerful because:

- It confronts us with the reality that we are not right with God.
- It convicts us of our guilt because of our sins and our sinfulness.
- It commands us to repent, to turn from our sins and to turn to God.
- It calls us to believe on Christ, trusting in His death and resurrection.
- It calls on us to be baptized and to commit to follow Christ as His disciple.
- It changes us radically by leading us to be spiritually born and thus becoming a new person.

The gospel is indeed powerful, and we should have confidence and boldness when we tell others. A great story out of baseball history illustrates the power of the gospel. It comes from *Illustrations for Preaching and Teaching: From Leadership Journal.* It was July 15th, 1986, and Roger Clemens, the sizzling right-hander for the Boston Red Sox was starting his first All-Star Game. He came to bat in the second inning nervous and uncertain. He had not been at bat in several years because of the American League's designated hitter rule. After taking a few unconfident practice swings, he looked out at the pitcher, Dwight Gooden, who had won the Cy Young Award. Gooden wound up and threw a white-hot fastball past Clemens. With a nervous smile on his face, Clemens stepped out of the box and asked catcher Gary Carter, "Is that what my pitches look like?" "You bet it is!" replied Carter. Although Clemens quickly struck out, he went on to pitch three perfect innings and be named the game's most valuable player. From that day on, he later said, he pitched with far greater boldness because of the assurance of the power of his pitching. Sometimes we forget how powerful the gospel is and how powerful the witness of the Holy Spirit is through us. Let us speak the gospel with boldness and confidence!

In regard to the pervasiveness of the gospel, the reason Paul was unashamed of it was because its extensiveness. He understood that the gospel is extended and available to all mankind. Paul knew it to be amazing and magnificent. God's plan and provision encompasses all sinful humanity from Adam to the last human to be born! It embraces all nations and ethnic groups. Paul was thrilled and motivated by this truth. When he comprehended the sweeping scope of the gospel, he was convicted of the compelling need for it to be proclaimed to the entire human race. That is the reason he was driven to declare it!

Another truth Paul felt resonating from the very heart of the gospel was its provision. Paul painstakingly presents humanity's sinful condition and guilt in Romans 1:18–3:20. In 1:18-32 he gives the historical account of how the nations, the Gentiles, departed from God in rebellion turning to immorality and idolatry. Then in 2:1–3:20 he indicts the Jewish people with their failure to keep the law and thus their guilt before God. He declares "There is no one righteous, not even one" (Romans 3:10)! Then concluding Paul pronounces the world, Gentiles and Jews, guilty before God:

> Now we know that whatever the law says, it says to those who are under the law, that every mouth may be stopped, and all the world may become guilty before God (Romans 3:19 NKJV).

The condition the apostle describes in Romans is a universal condition of humanity's unrighteousness before God. Humanity's desperate and crying need to become right with God is righteousness. Righteousness is what humanity lacks, and it is the only thing that will make human beings acceptable to God, who is holy.

Here is where God steps in to remedy the problem of our lack of righteousness. God made a way to provide *righteousness* for unrighteous humans. Since we cannot provide a righteousness of our own that is acceptable to God, if we are to become righteous, then God must provide us with a righteousness that will make us acceptable to Him. As we are about to discover, God has made that provision of righteousness through Christ.

How does God provide *righteousness* for sinful humans? In Romans 5, Paul calls the righteousness that God would provide for unrighteous people "the gift of righteousness" (Romans 5:17). Furthermore, he is very specific as to what this gift of righteousness is: it is "the obedience of one." He contrasts Adam's one act of disobedience or sin that plunged mankind into sin and brought death into the world with the one act of obedience by Jesus Christ. He declares that Adam's one act of disobedience made us unrighteous, but Christ's one act of obedience can make us righteous. And what was that one act of obedience? "He humbled Himself by becoming *obedient* to the point of death—even to death on a cross" (Philippians 2:8; emphasis added). Jesus not only obeyed God and His law by living a perfect, sinless life, but He also supremely obeyed the Father when He did the Father's will by going to the cross to give Himself as a sacrifice for the sins of humanity. Thereby He provided His own righteousness to be given to us or bestowed on us. The gift of righteousness is the righteous merits of the obedient life and obedient death of Jesus Christ—His perfection. We receive that *gift* of righteousness by trusting in Him by faith to save us from our sin and to make us right with God.

The Theme of Romans

Righteousness is the key word in Romans. In the King James Version, the words "righteous" or "righteousness" are mentioned forty-three times in Romans. The words "justify," "justified," and "justification" that mean "to be declared righteous" are mentioned fourteen times. All of these words come from the same root word in Greek and therefore form a word-group. The total number of times this entire word-group is used in Romans is fifty-seven times! In Eastern literature the more times a particular thing is mentioned, the more important the author believes it to be. Therefore, based on Paul's prolific use of the word-group for righteousness in Romans, our need for righteousness before God is obviously regarded as profoundly important!

Righteousness is mentioned as the primary theme in Romans 1:17 as Paul plainly sets forth his main proposition. A second text in Romans that also addresses this important theme is Romans 3:21–26. It begins with the second most-used phrase by Paul, "But now." It is making a strong statement of contrast to what had just been said regarding humanity's sinful condition of unrighteousness. After declaring: "There is none righteous, no not one," he introduces a great and powerful new reality. Romans 3:21 states: *"But now a righteousness from God, apart from law, has been made known, to which the Law and Prophets testify"* (NIV 1984; emphasis added).

No righteousness is possible to humans either through the law or by works. The law has condemned all of humanity. Now, however, in God's marvelous mercy and due to the generosity of His grace, a righteousness that originates with God and that is provided by Him for unworthy sinners has been made available by the redemption that is in Christ.

> And all are justified (declared righteous) freely by his grace through the redemption that came by Christ Jesus. God presented Christ as a sacrifice of atonement ("propitiation" in NASB), through the shedding of his blood—to be received by faith. He did this to demonstrate his righteousness, because in his forbearance he had left the sins committed beforehand unpunished; he did it to demonstrate his righteousness at the present time, so as to be just and the one who justifies (declares righteous) those who have faith in Jesus (Romans 3: 24–25 NIV).

The conclusion is that God demonstrated His justice by requiring redemption as a payment for sin and propitiation as the punishment of sin so that He could justly forgive sinners and declare them righteous. God has proven Himself to be just and righteous because the penalty of sin was paid for, thus satisfying the demands of God's holiness and justice. God demonstrates His righteousness because He does not overlook sin, and His justice is intact because He has made a way for sin to be paid for judicially (justification) and punitively (propitiation) so that He can be a just judge. Then wonderfully by redemption and propitiation, God becomes the justifier of those who trust in Jesus.

The result of accepting the righteousness that comes through faith is that one is "justified (declared righteous) freely by His grace." The word "freely" is a form of the Greek word "dora," a word that gives strong emphasis on the freeness of the gift. That's why the NASB translates the verse this way: "being justified as a *gift* by His grace through the redemption which is in Christ Jesus" (emphasis added).

One particular perspective of Romans is important in appreciating its theme. There is forensic or legal terminology throughout the book. The stage or setting of the book is a court of law. The forensic or legal words Paul uses include:

- "the law" (ος νομος)
- "guilty" (υποδικος = "under judgment; one who has lost his suit")
- "condemned" (or judgment) (κριμα = a legal, condemnatory judgmental decree)
- "justify; justified; justification" (δικαιαω =legal pronouncement of righteousness)

At an early age God began speaking to me thanks to my parents. After World War II our church denomination challenged parents to place their children in Sunday School starting in the Cradle Roll or Nursery Department. Young parents were challenged to keep them in Sunday School throughout their childhood. My parents enrolled me in the Cradle Roll Department of the First Baptist Church of Pelham, Georgia. The church had an outstanding Bible curriculum and program. Sometime around first grade we were taught and assisted in memorizing the Ten Commandments.

It was at Pelham Elementary School that my very first strong spiritual impression came. I was in the first grade. One day during recess God spoke plainly to my heart and mind. He impressed on me that He was holy and expected me to be holy. At that moment I made a commitment to Him that I would be holy, not like the other children. That commitment was soon and often broken. By second grade I was cursing and telling off-color jokes and stole two items on two different occasions. All the while the Holy Spirit was wielding God's holy law and piercing my soul with heart-wrenching conviction. On one occasion when I was being supervised by a neighbor while my parents were briefly away from our home, I fell off my bicycle and severely scraped my side. In panic I ran to our home rather than to a neighbor's home. Filled with fear I ran through our home in circles crying out: "God, please don't let me die! Please don't let me die!" I felt that hell would be my destiny if I died at that moment. On another occasion at age eight some boys and I were sitting around on a summer day cursing. Some were taking God's name in vain. When I started to open my mouth to do the same, the Third Commandment rang out in my heart and mind, "You shall not take the name of the LORD your God in vain. For the LORD will not hold him guiltless who takes His name in vain" (Exodus 20:7 freely quoted). I was under an enormous weight of guilt for my sin and sinfulness. The knowledge that I was not right with God struck fear in me continually.

During this period of my life, from age six to ten, there were moments when the Lord began preparing me for His call on my life. One of those moments occurred when I was in the second grade. One of the Bible class lessons was about Elisha, the man of God. A woman of Shunem, a town on the north side of the Valley of Megeddo, and her husband built a special room for Elisha so that he would have a place to lodge when passing through (2 Kings 4). Before I even knew of salvation in Christ, the Lord used the phrase "man of God" as something of a premonition of His call on my life to be a preacher of His Word and a pastor for His people. That phrase made a deep and correct impression on me. (The phrase "man of God" will be thoroughly explained in the last chapter of the book.)

My father had a new job offer, and our family moved thirty miles away to another town, Bainbridge, Georgia, where we began attending Calvary Baptist Church. The wonderful pastor of the church, Dr. Charles Bishop, preached the gospel plainly and powerfully. At age ten I heard and understood for the first time that Christ died on the cross for my sin and took my punishment so God could forgive me. To express the thoughts and emotions I experienced during that time is impossible. Instantly I knew that this was what my heart had been yearning for! My heart ran to Jesus! I took Him as my Lord and Savior with my whole heart! As I walked toward the front of the church to confess my faith in Christ, my guilt was lifted and my heart was set free. I experienced a new life with new desires and with a new orientation and purpose.

I've told you my story hoping that it may be helpful to you if you have not yet trusted Christ as your Savior and given Him your heart. Would you pray right now, and ask Jesus Christ to be your Lord and Savior? Admit that you are a sinner and thank God for His gift of forgiveness of your sin through His Son. If you accept Him now, you may want to write this date in your Bible as your "spiritual birthday." The first thing you should then do is to tell someone, anyone, that you have received Christ as your Lord and Savior. If you trust Christ now, your life will be changed forever for good. I know, because the Lord changed my life, and He will do the same for you.

Chapter 2

The Dynamic of Authentic Christianity

Discipleship — the Lost Secret of Authentic Christianity

The History of Discipleship
The Honor of Discipleship
The Hallmark of Discipleship
The Seven Principles of Disciple-Making
The Biblical Methods of Disciple-Making
Practical Approaches to Disciple-Making

Then Jesus came near and said to them,
All authority has been given to Me in heaven and on earth.
Go, therefore, and make disciples of all nations:
Baptizing them in the name of the Father,
and of the Son, and of the Holy Spirit;
Teaching them to obey all things that
I have commanded you.
And remember, I am with you always, to the end of the age.

Matthew 28:18–20

Discipleship – the Lost Secret
of Authentic Christianity

Jesus gave the Church the mandate to make disciples. It's known as the Great Commission. He then defined this as a two-step process: baptizing and teaching. The first phase of disciple-making is baptizing. The idea of this is evangelizing, that is, telling the gospel to someone and inviting them to trust Christ as their Savior. It also includes bringing a person to the point of a public profession of faith and public commitment to be a disciple of Jesus Christ. The second phase of making disciples is the ongoing teaching and training involved in developing a mature disciple.

The First Phase of Disciple-Making

There is much to be said about what a disciple is and what a disciple of Jesus Christ looks like. But before we consider that, we need to cover this first and critical phase of making disciples, evangelism and baptism. Without this phase in disciple-making, disciple-making dies. It ceases to exist. In today's church, however, bringing a person to faith in Christ and baptizing him is often where it also ends. We wind up with church members and not vibrant disciples.

Dr. J. I. Packer stated: "Go ye and make disciples was spoken to them (the apostles) in their representative capacity; this is Christ's command not merely to his apostles, but to the whole Church. Evangelism is the inalienable responsibility of every Christian community, and of each and every Christian. We are all under orders to devote ourselves to spreading the Good News, and to use all our ingenuity and enterprise to bring it to the notice of the whole world."

The evangelistic incentive is the glory of God. God is glorified by trophies of His grace, people who have been wonderfully delivered from sin and made the children of God. The evangelistic message is the gospel of God. The evangelistic agency is the Church of God. And the evangelistic dynamic is the Spirit of God.

The apostle Paul gives us a great example of evangelism. His aim was conversion. In 1 Corinthians 9:22 he said, "To the weak I became weak, in order to win the weak. I have become all things to all people, so that I may by all means save some." Paul's aim was conversion. While salvation is the work of God alone, conversion is the work of God and man laboring together (Luke 1:16; Acts 26:17; James 5:19). This means that evangelism is more than teaching and instructing. It is eliciting a response. It is not just informing. It is inviting (2 Corinthians 5:19). I love what J. I. Packer observed about this. "Paul sought to save men; and because he sought to save them, he was not content merely to throw truth at them; but he went out of his way to get alongside them, and to start thinking with them from where they were, and to speak to them in terms they could understand, and above all to avoid everything that would prejudice them against the Gospel. . . . his aim and object in all his handling of the Gospel . . . was never less than to win souls, but converting those whom he saw as neighbors to faith in the Lord Jesus Christ."

There are a number of approaches or methods of evangelism mentioned in the New Testament. These are listed and explained below:

- Casual Conversation – Greek: "laleo" meaning "to speak" (Acts 4:1, 31) To talk casually or to tell others; (*The Way of the Master* is a popular, contemporary way of doing this, as is also *Sharing Jesus Without Fear.*)
- Directed Evangelism – Greek: "evangelidzo" meaning "to teach" (Acts 5:42) Used by Christians in general, not just preachers; used in addressing individuals or groups.
- Doctrinal Presentation – Greek: "didasko" meaning "to teach" (Acts 4:2; 5:21, 25 & 28) Used primarily by the apostles; calls for greater skill and knowledge than the two methods already mentioned.
- Evangelistic Preaching – Greek: "kerusso" meaning "to cry or proclaim as a herald" (Acts 8:5-6) Used by Philip the evangelist, by Peter, and by Paul; this is the responsibility of certain gifted and called individuals.

- Authoritative Announcement – Greek: "katangello" meaning "to announce publicly." Implies authority, apostolic or missionary authority in nature; used especially by Paul.
- Personal Testimony – Greek: "martuero" meaning "to bear testimony or witness" (Acts 1:8; 1 Peter 3:15) To earnestly tell how the Lord brought you to faith in Christ and how the gospel has affected your life. This can be an easy and very effective method of sharing the gospel with others. Strong intellectual and emotional overtones are involved in this approach.
- In-Depth Dialogue – Greek: "dialegomai" means "to discuss with interaction" (Acts 18:11 & 19:10) To discuss extensively with interaction or in a dialogue fashion. This often involves apologetics. There are numerous good books on apologetics that can assist believers in using this approach. It is a time-proven missionary method used by both Paul and Apollos. When using this method, we must avoid allowing it to turn into an intellectual debate.

It is apparent that there are many approaches and methods of sharing the gospel and seeking to bring people to saving faith in Jesus Christ. Literature, technology, and other creative means may and should be utilized in evangelism. There are also a number of excellent programs to use in training people to evangelize.

The Second Phase of Disciple-Making

After evangelizing and bringing people to the confession and commitment involved in baptism, we are then ready for the second phase of disciple-making. The process of teaching and training needs to begin immediately while the new believer's faith and commitment are fresh.

However, in many cases, especially in recent times, we as the Church of Jesus Christ have been more effective in evangelism than we have been in the teaching and training phase of disciple-making.

And tragically, genuine disciple-making is virtually absent from the contemporary church scene due to the following.

The church continues to shrink in the United States for a number of reasons:

> ➤ It lacks relevancy due to moral duplicity.
> ➤ It equates intellectual assent with faith.
> ➤ It is more concerned with style rather than substance.
> ➤ It panders to a consumer mentality.
> ➤ It defines success primarily by numbers.
> ➤ It produces more consumers of religious goods and services than disciples.

In *Not a Fan—Becoming a Completely Committed Follower of Jesus*, Kyle Idleman says, "My concern is that many churches in America have gone from being sanctuaries to becoming stadiums. And every week all the fans come to the stadium where they cheer for Jesus but have no interest in truly following Him. The biggest threat to the Church today is fans calling themselves Christians when they aren't actually interested in following Christ. They want to be close enough to Jesus to get all the benefits, but not so close that it requires anything from them."

Dietrich Bonhoeffer, the famous Lutheran pastor who took his commitment to Christ seriously and as a result lost his life to the Nazis during World War II, states in his book, *The Cost of Discipleship:* "Christianity without discipleship is always Christianity without Christ."

A faith that separates salvation from discipleship is not the faith of the New Testament! This does not mean that we cease to preach the gospel of pure grace, for grace is the heart and essence of the gospel. It does mean, however, that we renounce the idea of a faith that then results in no fruit and that demands no discipleship. Remember, the vines that bear no fruit are cut off and thrown into the fire to be destroyed (John 15:1–6). If there is no fruit, one is probably not a Christian and therefore is not really saved.

Faith without obedience is not real faith at all. It is nothing more than an intellectual acceptance or sentimental attachment (James 2:14–17). That kind of faith is a sham! The faith taught by Jesus ultimately embraces a lifelong abandonment of self that forsakes the world to follow Him whatever the cost or destination (Matthew 16:24 & 19:21; Luke 14:26–27, 33).

The History of Discipleship

1. Jesus called His disciples to Him and chose twelve to be apostles (Luke 6:13).
2. He later appointed seventy others out of His disciples (Luke 10:1).
3. In the Great Commission Jesus commanded the eleven apostles and about five hundred disciples to make disciples (Matthew 28:16–20; 1 Corinthians 15:6).
4. Approximately one hundred and twenty disciples were gathered in the Upper Room in Jerusalem when the Holy Spirit came to fill them (Acts 1:15 & 2:1–4).
5. On that same day about three thousand were saved and added to the disciples (Acts 2:41).
6. Later on Solomon's Porch about two thousand more were added to the number of disciples, swelling their number to approximately five thousand five hundred (Acts 4:4).
7. The number of disciples continued to increase greatly in Jerusalem (Acts 6:7). One biblical scholar has estimated that the number of disciples had increased to twenty thousand by the time of Stephen's stoning in Acts chapter 8.
8. While yet unsaved Saul, who was later called Paul, was threatening the disciples of the Lord (Acts 9:1, 9).
9. The disciples were first called Christians at Antioch (Acts 11:26 - see 1 Peter 4:16 for the context of the pejorative use of the word "Christian").
10. Paul and Barnabas made many disciples at Derbe and strengthened the souls of the disciples at Lystra, Iconium, and Antioch (Acts 14:20).
11. Paul went throughout Galatia and Phyrgia strengthening the disciples (Acts 18:23).

The Honor of Discipleship

Jesus called His disciples: "Come and follow Me."

What Is a Disciple?

The very first indication we have of what a disciple is comes from Christ calling people to be His disciples. The concept of discipleship is clearly and distinctively demonstrated and illustrated in the twelve He chose and their relationship with Him. Since we have more specific and detailed information about these disciples than about any others, we can use what we observe about them to arrive at conclusions as to what discipleship is.

The following are the basic, important principles of discipleship that we learn from observing the relationship of the twelve apostles to Christ. These principles were not only true for Christ's disciples He made while on earth, but they are also true for us today. As you read these principles, think first of how they applied to the twelve apostles, and then apply them to yourself as a disciple of Jesus. Those principles are:

1. We are called into a life-changing relationship with Christ (2 Corinthians 5:17).
2. We are called to an identification with and loyalty to Christ (Matthew 10:32–33).
3. We are called to follow Christ and to learn from Him (Matthew 11:28–30).
4. We are called to emulate Christ or to follow the pattern of His life (1 John 2:6).
5. We are called to represent Christ by our life and witness (2 Corinthians 5:19–20).
6. We are called to serve Christ in His Great Commission enterprise (Matthew 28:18–20).

We have just observed what a disciple is. This can be represented and remembered by the acronym "LIFERS." The principles or characteristics of disciples or lifers are:

L   Life-changing relationship
I   Identification with Christ
F   Following Christ
E   Emulating Christ
R   Representing Christ
S   Serving Christ

As we consider each of these principles carefully, we can see fleshed out before our eyes what a true disciple looks like.

Life-Changing Relationship

First, we are called into a life-changing relationship with Christ. Discipleship is a transformational relationship. This transformation begins with a spiritual birth that establishes the new relationship with Christ. Jesus explained that just as we had a physical birth, we must have spiritual birth in order to be part of His kingdom. And He said that the spiritual birth occurs as a miracle of the Holy Spirit transforming us when we believe on Him (John 3:1–16). It is a miracle that occurs in our inner being. We are given a new, spiritual life that is different from living life on a physical and sensual level.

This life-changing relationship does not, however, end with a spiritual birth. The transformation continues as a process of learning and growing because of our relationship with Jesus. This is evident in the lives of the twelve. And it is evident in all true believers today. More about this transformation will be presented when we consider the Christian's character and character development in a later chapter.

Identification with Christ

A second principle is an identification with and loyalty to Christ. It is particularly and initially established by the baptism of the new believer in Christ. The baptism of a believer in Christ is an open and public confession of his faith in Christ. His baptism brands him as belonging to Christ, as one of His disciples! In principle, baptism is, therefore, not only a confession of faith but is also a proclamation of a person's commitment to follow Christ as one of His disciples.

Baptism is a confession of one's faith in Christ, but it is also a commitment to be and to live as His disciple. This second significance of baptism is often not recognized and not taught in contemporary American Christianity. Much more will be said about baptism in the chapter *The Doctrines of Authentic Christianity.*

Following Christ

We are also called to follow Christ and to learn from Him. One important emphasis of discipleship is the concept of apprenticeship. In New Testament times a mentor taught a disciple how to fulfill a profession or do the work of a trade.

Discipleship demands attentiveness and the development of knowledge and skills. It is intentional and requires dedication to the goal and achievement of proficiency and competency. It is a maturing process of growth and development toward practical achievement of skills, usefulness and productivity. It is a calling to take seriously. It can be measured by increasing fruitfulness over time.

Emulating Christ

A fourth principle is we are called to emulate Christ or to follow the pattern of His life. Christ is more than a good example for a disciple. He is to be our pattern. We are called to walk as He walked. That means we are to live as He lived (1 John 2:6). This means emulating His character and philosophy of life.

Jesus's character included characteristics such as love, humility, compassion, commitment to truth, hatred of evil, mercy, forgiveness, kindness, patience, gentleness, generosity, endurance, peacefulness, meekness, faithfulness, and self-control. His philosophy of life focused on glorifying His Father, making Himself a slave to do the Father's will, and selflessly and sacrificially serving others out of genuine love for them. An authentic disciple will develop this philosophy and these goals and choose to pursue them in his life.

Representing Christ

Jesus said to his disciples: "You are the light of the world. A city on a hill cannot be hidden. Neither do people light a lamp and put it under a bowl. Instead they put it on its stand, and it gives light to everyone in the house. In the same way, let your light shine before men, that they may see your good deeds and praise your Father in heaven" (Matthew 5:14–16 NIV). Disciples become Christ's representatives on earth (2 Corinthians 5:19–20). We are to represent Him, His redemptive work, and His teachings to the world. We are, in fact, His ambassadors. We are to be His witnesses to all people and to the most remote places of the earth (Acts 1:8). Representing Him requires that we conduct our lives with integrity and dignity so that as His ambassadors we represent Him honorably.

Serving Christ

We serve Christ in two ways. First we serve Him when we serve others. This starts in the local church. Every disciple is called to be actively involved in ministry of some kind in order to assist in meeting the needs of other believers in the local assembly (1 Corinthians 12:11–26; Ephesians 4:11–16). This is a key to being a functioning part of the body of Christ. As we serve one another we serve Him (Matthew 10:42)!

But we also serve those who are outside the Christian family, those who are not believers in Christ. A disciple should love like Christ loves and should make himself available to meet the needs of others in small and large ways. This requires discernment and sensitivity to the leading of the Holy Spirit.

Serving the Lord also includes involvement in His Great Commission. We are to testify to others about the good news, to help those who accept Christ to be baptized, and then to teach them to obey all that Jesus commanded. This is the calling of every disciple. It is a critical part of serving Christ.

The Fascinating Story of a Fisherman's Call to Follow Christ (John 21)

"Follow me," he told them, "and I will make you fish for people!" (Matthew 4:19) The story we are entering into involves the one and only miracle performed by Jesus after His death and resurrection. But the story has a very special background to it that occurs at the very outset of Jesus's ministry. In order to know the whole story, that is where we must begin.

During the earliest days of Jesus's ministry, He was teaching along the shore of the Sea of Galilee. A large crowd was gathered early that morning to hear Him. The crowd was apparently so large that it was going to be difficult for all of them to hear His teaching. Two boats were nearby with fishermen who had already become acquainted with Jesus. Asking a favor of the fishermen, He requested that they take Him out on the lake in their boat a little distance from shore so He could teach the people and they would be able to hear Him.

After He finished teaching they took Him to shore. Knowing that the fishermen had been fishing all night and had caught nothing, Jesus told them to go out away from shore into deeper waters and to let down their nets. Not expecting to catch anything, they complied reluctantly. But then, to their astonishment, they hauled in such a load of fish that it required two boats and all the men in them to haul in the catch of fish! The massive weight of the fish almost broke their nets!

Peter, the leader of the group of fishermen, came to shore and ran up the sandy beach to Jesus, fell down at His feet and said, "Depart from me, O Lord, for I am a sinful man." He was overwhelmed by the sovereign power of Jesus. With reverent fear he was humbled to be in the presence of one so awesome. That day Jesus called four fishermen—Peter and Andrew and James and John—to follow Him and promised that He would make them fishers of men. Having seen His power and being compelled by His challenging call, they became His devoted followers that day.

Now let's fast forward. A little more than three years have gone by and Jesus has completed His ministry, has died and has risen. Forty days elapsed between His resurrection and when He ascended to heaven. During those forty days He showed Himself alive to many witnesses at various times and locations. Several of these occasions included His appearances to the apostles themselves, Peter among them. Many of the appearances occurred during the first ten days, but then the number of Jesus's appearances became fewer and fewer. It was longer between His appearances as if He was preparing His disciples to live life without His physical presence with them.

Without Jesus with them, they began to feel lonely and forsaken, and they lost a sense of purpose and hope. For Peter, however, it was even worse. He was grappling with feelings of failure and regret from having denied the Lord Jesus three times the night of His trial, the night before His death. That night of the trial, as soon as Peter had denied the Lord the third time, Jesus looked at Peter. Then just as He had foretold what would happen, a rooster crowed as a reminder to Peter of Jesus's prediction. Peter would never forget that look of hurt and sorrow in Jesus's eyes. It had haunted him almost every day since then.

In his state of despair, Peter decided to return to his old and beloved occupation—fishing. It was his comfort zone and his comfort. In our imagination we can hear him saying to the other apostles, "Guys, I'm going fishing." And since they were so accustomed to following Peter as their leader, they decided to go with him. It's not unlikely they were each dealing inside with the ache of missing Jesus and wrestling with what the future would hold. Therefore, discouraged, weary and confused, they all went fishing.

They had fished all night on the Sea of Galilee and had caught nothing. It must have been a beautiful sight of first light on the sea, although they were undoubtedly exhausted. They probably felt as empty inside as their nets literally were. Then they observed a man on the shore. He called out to them and asked if they had any food. When they replied that they had caught nothing, He spoke to them with an extraordinary power of suggestion. He told them to cast their nets on a certain side of the boat. Weary and worn out, they probably felt annoyed by the stranger's suggestion. As if too tired to argue with Him, they threw their nets out once more. Imagine their amazement at what happened next. They caught a huge, unbelievable load of fish! It was déjà vu! It was the same miracle Jesus performed when He called four of them to be His disciples!

In that moment, John, one of those four fishermen Jesus had called, looked at Peter and said with uncontrollable excitement, "Peter, it's the Lord!" Peter could hardly believe it. Just like before, he could not wait to get to Jesus, but this time it was a feeling of indescribable joy. His heart pounding in his chest, he took off his fisherman's overcoat and dove into the water and swam to shore. There in the glow of the early dawn, with a chilly breeze blowing, Jesus had a fire of coals with bread and fish on the fire. Breakfast was ready, and these weary fishermen were ravishingly hungry. You know it tasted good!

Have you ever had fresh fish for breakfast? Early in my years of being a pastor, one of the men of our church took me far back into the mountains of north Georgia to fish all night. Near dusk we met some good mountain people with whom he had had some business dealings. They knew the river and took us with them. We were below a dam and waded out waist deep to chest high into the middle of the river, and each of us sat on a huge flat rock separated from the others and fished all night in the dark with only the thin light of the moon to help us see. It was calm and serene as we were separated at such a distance that we could not communicate with each other. At first light the next morning, we waded back to shore and cooked fish for breakfast. The morning air was chilly, and I was hungry. I believe that was the best fish I ever ate! There is nothing like being really hungry after fishing all night, coming to shore in the cool crispness of the morning and cooking and eating fresh fish by a warm fire!

Let's return to our biblical story. The rest of the disciples on the boat arrived ashore. They were together again with Jesus and enjoying the fellowship of their group being reunited. As they finished their meal, they were all sitting around the fire in silent contemplation. They were savoring that moment of quiet serenity in Jesus's presence. Meanwhile Peter was gazing into the "fire of coals." "Fire of coals" is the literal rendering of the Greek word in the text. Interestingly, the only other place this particular Greek word is found in the New Testament is when Peter was in the courtyard of Caiaphas's house, the home of the high priest, the night he betrayed Jesus. And that night he had warmed his hands by a "fire of coals." When we stare into orange-hot coals and flickering flames of a fire, our minds tend to muse. Peter must have been staring at the hot coals remembering and reflecting on the night when he had betrayed the Lord.

Peter was mesmerized by the fire, but Jesus interrupted his thoughts with the question, "Simon, son of Jonah, do you love Me?" Simon was Peter's real name. At that moment, the question drove deeply into Peter's heart. It was a pointed and powerful question. Two more times He asked Peter that poignant question. Peter hesitated in answering each time. But each time Peter responded, "Yes Lord. You know that I love You." Peter's three confessions of his relationship to Christ were the antithesis of his three denials of his relationship to Jesus on the night of His betrayal.

Although this had to be painful for Peter, this was the Lord's loving way of restoring Peter back into fellowship and favor. It was not that Jesus needed this, but that Peter needed it. He needed to make his confession of love for Jesus three times for spiritual restoration and ability to leave his failure behind. Overcoming the guilt of his past failure was essential for him to be ready to take on the important and crucial ministry Jesus had for him in the near future.

During one of the questions, Jesus asked Peter something very significant. He asked him if he loved Him more than these, probably meaning the fish. In other words, did Peter love Jesus more than he loved his past life and enjoyments? Peter must have loved being a fisherman. Or, to put it another way, Jesus was asking Peter if he loved Him enough to once again and permanently leave his old occupation, to give up his own plans and his old life to follow Him and His plan. Did Peter love

Jesus enough to sacrifice his own will and purpose to fulfill the Lord's purpose for his life?

In all three questions, Jesus was not only *restoring* Peter, but was also *re-commissioning* him. Remember the miracle performed by Christ when He first commissioned Peter and called him to be a fisher of men? It involved an overwhelming catch of fish. Now after performing that same miracle again, Jesus recalls and re-commissions Peter. After Peter responds positively, although weakly, to Jesus's question by saying, "Yes, Lord, You know that I love You," Jesus instructed him to feed His sheep. In essence, Jesus was saying, "Peter, if you truly love me, serve Me by taking care of My people for me."

In the passage Jesus also made Peter aware that there would be sacrifice and suffering involved in following His call. He would have to pay a high price to serve Jesus. So Peter said, "Lord, what about these other disciples?" And Jesus said to him, "Don't worry about my plan for them - about whether they suffer or do not suffer. Peter, *you* follow me!"

It is a heart-wrenching story. Imagine how conflicted Peter must have felt that morning on the shore of Galilee. He had failed the Lord, but the Lord still wanted his love and wanted him to serve Him! For Peter, it was intimately up close and personal. For Peter, discipleship was about his love for Jesus and his devotion to Him. His discipleship had nothing to do with what others would do or would not do. It had nothing to do with what cost other disciples might not have to pay in suffering. It had nothing to do with the fame or fortunes of other disciples. It was strictly, and very personally, between Peter and Jesus. Wow — what a powerful moment!

The Lord was inviting Peter into a love relationship that would compel him to move forward in serving Him and to endure any and every trial, hardship, wound, rejection, disappointment and pain. For Peter, it was about forsaking his own plans and pleasures, like being a fisherman, and about serving the Lord in a wholly dedicated fashion. For Peter, discipleship was about being willing to suffer and die if necessary to be a faithful follower of Christ. It would require that he would never deny Jesus again under any circumstances. For Peter, it was about devotedly following Jesus until the day he would die. Peter was a LIFER!

The greatest lesson of this story is that the one and only thing that would keep Peter faithful to this calling through thick and thin, and for the long haul of life, was love for Jesus. "Simon, son of Jonah, do you love me? *Then* feed my sheep!" It was Peter's love for Jesus that would continue to motivate him throughout his life and would sustain him to the end. And that is the one and only thing that will keep you and me faithful in following the Lord Jesus and serving Him all the days of our lives – our love for Him!

What is discipleship about to you? Put your name in the blank: Jesus is asking you, "_____, do you love me? _____, if you love me it means you will serve me. If you love me it means you may have to suffer for my name's sake. _____, do you love me enough to follow and serve me until the day you die?" It is up close and personal for you like it was for Peter. It is just between *you* and Jesus. Do *you* love Him? Will *you* serve Him? Will *you* be faithful to Him through thick and thin? Will *you* serve Him until you draw your last breath? This is what Jesus very personally wants from you, and from me.

Clearly, this is not only what discipleship was for Peter, but also what it is for you and me. There is only one thing that will cause us to continue throughout our life living for the Lord, selflessly serving Him, sacrificing our plans and pleasures to follow Him, to pursue His will for our lives, and to suffer for Him. And that one thing is love–love for Jesus! It is our relationship with Him that drives us. The one thing that will motivate us to faithful discipleship throughout life's journey is to love Him because He first loved us. That was Paul's motive, too. In Galatians 2:20, he says about the Lord Jesus, "Who loved *me* and gave Himself for *me*" (emphasis added). It was Paul's passion to know Christ in the intimacy of a relationship with Him!

> More than that, I also consider everything to be a loss in view of the surpassing value of knowing Christ Jesus my Lord. Because of Him I have suffered the loss of all things and consider them filth (rubbish or trash), so that I may gain Christ (Philippians 3:8).

Not only do you and I have the assurance that Jesus loved us and died for us, but Revelation 1:5 explains: "Now to him who *loves* us and has set us free by his own blood" (emphasis added). Here is the one and only place in the New Testament that says in the present tense, right now, that Jesus loves us! His continuing love also motivates us to love Him back, to live for Him and serve Him.

Peter learned the lesson, and history tells us the rest of the story—how he responded remarkably to it. Because of his love and devotion to Jesus, thousands heard him preach on the Day of Pentecost and believed in Jesus and in His power to save! Then Peter preached to a more modest-sized group of Gentiles at the home of Cornelius, and that opened the door for millions upon millions, and perhaps billions of Gentiles to believe in the Lord Jesus Christ.

As Jesus indicated to Peter that morning when they ate breakfast together on the shore of Galilee, His plan for each disciple's life is different and unique. Each of us should seek and pursue the personal plan and mission He has for us, regardless of what others may do. Like Peter, discipleship for *you* is one-on-one, up-close and personal with Jesus. Are *you* going to love Him supremely, stand up for Him boldly, serve Him faithfully, and follow Him until the day you die?

The Seven Principles of Disciple-Making

A disciple is one who follows Jesus and leads others to do likewise. It is not enough to be His disciple. He has called us to make disciples! The primary purpose of the whole hurch is to make disciples out of every ethnic group in the world. It is to make a disciple out of each and every person who is willing to trust in Christ and to follow Him.

> Then Jesus came near and said to them, "All authority has been given to me in heaven and on earth. Go, therefore, and make disciples of all nations, baptizing them in the name of the Father and of the Son and of the Holy Spirit, teaching them to observe everything I

have commanded you. And remember, I am with you always, to the end of the age" (Matthew 28:18–20).

Discipleship is extremely important as it has been modeled and practiced by Jesus Himself and has been commanded by Him. The solution to the general weakness in the affluent church in Western culture is spiritual depth. And spiritual depth is just what we defined as being like Jesus.

The Great Commission is more about depth than about strategy or technique. Fostering spiritual transformation is the primary and exclusive work of the church. The evidence of being a follower of Jesus is following Jesus. It is about commitment and passion in seeking God's will and then following His direction.

The big question is, *"How do we make disciples?"* We will soon examine some specific, practical methods of making disciples. However, first, it is important to understand the philosophy or principles behind disciple-making.

Principle # 1 – Discipleship Is Intentional

First, discipleship is intentional on the part of the disciple-maker. But it must also be intentional on the part of the new or immature disciple. For him, discipleship must be a definite and distinctive answering of a personal call to follow Jesus.

To make a disciple then, our first task is to help a person recognize that Jesus is calling them personally to make a commitment to follow Him. Each individual must choose to follow Christ and thus be His disciple. When Jesus encountered Matthew the tax collector and called him to follow Him, Matthew did so immediately. When He called four fishermen named Peter, Andrew, James, and John to come and follow Him, they chose to be his disciples, left their nets and followed Him.

When we choose to be Christ's disciple, it does not necessarily mean a change in vocation or home location. It simply means that we will follow Him in our lives to go where He wants to take us, to learn what He wants to teach us, and to become what He wants us to become.

> Then, moving on, He saw Levi the son of Alphaeus
> sitting at the tax office, and He said to him, "Follow
> Me!" So he got up and followed Him (Mark 2:14).

As in the case of Levi, whom most of us know better as Matthew, Jesus tapped him on the shoulder and invited him to follow Him. Jesus's call was intentional, and the way He tapped or called Matthew required that Matthew's decision be an intentional one to follow Him. Like Jesus, we must tap people, and extend Jesus's call to them. Jesus prayed all night before choosing His disciples, and we should pray for the Spirit's leading as to who we should tap and explain the call to.

To make disciples, we must share with them the importance and power of Christ's call, and we must help them see the long-term vision of what following Jesus is about. When Jesus called His disciples, He had a vision for their lives, and they were aware that He had a vision for their lives. He was going to train them to become something special. This is the vision we must share with those we disciple. It is the vision we must instill in them. It is the vision they must catch from us. If it is not the obvious feature of our lives, then they will not be affected. Only a fire in you can ignite a fire in another. Jesus had a fire in His life, a fire of vision of the Father's will for Himself, and He in turn called His disciples to receive that same kind of fire in their lives.

Making disciples requires that we see the potential in people's lives. It also necessitates that we understand they will miss enormous blessings in this life and eternal reward in the life to come if we do not inspire them to follow Christ as His disciple. Since discipleship is intentional, it means that we must do as Christ did, and tap people. We must issue the challenge to them to enter the process of following Christ as His disciple. We must engage them and give them the opportunity to make that decision to become involved in active discipleship growth.

Principle # 2 – Discipleship Is Sacrificial

Jesus calls us to deny ourselves the right to be in charge of our own lives. He has already modeled this for us. We must explain this to anyone we wish to disciple. They must be willing to surrender their lives to truly follow Christ. Discipleship requires a high level of commitment. Being a Christian is not fun and games or an easy road. It is therefore necessary to assist those we disciple to understand the commitment they are making. They must know that discipleship is a journey and that it will require devotion to Christ and determination to endure and to persevere.

> Jesus said to His disciples, "If anyone wants to come with me, he must deny himself, take up his cross, and follow me" (Matthew 16:24).

But while explaining to potential disciples the commitment required, we should also cast a vision in their minds of the rewards. Although demanding and difficult at times, following Christ in life is richly and profoundly rewarding. It gives the individual believer a life of faith-adventure with Christ. It results in God's blessings on marriages and families. It builds strong character. It develops wonderful relationships with those who journey together as disciples. It produces fruitfulness in impacting the lives of others for time and eternity. It leaves a lasting legacy behind and enters an eternal legacy after this life.

One of the great privileges of my life was working with the chairman of the deacons of the first church I served as pastor. Olin Cantrell had a fourth grade education, but that didn't stop him from being a great servant of the Lord and a man highly admired in the community. Accepting Christ as a young couple, he and his wife Amy served the Lord in incredibly sacrificial ways. Every Sunday morning for over thirty years Olin went to the prison where he was the volunteer chaplain and taught Bible classes. Afterward he went home for breakfast and then to our church where he taught our main adult Bible class. After our worship service it was home for Sunday dinner and then back to the prison to preach for a church service that inmates and their families attended. There were many prisoners who accepted Christ over the years and many were transported to our church to be baptized.

Every time the doors of the church were open, Olin and Amy

were there. Another deacon in our church who worked at the same textile mill with Olin informed me that that Olin turned down double time pay many times, and one time even triple time pay, just to be in church. And Olin was the kind of man who never told anyone! Yes, they also sacrificed some of the finer things of life in order to support the ministries of the church.

Olin and Amy opened their modest home to host and entertain many evangelists and missionaries. And Amy was an amazing cook. She always set wonderful food on the table, although she worked a full-time job as a short-order cook at a local restaurant. Her north Georgia red-eye gravy, country fried ham and biscuits were "to die for!" Amy taught Bible classes, worked in our Vacation Bible School, and did everything she could to support her husband as they served the Lord. Her personality was magnetic, and the church could only hold about half of the people who came to pay their respects at her funeral service.

Olin and Amy Cantrell were very ordinary people, but by living faithful and sacrificial lives one day at a time they were genuine disciples who had an impressive witness and left an impactful and lasting legacy. They were ordinary people who served the Lord in extraordinary ways! What kind of disciple are you? Are you living a faithful and sacrificial life for your Lord who gave His life for you?

Principle # 3 – Discipleship Is Relational

Discipleship is relational as we observe firsthand the interaction of Jesus with His disciples in the Gospels.

He said to them, "I have called you friends" (John 15:15).

He prayed with them, ate with them, traveled with them, ministered with them, and even washed their feet in an act of love and humility. Discipleship is relational!

To disciple other people, we must enter into a relationship with them and spend time with them. We must share our lives with them and be open to them sharing their lives with us. This is a powerful dynamic!

God uses those who are willing to be humble and to meet others on the same level. While it is true that the one who disciples a young disciple may be at a much higher level of maturity and knowledge, he must meet the young disciple on his level. It must be a brother to brother or sister to sister relationship. Mentoring is different as it is more a father to son or mother to daughter relationship.

Discipleship requires that the young disciple have a humble and submissive spirit. When he does, he will be teachable and will grow. A leader must gain the love and respect of those he would disciple in order to be successful in teaching and training them. Only then will there be an openness of spirit to receive a transfer of living truth.

On the other hand, anyone who is interested in growing as a disciple must be willing to commit himself to be taught and to be held accountable to grow spiritually. A man who was young in the faith and was a member of a church I served as pastor came to me with sincere, humble and passionate desire and said, "Pastor, I want you to teach me. If you see anything in my life that is displeasing to the Lord, please rebuke me. I want to grow and become a servant for God." A disciple will grow when he has a heart of humility and a teachable spirit. And that brother grew!

Principle # 4 – Discipleship Is Transformational

Discipleship is a process of transformation of character into Christ-likeness. Therefore, those who disciple others must model Christ-like character and must teach and train other disciples in living out Christ-like character. There are some good books to utilize in this process. We will address it more thoroughly in a later chapter on *The Deportment of Essential Christianity – Character and Conduct.*

> It is enough for the disciple to be like his teacher, and the servant like his master (Matthew 10:25).

Principle # 5 – Discipleship Is Communal

Spiritual growth and discipleship are fostered by a disciple's spiritual connection and interaction with other disciples in the context of loving and learning from one another. It is therefore necessary that those who disciple others teach them that they must become a part of and participate in a church body or a church group, a community of disciples.

The redwood trees of California illustrate the necessity of discipleship in connection and interaction with other disciples. I have personally visited a redwood forest in Northern California, and the sight of the redwoods is stunning. The redwood tree species contains the largest and tallest trees in the world. No one has ever successfully painted or photographed a redwood tree. The feeling they produce is not transferable. Observing them creates silence and awe. Someone has commented on Wikipedia that, "It's not only their unbelievable stature, nor the color which seems to shift and vary under your eyes. No, they are not like any trees we know. They are ambassadors from another time." The average age of the redwood trees is 500–700 years old. The tallest known redwood tree is 379 feet tall. But here is the kicker. Redwoods do not have a deep tap-root to hold them up despite many of them standing 200–300 feet tall or taller. What is the secret power that holds them up? Their root systems are intricate and are connected to one another like an underground web. That connection of their roots is literally what holds them up and sustains them! No redwood grows alone. They require multiple trees to connect in their root system. And so it is with disciples of Jesus Christ!

> For the training of the saints in the work of ministry, to build up the body of Christ, until we all reach unity in the faith and in the knowledge of God's Son, growing into a mature man with a stature measured by Christ's fullness. Then we will no longer be little children, tossed by the waves and blown around by every wind of teaching, by human cunning with cleverness in the techniques of deceit. But speaking

the truth in love, let us grow in every way into Him
who is the head—Christ. From Him the whole body,
fitted and knit together by every supporting ligament,
promotes the growth of the body for building up itself
in love by the proper working of each individual part
(Ephesians 4:12–16).

Principle # 6 – Discipleship Is Purposeful

The purpose of discipleship is to become a trained and useful tool
for Christ to serve Him by doing ministry for Him. To disciple, we must
assist the young disciple in discovering his spiritual giftedness and in
becoming involved in ministry to others.

And He personally gave some to be apostles, some
prophets, some evangelists, some pastors and teachers,
for the training of the saints in the work of ministry, to
build up the body of Christ, until we all reach unity in
the faith and in the knowledge of God's Son, growing
into a mature man with a stature measured by Christ's
fullness (Ephesians 4:11–13).

Principle # 7 – Discipleship Is Missional

The culminating goal and purpose of discipleship is for the disciple
to make other disciples. The disciple must become a disciple-maker to
fulfill his ultimate role and for the world to be reached for Jesus Christ.
Only as each disciple does his or her part to make disciples can the Great
Commission of making disciples of all nations or ethnic groups be fulfilled.

Disciple-makers must assist the one they disciple in finding someone
else who they can disciple. As disciple-makers, we must also assist our
disciple in training him to make other disciples. He has observed you in
this process. Then let him assist you in making a new disciple. Finally,
you observe and assist him as he makes a new disciple.

You did not choose Me, but I chose you. I appointed
you that you should go out and produce fruit and that
your fruit should remain (John 15:16).

As the Father has sent me, I also send you (John 20:21 -
See also Matthew 28:18–20; Mark 16:15; Luke 24:46–
49; & Acts 1:8).

Are you a true disciple of Jesus? Are you a disciple of Jesus who
has not been following Him closely? Would you at this moment bow
your head in prayer and rededicate your life to follow Christ more
faithfully? Have you been a disciple for years yet never been a disciple-
maker? Are you willing to dedicate yourself to learn to become a
disciple-maker?

The Biblical Methods of Disciple-Making

Follow-Up or Basic Discipleship

While the first phase of disciple-making is evangelism, the
second one, and critically important, is what some call "follow-up"
or "basic discipleship." Follow-up is taking a new Christian, someone
who has recently accepted Christ, or a new couple that have recently
accepted Christ, and teaching them the basics of the Christian life. I
have personally done follow-up many times and have trained people
in churches I have served to do it as well. Follow-up is simple, easy,
extremely effective and richly rewarding for everyone involved.

So how do you do follow-up? There are a number of great resources
that are great tools to use. Evangelist Steve Hale has produced an
excellent booklet for this purpose. You will need to contact his ministry
directly to acquire it. I also have a follow-up booklet called *How To Live
the Christian Life*. Booklets such as these address subjects like assurance
of salvation, baptism, the importance of being an active part of a church
family, prayer, reading the Bible devotionally, dealing with temptation,
stewardship, and sharing the gospel with others.

Follow-up is usually most effective when an individual or couple teaches a new Christian or a new Christian couple. It is best to meet weekly for about an hour in the home of the new Christian. It requires only about a seven- to eight-week commitment. The effectiveness of this ministry in grounding the new Christian is crucial. Significant results are almost always produced by follow-up, and richly-rewarding relationships grow out of it.

Transformational Discipleship Groups

This kind of discipleship group is pictured by the relationship Jesus had with three of the twelve —Peter, James, and John. Jesus spent intimate time alone with them. There is extraordinary transformational power in a group of this size (no more than four). Some discipleship experts have recognized the special dynamic of a group of no more than four. I have personally led a number of intimate discipleship groups of this size and chose to call them "transformational discipleship groups." Watching how God works in the lives of individuals in these groups and sharing in their fellowship and growth is encouraging and inspiring. At the same time, the experience has also challenged and strengthened me in my walk with the Lord. It has thrilled me to see mediocre, shallow, and sometimes struggling believers become strong, grounded believers who are excited, strong, and stable.

In forming an intimate or transformational discipleship group, you may have one mature believer leading two or three immature believers who are ready and willing to grow, or a group may be composed of two mature believers with two immature ones that are ready and willing to grow. In that case, one of the mature believers must be the leader with the other mature believer assisting and the two of them co-leading. All four individuals in this intimate group setting will benefit from this relationship.

Because the group is so small, true openness about their lives can be freely expressed when there is a group commitment to strict confidentiality. Meeting weekly for interactive Bible study, prayer, and sharing about their lives makes for a dynamic and transformational environment.

In forming transformational discipleship groups, several practical tips might prove helpful. First, Gary Ogden's discipleship manual or workbook, *Discipleship Essentials*, is an excellent tool for this purpose. A meeting place can be either in a home or at church. The time allotted for the meeting should not be less than one and one-half hours weekly.

How do you start a group? First pray for several weeks and think about people who may be ready to grow spiritually but just need the right opportunity and invitation. Then personally invite several people to a no-obligation, introductory meeting to learn more about the opportunity.

In your introductory meeting, explain the spiritual and practical benefits of being part of a discipleship group. When possible, utilize testimonies of past leaders and participants. Assure them that as the process moves along they will build strong, deep, satisfying relationships with those in the group. They also may find that their relationships with family and others may be greatly improved because of their spiritual growth. Most of all, their personal relationship with the Lord will come to life for them. They will probably experience a more intimate relationship with the Lord.

It also may help to explain the purpose of the groups: to stimulate, support, and hold one another accountable in a process of spiritual growth. Let them know that in the process of discussing the study materials, praying together and sharing about their lives, they will encourage and bless each other.

They also need to know the commitment that they will be making. It will be a covenant they will sign and date stating that they will commit to be very regular and faithful in attending the weekly meetings, in studying the discipleship materials weekly, and in keeping in strictest confidence the personal matters discussed in the meetings. This kind of pledge or commitment is included in Ogden's workbook, *Discipleship Essentials*. Make sure they understand that they are also committing to seriously consider leading or co-leading a new transformational discipleship group after finishing with the group they are now starting with. You should also tell them how long the time commitment is for meeting with the group.

Let them know that no one is expected to talk about intimate details of their lives, but that sometimes that may be done voluntarily. This will be an opportunity to pray together for the Lord's help and guidance and to support a group member that may be facing some challenging circumstances or even a crisis.

Finally, those considering becoming a part of the transformational discipleship group will need to know the nuts and bolts of how the meetings work. There are normally three elements to the meetings: Sharing about your week and your walk with the Lord, discussing the discipleship material you have been studying during the week, and praying together. If you are using *Discipleship Essentials*, you may want to explain that the book has 25 lessons and you will study half the lesson per week. *Discipleship Essentials* has a natural break in all lessons that ends just before the "Reading" for the first half of the lesson and begins with the "Reading" for the second half of the lesson. With 25 lessons, taking half a lesson per week, and canceling a few times due to holidays or inclement weather, you are looking at a little over one year to complete the group's time together.

One very important thing you must do is to emphasize over and over again that this is not a class. It is a transformational discipleship group, growing and doing life together. A class implies learning facts and information. Calling your group a class would encourage a mindset of learning facts and information rather that aiming at transformation of life. This important point cannot be overemphasized. You must cultivate a mindset that this discipleship group is about spiritual growth.

I believe that this approach to disciple-making has more potential than anything else to make the greatest impact in the individual lives of believers and in the local church too. This approach can transform not only individuals, but also churches! After you start your group, it will be a joy to watch as those in the group bond, members of the group open up to one another, feel connected in their life-walk to one another, and pray for one another. Few experiences in life can compare to the enriching and fulfilling results of being part of this kind of discipleship group. These relationships will often last decades after the group stops meeting.

Many churches use small group ministries as a support and growth network for their churches. There are some good benefits with the ministry of small groups; however, there are even greater benefits with intimate transformational discipleship groups due to the dynamics produced by the size of the group. Both kinds of ministries can certainly be used effectively. Some people who are not ready to make the commitment to be involved in transformational discipleship may feel the need of fellowship and the support of a small group and may feel more comfortable in a group that size.

Another effective disciple-making option is the Alpha Course, which introduces never-churched and un-churched people to the basic truths of the gospel. Many churches have used this program with great effectiveness.

A disciple-making program that is another option is called MasterLife, a Lifeway book series that is effective, according to Leland Hamby, senior pastor of Alhambra Baptist Church in California. His church has used MasterLife for more than twelve years and has found it productive in producing disciples. And, of course, there are other programs that certainly may also be effective in producing disciples. The important thing is to be committed to making disciples and to find what works for your church. Then establish it as a ministry.

Leadership Training

A leadership group is demonstrated for us by the twelve apostles. This core group represents those who have potential to be leaders and to serve in significant ways. They are to be taught and trained (Ephesians 2:20). In training leaders, you may want to consider the workbook, *Leadership Essentials*, by Gary Ogden. Another book with a solid, biblical philosophy on leadership is *Spiritual Leadership – Moving People on to God's Agenda* by Henry Blackaby and his son, Richard Blackaby. *Spiritual Leadership – an Interactive Study* is the workbook that accompanies their book. J. Oswald Sander's book *Spiritual Leadership – Principles of Excellence for Every Believer* is a classic on the subject.

Mentoring

The last model of disciple-making is mentoring. This is seen in the apostle Paul. Paul mentored Timothy and Titus one-on-one. They were probably not the only ones he did this with, but they are the ones most observable in his writings. Mentoring has to do with developing someone else to be the same in calling, function, and ministry just like your own. It is much like training an apprentice for a vocation.

There are more great resources both for disciple-making and for mentoring. Some of these are provided in Appendix A.

"While you are going, make disciples!" (Matthew 28:19)

Chapter 3

The Doctrines of Authentic Christianity

The Seven Foundational Convictions of Authentic Christianity

There Is:

One body,

One Spirit,

One hope of your calling,

One Lord,

One faith,

One baptism,

One God and Father of all.

Ephesians 4:4–6

Believing Christianly

71

The Truths That Unite Us

The Seven Foundational Convictions
of Authentic Christianity

My quest to discover the essential beliefs of the Christian faith began years ago with a question from a member of my congregation: "Pastor, what are the beliefs that must be held by a church for it to be a Christian church?" This question both challenged and intrigued me. I was aware that there were varying opinions regarding what doctrines are basic to the Christian faith. The question that captivated my imagination was, "Which doctrines are *authoritatively* basic or essential to the Christian faith?" I asked myself, "Does God somehow convey to us specifically and clearly those beliefs that are required and basic to Christian faith?" Years later I was to discover that He has!

Why is it important to identify and to define the essential beliefs of Christianity? It is important because in a world of confusion of doctrines, dogmas, philosophies, religions, heresies, and cults, the essence of Christianity has often become obscured or distorted. The result is a prevailing ignorance, deception, and uncertainty. What an individual or a society believes is important because it defines and determines who we are. Our beliefs or worldview influences our character and shapes our culture. The impact of beliefs affects individuals and nations and determines their ultimate destiny.

The essential truths of Christianity form a standard of measurement, a rule by which every church or organization that claims to be Christian can be evaluated. This means that there is an objective standard by which every religious sect, cult, or group may be judged to determine whether it is Christian in its teachings or whether it fails to be genuinely Christian.

The essential Christian doctrines are not stale creeds. They are dynamic truths that transform and motivate true Christians to live differently. They are truths that require action and compel a life of commitment. Our lives must be built on them, must reflect them and testify to others about them.

Defining the essential beliefs does not reduce Christian faith to its lowest common denominators. Instead it boils Christian truth down to its most potent ingredients. In 1995 my wife and I toured the countries of Jordan, Israel, and Egypt. While in Cairo, Egypt, we visited a store for tourists that sold exotic fragrances. The perfumes were expensive because they had no alcohol in them. They were the pure essence with nothing added. These perfumes of pure substance were indivisible because if any element would be removed from them then they would cease to be the substance and essence that they were. The same is true for the essence of Christianity. These perfumes were potent in fragrance. Christianity in its doctrinal essentials or essence is both irreducible and potent.

The essentials, according to Paul, both require and encourage the unity of all true Christian believers (Ephesians 4:1–6). In fact, the context in which these doctrines are given to us is one where Paul is appealing for unity in the local church of Ephesus. He continues in this same chapter to insist that the essential truths are necessary to the spiritual growth of believers individually and corporately and that they provide stability, strength, and protection in the face of false teachings (Ephesians 4:13–15). They also promote holy living and empower the Church in its spiritually militant battle against the forces of darkness (Ephesians 6:11–16).

Christ and His redemptive work are the heart and core of Christian truth and God's revelation to man. And, as we will see, the triune God permeates and animates the entire body of Christian truth.

There Is One Final, Written Revelation from God
The Holy Scriptures

There is one essential element of Christian faith that is already established and assumed prior to the New Testament. In fact, it probably was not considered a doctrine by the Jews and early Christians. This early Christian essential was belief in the Holy Scriptures as the written revelation from God. It was the authoritative, revered, and holy *medium of doctrine*, not itself a doctrine.

It is almost impossible to adequately express the reverence that Jews of both the Old Testament and the New Testament eras had for the Old Testament scriptures. God had spoken! His Word is proclaimed: "Thus says the LORD!" This is *God's* revelation through His Word, the Holy Scriptures. The most basic and staunchest conviction of all Christian truth begins with the accepted premise of the divine inspiration and authority of the Scriptures. Without this, all other doctrines have no foundational authority supporting them. Without this, all doctrines become simply human choices and conjectures.

> And that from childhood you have known the sacred Scriptures, which are able to instruct you for salvation through faith in Christ Jesus. All Scripture is inspired (literally "God-breathed" - Greek: "theopneustos" θεοπνευστος) by God and is profitable for teaching, for rebuking, for correcting, for training in righteousness (2 Timothy 3:15–16).

> First of all, you should know this: no prophecy of Scripture comes from one's own interpretation, because no prophecy ever came by the will of man; instead, moved by the Holy Spirit, men spoke from God (2 Peter 1:20–21).

Psalm 119:89 declares, "Forever, O LORD, Your word is settled in heaven" (NASB). "Jesus said, 'For truly I say to you, until heaven and earth pass away, not the smallest letter or stroke shall pass from the Law until all is accomplished'" (Matthew 5:18 NASB). He also stated: "Heaven and earth will pass away, but My words will not pass away" (Mark 13:31 NASB).

The very nature of the Scripture, the Holy Bible, is that it is God's revelation to man. This is a compelling suggestion to us that God wanted to preserve His revelation so that all people could know it.

The purpose of the Holy Scriptures is that people might know about God and might have the opportunity to know Him in a personal relationship. Scripture explains to us what God is like. It describes His character, wisdom, and power. The Bible makes definitive statements about God and also tells us some of His names. Those names reveal to us a great deal about Him. Holy Scripture declares His creative works so that we might see His wisdom and power visibly demonstrated. They chronicle His relationship with individuals so that we might understand the kind of relationship He wants with us.

The Bible reveals God's involvement in human history as He deals with the nations. It reveals His compassion and forgiveness in His Son because the Father sent Him to become a human being and to minister to hurting and helpless people. It declares His holiness and justice in view of sin and His wrath and judgment against it. The Bible also reveals His love, mercy, and grace through the voluntary suffering and death of His Son for the sins of the world.

God's Word demonstrates God's plan for the present age through His gracious work in calling out from among the nations a people to bear His name and through whom He will be glorified (Acts 15:14). This group of people is the Church. Thus God not only embraces the Jewish nation but also the Gentiles in His expansive love for all of mankind. Furthermore, Holy Scripture helps us understand God better by telling us His plan for the consummation of earthly history. The Word of God also gives us glimpses of His plans for eternity to come.

Unless you have a firm conviction that the Bible is the inspired and authoritative Word of God, you have no sure foundation of faith to build on. The Bible is either a creative work of man's imagination or it is a work so guided by the Spirit of God that it is God's Word and revelation even though He used human agents to write it. After enjoying the following wonderful poem by the great reformer, Martin Luther, we will turn to the essential truths of Christianity as given in Ephesians 4:4–6.

God's Unchanging Word
Martin Luther

For feelings come, and feelings go, and feelings are deceiving;
My warrant is the Word of God, naught else is worth believing.
Though all my heart should feel condemned
by want of some sweet token,
There is one greater than my heart whose Word cannot be broken.
I'll trust in God's unchanging Word 'till soul and body sever –
For though all things shall pass away, His Word will stand forever!

How Do We Determine Which Doctrines Are Essential to Authentic Christianity?

The cardinal question in identifying the essential doctrines of Christianity is how do we authoritatively decide which doctrines are essential and which are not? The answer cannot rest on human opinion because human opinion lacks divine authority. Perhaps that is why God has made the identification of the essential doctrines simple and clear in His Word.

God has revealed the essential truths to us in Ephesians 4:4–6. In this passage, Paul is pressing a practical principle of what unites all Christians and should therefore call all to a practical unity in the local church. It is no coincidence that the Holy Spirit directed Paul to write this Scripture because in it we are given the entire body of essential Christian convictions or beliefs.

The seven spiritual truths, doctrines, or convictions that form the body of essential Christian belief are:

1. *one body,* (the Church)
2. *one Spirit,* (the Holy Spirit)
3. *one hope of your calling;* (Eternal Life, Resurrection, Immortality)
4. *one Lord,* (Jesus Christ)

5. *one faith,* (the Gospel)
6. *one baptism;* (Confession of Faith – Commitment to Discipleship)
7. *one God and Father of all* (God the Father)

One Body - The Church

It is natural that Paul would begin with this unifying truth in pressing his appeal for unity in a local church. We are one in Christ, and therefore that unity should not be violated or harmed. That is why unity should be carefully and diligently preserved in the local church, but also in spirit in the universal Church as well. The phrase "there is one body" indicates both uniqueness and unity. The body is one and thus united in Christ in a number of ways:

- *Functionally* in the use of the spiritual gifts in maintaining and building up the body (1 Corinthians 12)
- *Organically* in its shared life in Christ and the relationship of the members of the body to one another (Ephesians 4:16 & 5:30)
- *Relationally* in the relationship of all of its members to the Head (Colossians 1:18)
- *Authoritatively* in relationship to its Head (Ephesians 5:23–24)
- *Sympathetically* or emotionally in the love Christ has for all members of the body and thus the love they should have for one another (Ephesians 5:29)

Every New Testament truth about the Church is spoken in this brief phrase, "one body." We as believers are the Church. The Church is not an institution, an organization, or a denomination. The Church is the spiritual body of Christ. This is a doctrine that is essential to Christianity in several ways. It is essential because God ordained the Church as His great mystery that would be ultimately revealed, and He appointed the Church to be the Bride of His Son. The Church is essential as God's present program in and for this world.

The Church is, first of all, the planned mystery of God that was hidden from previous ages and generations. The Church was born in a moment of history on the day of the Feast of Pentecost (Acts 2), and God has revealed the Church in this present age (Ephesians 3:1–11). Jesus gave the apostles teaching that anticipated the Church as He spoke about it in the future tense in Matthew 16:18. However, Jesus gave no specific truth about this mystery except for certain principles that would be involved in it (John chapters 14–16).

The mystery of the Church was also anticipated by the Abrahamic Covenant. It promised that in Abraham's seed all nations or families of the earth would be blessed (Genesis 12:3). In fact, God established the nation of Israel as His representative to the nations of the world suggesting God's perpetual interest in all peoples of all nations for all time (Exodus 19:5–6). The prophet Isaiah announced that all flesh would see the glory of the Lord (Isaiah 40:5), and he announced that the servant of the Lord would bring forth judgment to the Gentiles and would be the light of the Gentiles (42:1, 6).

The Church was created by the redemptive work of Christ, bringing both Jew and Gentile together into one reconciled and united body (Ephesians 2:11–16 & 3:6). The Church has thus become a new and unique people of God similar to, but distinct from, the Jewish nation (1 Peter 2:9–10). Paul distinguishes the Church as a group in 1 Corinthians 10:32 when he says: "Give no offense to the Jews or the Greeks (Gentiles) or the church of God." In Revelation 21 we discover the image of the two distinct peoples of God - Israel and the Church. In the description of the New Jerusalem, the gates have inscribed on them the names of the twelve tribes of Israel representing the Jewish nation as the people of God. The foundations of the walls have the names of the twelve apostles representing the Church as the people of God. Both peoples of God - Israel, Jewish believers from the Old Testament era, and the Church, Jewish and Gentile believers from the New Testament era - will share in the eternal Kingdom of God!

The Church was created through the agency of the Holy Spirit. He places all believers into union with Jesus Christ and lives in all believers as the Spirit of Christ, or Christ in them (1 Corinthians 12:13 & John 14:20). Therefore, it is actually in the person of the Holy Spirit that Christ lives in believers. Since the Father, Son, and Holy Spirit are one in three and are three in one, each member of the Godhead, though distinct, also represents the presence of the other members of the Godhead. Therefore, the Holy Spirit indwelling the believer is essentially the same as Christ indwelling the believer. Thus, the Church is not a human organization but rather a spiritual organism indwelt by the Holy Spirit (1 Corinthians 3:16–17; Note that "you" in these verses is plural, not singular; See also Ephesians 2:19–22). The Church is a living, corporate Temple being built by Jesus Christ with Him as the chief cornerstone or keystone (1 Peter 2:4–8).

The Church is the espoused, "betrothed," or "legally married without the marriage being yet consummated," Bride of Christ (2 Corinthians 11:2). She is loved by Him and will be presented to Him for intimate consummation of marriage, an eternal and intimate relationship (Ephesians 5:25–27). Christ, and Christ alone, is the head both of His Body and of His Bride (Ephesians 1:22-23).

The Church is also the spiritual army of Christ (Ephesians 6:10–18). The Church has been authorized and commissioned with an urgent and crucial task of universal proportions (Matthew 28:18–20). This task is known as the Great Commission. The Church has been given an invaluable gift, the Holy Spirit, to help in this task (Acts 1:4–8 & 2:1–4). She has been given a clear command by Christ Himself to carry out this commission (Matthew 28:18–20). Christ has promised that He would build His Church (Matthew 16:18) through His power and involvement, and this occurs as His Body carries out this Great Commission. The fulfillment of this commission will necessitate spiritual warfare in spiritual conflict with spiritual powers that are enemies of God, of Christ, and of God's people. Those enemies will wage war against the advancement of the gospel, the Church, and the coming kingdom (Matthew 16:18; Ephesians 6:10–18).

The Church is destined to be purified and presented in perfection as Christ's Bride, to be forever wedded to Him (Ephesians 5:25–27). She is also destined for ultimate victory and enthronement with Christ (Revelation 1:6; 19:6–8 and 20:4).

The sad truth is that fracturing the Church into many *opposing* denominations and sects is one of our adversary's highest priorities.

Hostilities between denominations that all believe in the essential Christian truths is detrimental to the unity that Christ desires and prayed for the evening before His death (John 17, especially verses 11, 21 and 23). We do not have to agree with every theological point to accept and love one another or to work effectively together for the cause of Christ. Believing the essential truths of the Christian faith should unify and unite us to love one another and to strive together for the advancement of the gospel and the expansion of the kingdom of Jesus Christ.

The Church's Calling

The Church Is Called in One Body

Colossians 1:15 speaks of the Church as being "called in one body." To appreciate the significance of this truth, consider what it means when a person is called of God to preach. God's calling is a powerful and compelling thing. The responsibility of being called of God to preach is expressed by Paul as he said: "Woe unto me if I do not preach the gospel!" The Church is called of God – each and every one of us! It means: (1) that we as the Church are specifically chosen by God (2) that God has a plan, purpose, and destiny for the Church, and, (3) that Christ has charged His Church with a sacred mission.

The Church Is Called to Be Holy

The Lord "has saved us and called us with a holy calling" (2 Timothy 1:9 NASB). In 1 Corinthians 1:2, Paul addresses his letter to the Corinthians: "To the church of God which is at Corinth, to those who have been sanctified in Christ Jesus, saints ('holy ones') by calling" (NASB). To the Thessalonians he declared: "God did not call us to be impure, but to live a holy life" (1 Thessalonians 4:7 NASB). Peter calls the Church "a holy nation" (1 Peter 2:9).

The word holy means sacred or consecrated. It means separated from that which is profane or ordinary. It also means hallowed. Jerry Bridges in his book, *The Pursuit of Holiness,* states: "Though we often think of holiness in a more narrow sense of separation from impurity and moral evil, in its broader sense holiness is separation to the will of God in whatever God directs."

Holiness is the consecration of our lives as they are set apart for God's holy purposes and to be lived for Him (Romans 12:1). This holiness or consecration includes a dedication to purity and separation from sin (2 Corinthians 7:1). When a believer separates himself to God, he leaves sinful living and sinful choices behind. Beyond that, holiness is also doing right or righteous conduct (Titus 2:12). This includes much more than abstaining from things we should not do, from overt sins. It also includes doing things we should be doing like serving the poor, telling the good news, generously giving of our time and our resources to serve and glorify God. The average Christian sins much more in this way than sinning overtly. Ultimately, holiness is the very expression of godly character (Ephesians 4:24).

The Bible challenges us: "discipline yourself for the purpose of godliness" (1 Timothy 4:7 NASB). It also commands: "Pursue peace with everyone, and holiness - without it no one will see the Lord" (Hebrews 12:14).

The world distracts disciples with its allurements and entertainment. It seduces disciples with the temptations of the flesh, with materialism, with values fostered by pride in achievement, and with fame and fortune. The fallen kingdom of this world and the kingdom of Jesus Christ are kingdoms in conflict. Believers may often attempt to straddle the fence between the world and Christ, but they do so to their own peril, and it will not work. Those who profess faith in Christ must choose who they are going to love and be loyal to, Christ or the world. A true disciple chooses loyalty to Christ.

Christian, you are called to be holy! Local church, you are called to be holy! The Church, corporately, all of God's people, is called to be holy. In Peter's first epistle, God's Word exhorts us: "But as the One who called you is holy, you also are to be holy in all your conduct; for it is written, Be holy, because I am holy" (1 Peter 1:15–16; cf. Leviticus 11:44–45; 19:2; 20:7).

The Church Is Called to Peace

God is "the God of peace" (Romans 15:33 & 16:20; Philippians 4:9; 1 Thessalonians 5:23; Hebrews 13:20). Jesus Christ has given us peace and has called us to be peacemakers (John 14:27; Matthew 5:9). The gospel or good news is "the gospel of peace" (Romans 10:15; 2 Corinthians 5:18). One aspect of the fruit of the Spirit is peace (Galatians 5:22; Romans 14:17). Christians are commanded to be at peace with one another (2 Corinthians 13:11; Colossians 3:15). Christians are commanded to do all in their power to live peaceably with all people (Romans 12:18; Hebrews 12:14).

God has called us to be at peace as Christ's Church. This means that we should not be rancorous, belligerent, pugnacious, and unnecessarily divisive. The Church, all true believers placed by the Holy Spirit into the Body of Christ, should stand firmly, uncompromisingly, and vigorously, though in a patient and loving spirit, for the essential or fundamental truths of the Christian faith, for the inspiration and authority of the Word of God, for the gospel of Jesus Christ and for moral righteousness. However, when secondary doctrines and other differences of opinion are in view, we should always address our disagreements with respect and brotherly kindness. It would be destructive to view other believers with differing opinions on secondary issues as enemies when in fact they are a part of the beloved body of our precious Lord. We should not be at war with one another over non-essential matters. It shatters the peace of the Church, hinders its effectiveness, and diminishes its testimony before the world.

The gospel and its claims that Christ is the one and only Savior will always create division because rebellious sinners will reject Him, will chaff against Him, and will resist the message concerning Him. The world will also militantly oppose the moral standards of God's Word. Division is unavoidable in such cases. However, Christians should not be divisive when it is not required. Neither should we be disrespectful and hostile even when division is necessary. Our spirit should be one of peace, respect, gentleness, and kindness toward all. Because our God is "the God of peace" we should be a people of peace.

This means that unity, true unity of spirit and of purpose, should be one of the very highest values of each and every disciple and of each and every local church. Unity is stressed by the term "one body" (Romans 12:4; 1 Corinthians 12:13; Ephesians 4:4). This means that no division should exist within the body, but rather equality, forgiveness and tolerance (1 Corinthians 12:25–26; Galatians 3:27–28; Romans 1:14). This is true both for the universal Church and also for each local church. The stress is on unity of purpose and spirit. There should be no politics and no partisanship in the church. God has called His people to peace – to be at peace with one another (Ephesians 4:1–3; Philippians 1:27 & 2:1–4). Politics is fractious, divisive, and discordant. It has no place in the local church. It is destructive to the spiritual health of the believers in the local body and to the public testimony of the church! Discord and division tarnish all that the Church represents as the Body of Christ.

Discord within the local church is usually caused by selfish ambition or a quest for power and control. The New Testament strongly denounces this kind of behavior in the church. Sadly, there are always people who demand that they have their way. In order to get their way, they will create division to force the church to comply. When this occurs, divisions are developed, hard feelings are formed, the work of the Holy Spirit is stifled, and the progress of the ministry and mission of the church comes to a standstill. And often many members are severely spiritually wounded in the process. This discord is one of Satan's most effective tools.

God gives a stern and terrifying warning to those who willfully damage and destroy the local church by causing division.

> Don't you know that you yourselves are God's temple and that God's Spirit lives in you? If anyone destroys God's temple God will destroy him; for God's temple is sacred, and you are that temple (1 Corinthians 3;16-17 NIV).

In that context the local church is God's temple (cf. Ephesians 2:19-23). Too many Christians do not grasp how sacred both the local church and the universal Church are, and how detestable it is for people to perpetuate problems, divisions, and disturbances that fracture and destroy its unity. The Church is precious to God, and the local church is a microcosm of the universal Church. Both should be cherished as precious, and they must be protected from destructive strife and division.

The Church should have no ethnic or racial distinctions, Jew or Gentile, no class or social distinctions, slave or free, no gender distinctions, male or female, and no educational or cultural distinctions, Greek or barbarian (Colossians 3:11). Each member is to be fully received and highly valued.

The Church Is Called to Suffer

> For you were called to this, because Christ also suffered for you, leaving you an example, so that you should follow in His steps (1 Peter 2:21).

Moody Magazine in its January/February 1999 edition states that every hour seventeen Christian believers die for their faith. The New York Times reported that one Nigerian lay preacher, when speaking to a suburban Denver congregation, described how he was tied to a tree and stoned by neighbors who claimed he had insulted their prophet Mohammed. More Christians have been killed for their faith in the last one hundred years than in the nineteen hundred years that preceded them. Voice of the Martyrs is a charity that ministers to the families of believers who have been martyred for their faith. Their website is well worth visiting in order to learn more about the persecution and suffering of Christians all over the world.

We live in a culture that craves self-indulgence and shrinks from suffering. Yet those of us who are Christ's disciples and called to follow Him are called to suffer for Him. The Church is called to suffer. We must do this as necessary for the sake of our Lord Jesus Christ. Satan and his godless world-system will persecute us and attack us, but we are to bear it for the cause of Christ and for His glory. We should expect it and should even embrace it.

The apostle Peter, in his first epistle, says a great deal about the believer's suffering. He uses the words "suffer" and "suffering" seventeen times! Peter admonishes us, "But if anyone suffers as a Christian, he should not be ashamed, but should glorify God with that name" (1 Peter 4:16). Joni Erikson Tada, a paraplegic who is a Christian and has a wonderful spirit, has said, "Joy is not the absence of suffering. It is the presence of the Lord." No one likes suffering, but if we are called to serve Christ in this way, we must do it with joy in our hearts, for it is an honor that associates us with Christ Himself.

Paul expresses this privilege we have to suffer for Christ's sake when he says, "For it has been given (or 'granted') to you on Christ's behalf not only to believe in Him, but also to suffer for Him" (Philippians 1:29). Of the early Christians it is said "they went out from the presence of the Sanhedrin, rejoicing that they were counted worthy to be dishonored (NASB – 'to suffer shame') on behalf of the name" (Acts 5:41). Paul said "that you may be counted worthy of the kingdom of God, for which you also suffer" (2 Thessalonians 1:5).

Sergei Omelchenko, a Christian from Ukraine who was persecuted under the former Soviet Union, declared: "Suffering has its own goal." Missionary Ronnie Bragg who served as a missionary for many years in Senegal, West Africa, stated that, "The world is only blessed by sacrifice."

To His disciples, Jesus said: "Are you able to be baptized with the baptism with which I was baptized? Whoever will follow me, let him take up his cross!" The cross we are to take up certainly symbolizes suffering that we must endure.

Today there are more than thirty countries where Christians are being severely persecuted, tortured, and killed. In Egypt, the Muslim Brotherhood and other militant Muslim groups are destroying churches and killing Christians. In other countries such as Afghanistan, Pakistan, and Somalia, the same actions are transpiring. In some places in India, Christians are persecuted and their churches destroyed by Hindus. In China, Christians in house-churches are persecuted, and their worship and witness is suppressed by the Communist government. Even in the United States, churches that defend biblical truth are increasingly under pressure and the threat of legal sanction. It is not difficult to imagine that such opposition might continue to increase here to the point of Christians being imprisoned for their convictions. These are only a few examples of the Church's suffering as she fulfills her calling to follow Christ.

Jesus said that no man could be His disciple unless he denies himself, takes up his cross, and follows Him (Mark 8:34). The Lord Himself also promises, "Blessed are you when they insult you and persecute you and falsely say every kind of evil against you because of me. Be glad and rejoice, because your reward is great in heaven" (Matthew 5:11–12).

If persecution comes, will you take up your calling to suffer and to do it for Jesus Christ willingly and gladly, and even if necessary, to the point of death? How will you answer that question in your own heart? How do you answer it in your spirit before Christ?

One Spirit - the Holy Spirit

It is of great importance that each believer understands and embraces the person, the real personality, of the Holy Spirit. He is God and is to be loved, admired, and worshiped. There are numerous evidences and proofs of the person or personality of the Holy Spirit. They are listed below:

First, there are names for the Holy Spirit that strongly imply personality. He is called "the Comforter" or "Helper" (John 14:16 & 16:7). This word means "one who is called to your side." In 1 John 2:1, the very same word is used of Jesus Christ. Jesus stated that the Holy Spirit was to come and take His place in guiding and helping us (John 14:16).

In addition, personal pronouns are used of the Holy Spirit (John 16:7, 8, 13–15). Twelve times in these verses the Greek masculine pronoun *ekeinos*, "that one" or "He," is used of the Spirit. That is especially remarkable because the pronoun should ordinarily be neuter to match the neuter noun "Spirit." This is a very strong indication of the Holy Spirit's personality.

In addition, the Holy Spirit is identified with the Father, Son, and Christians in such a way as to indicate personality:

- The Baptismal Formula   Matthew 28:19–20
- The Apostolic Benediction   2 Corinthians 13:14
- Identification with Christians   Acts 15:28

Another proof of the personality of the Holy Spirit is that personal characteristics are ascribed to the Holy Spirit.

- Knowledge and insight   1 Corinthians 2:10–11 & 1 Peter 1:11
- His will in giving spiritual gifts 1 Corinthians 12:11
- Mind – thought and purpose Romans 8:27 – cf. verse 7

One of the greatest evidences is that personal acts are ascribed to the Holy Spirit.

- The Spirit speaks   Revelation 2:7 & 1 Timothy 4:1
- The Spirit intercedes in prayer Romans 8:26
- He calls men for a mission   Acts 13:2, 16:6–7, 20:28

And finally, the Holy Spirit is susceptible to personal treatment.

- He may be grieved   Ephesians 4:30
- He may be insulted   Hebrews 10:29
- He may be sinned against   Matthew 12:31–32
- He can be lied to   Acts 5:3

From the very outset of Scripture, the Holy Spirit is visible in the Old Testament to the perceptive spiritual eye. The usual expression or designation for the Holy Spirit in the Old Testament is "the Spirit of God." He is seen at work in the work of creation (Genesis 1:2; Job 26:13). Perhaps the primary work of the Holy Spirit in the Old

Testament is the work of divine revelation through prophecy and in particular in inspiring the writings of the Holy Scriptures. The book of Ezekiel is a great illustration of this truth in terms of revelation being given to Ezekiel the prophet to write down (Ezekiel 2:2; 8:3; 11:1, 24). The Spirit came mightily on King Saul, and he prophesied (1 Samuel 10:6, 10). The apostle Peter clearly and specifically explains the work of the Holy Spirit in producing the sacred scriptures (2 Peter 1:20–21).

Millard Erikson in *Christian Theology* states, "Yet another work of the Spirit of God in the Old Testament was in conveying certain necessary skills for various tasks." The construction of the Tabernacle and the Temple were enhanced by the Spirit's work in equipping men with what appears to be supernatural wisdom and skill in their artisanship to perform their important tasks.

In terms of other works of the Spirit, it would appear that He endowed certain men with extraordinary wisdom for administration. This appears to be true of Joseph (Genesis 41:38). Perhaps this was also true for Joshua (Deuteronomy 34:9). Some leadership abilities also seemed to accompany the anointing of Israel's earliest kings for them to be able to lead the nation. An example was when David was anointed, as the Scripture says, by the Spirit of the LORD coming mightily upon him (1 Samuel 16:13).

Perhaps one of the most exciting and intriguing revelations about the Holy Spirit is the anticipation of His work in and alongside the coming Messiah (Isaiah 11:1–5; 42:1–4; 61:1–3). And finally, the Old Testament anticipates the future outpouring of the Holy Spirit on the Day of the Feast of Pentecost (Joel 2:28–29; cf. Acts 2:1–4 & 16–-21).

Millard Erikson says: "When we examine Jesus's life, we find a pervasive and powerful presence and activity of the Spirit throughout." And he is right! At the moment of Jesus's conception, the Holy Spirit came upon Mary and the power of the Highest overshadowed her so that the One to be born of her would be called the Son of God (Luke 1:35). Then, at the inauguration of His ministry as the Messiah, the Spirit descended on Jesus like a dove as Jesus was baptized in the waters of the Jordan River (Matthew 3:16). Jesus returned after His temptation in the power of the Spirit to initiate His ministry (Luke 4:14). By the

Spirit of God He cast out demons (Matthew 12:28). He rejoiced in the Holy Spirit seeing the blessing and power that was on His disciples whom He had sent out to preach, heal, and cast out demons (Luke 10:21). Then, in the very final hours of His life, came the moment when Jesus offered Himself as a sacrifice "through the eternal Spirit" (Hebrews 9:14). And finally, it was the Holy Spirit who raised Jesus from the dead (Romans 8:11).

The blessed Holy Spirit encompassed Jesus and supported Him in every moment throughout His life and raised Him from the dead. All of this is a testimony and seal of the Father's approval and affirmation of His Son as Messiah and also of His life and ministry. This testimony and seal was given in the manifest presence and power of the Spirit in and on the life of Jesus.

The Coming of the Holy Spirit

The coming of the Holy Spirit is recorded in Acts 2:1–4. The Holy Spirit was sent by the Father and the Son to finish the work God had begun in Christ and to fulfill God's purpose for the earth and for mankind. There are some monumental implications regarding the Spirit's coming. As we will see, the coming of the Holy Spirit initiated a new relationship, inaugurated a new age, and empowered a new movement.

1. The Coming of the Holy Spirit Initiated a New Relationship

During Old Testament times and during Jesus's ministry, the Holy Spirit never came to live in people. He would come "upon" people to give them special power to accomplish particular, important tasks. So His coming to live and abide in believers was a major change. Richard Longenecker says in *The Expositor's Bible Commentary*: "The relationship of the Spirit to the members of the body of Christ became much more intimate and personal at Pentecost, in fulfillment of Jesus's promise."

Jesus described this new relationship in new teachings He gave to

His apostles the night before His death. These teachings are found in John chapters 14–16. The teachings let the apostles know that a new relationship would exist, and He described what that relationship would be like:

a. A Relationship of Indwelling
b. A Relationship of Intimacy

Jesus also described for them the nature and quality of this new relationship:

- An Experience of Life – John 14:20 & 15:1–8
- An Experience of Love – John 14:21 & 15:9–10
- An Experience of Learning – John 14:26 & 16:12–15
- An Experience of Peace – John 14:27 & 16:33
- An Experience of Joy – John 15:11 & 16:22–24

2. The Coming of the Holy Spirit Inaugurated a New Age

His coming marked the beginning of the spiritual kingdom, the Church (Joel 2:28–29; 1 Corinthians 12:13; Romans 14:17; Colossians 1:13).

a. The Age of the Church as Distinct from Israel

The Church was a mystery, but was created in time after Jesus made it possible by His blood or sacrifice. It was the creation of a new people of God, Jews and Gentiles bonded together as the body and Bride of Christ (Ephesians 2:11–22).

b. The Age of Grace as Distinct from the Law

The Feast of Pentecost was for Judaism the day of the giving of the Law. The fact of the Spirit's coming on this very day, represents the beginning of a new age or dispensation.

The Law was given through Moses, but grace and truth came into existence through Jesus Christ (John 1:17).

To understand the new age or dispensation of grace, simply put, some of the salient features are: Grace is a pardon, a position, a power, and a provision.

Grace is a *pardon* for sin through Christ (Acts 13:38–39).
Grace is a *position* of favor in Christ (Romans 5:2).
Grace is a *power* to live victoriously through Christ (Romans 7:24–8:4).
Grace is a *provision* of eternal blessings because of Christ (Ephesians 2:7).

3. The Coming of the Holy Spirit Empowered a New Movement

The very language of the event of the coming of the Holy Spirit clearly declares that His coming is about a new, epic mission. Notice in Acts chapter 2 the expressive and dynamic language and its symbolic emphasis:

a. Like a rushing wind = *power!*
b. Tongues of fire = *purging!*
    A purging for mission - cf. Isaiah 6 and Isaiah's call to mission
c. Speaking in other tongues (languages) = *proclamation!*
    This picture comes from the Old Testament when the Spirit came upon persons and they prophesied.

All of these statements or pictures represent a new mission that these new believers individually, and the Church corporately, are called to. The Holy Spirit's coming empowered the spread of the gospel. Jesus told His disciples just before His ascension, "But you will receive power when the Holy Spirit has come upon you, and you will be My witnesses in Jerusalem, in all Judea and Samaria, and to the ends of the earth"

(Acts 1:8). Acts 4:33 states: "And the apostles were giving testimony with great power to the resurrection of the Lord Jesus, and great grace was on all of them." His coming also empowered the growth of the Church. It was His power that gave birth and growth to the Church as recorded and pictured in the book of Acts.

Do you love, appreciate and worship the Holy Spirit as one of the persons of the being of God? Are you grateful that He lives in you, is present with you to support, strengthen, and guide you? Do you recognize and rejoice in the new age of grace and all that means to you because of the coming of the Holy Spirit? Are you engaged in the mission of spreading the gospel and growing the Church?

Now that the Holy Spirit has come, one of His great works is engaging in a universal work of convicting and convincing all people of sin, righteousness, and the coming judgment (John 16:8). This is no small task or undertaking! However, as the infinite and all-present God, He fulfills that ministry to bring the world to recognize its dire and desperate need of a Savior.

When the Holy Spirit has brought conviction to a person's heart and that person responds in repentance toward God and in faith in the Lord Jesus Christ, the Holy Spirit regenerates that person. That means He gives and produces new life in a person in that very moment they receive Christ as Savior. That person then becomes a new creation or new person in Christ. This is also called the spiritual birth, new birth, or being "born again" (John 3:3–8; Titus 3:5). Regeneration is the transforming work of the Holy Spirit within the life of the believing sinner giving him a new nature, the nature of God (1 John 3:9 & 2 Peter 1:4). The old nature remains also for now, but there is a new and different person due to having the new or divine nature. The Holy Spirit also seals the new believer, indicating the security and safe-keeping of the believer (2 Corinthians 1:22; Ephesians 1:13–14 & 4:30).

After the initial work of salvation, the Holy Spirit continues His work in the believer's life. This continuing work is called sanctification (2 Thessalonians 2:13; 1 Peter 1:2). This work of sanctification is performed through various ministries of the Spirit in the believer's life. The Holy Spirit opposes the desires of the flesh or sinful nature and opposes sin in the believer's life (Galatians 5:16–17). He aids the believer in overcoming these by applying the union of the believer with Christ in His death and resurrection so that the believer experiences the power of having died with Christ to sin and being raised with Christ with new life (Romans chapters 6 & 8). When a believer chooses to yield to temptation and sins, the Holy Spirit convicts the believer and points the believer through God's Word to the specific point of his problem and need (Hebrews 4:12–13).

The blessed Holy Spirit aids the believer in several ways. He assists and directs us in our praying (Romans 8:26). He also teaches us and guides us into all truth (John 14:26 & 16:13–15; 1 John 2:27). Spiritual giftedness for ministry is given by the Spirit to each believer uniquely (1 Corinthians 12:4–11). And He also empowers us in our witness of Christ (Acts 1:8).

And finally, and of great importance, is the ministry of the Holy Spirit in transforming us into the likeness of Jesus Christ, God's Son (2 Corinthians 3:17–18). For now the Spirit's work is progressive in transforming us in stages or progressions "from glory to glory." Ultimately, that particular work will be completed and perfected by the Spirit when He raises us from the grave and transforms us completely into the likeness of Jesus Christ (Romans 8:11, 18, 23; cf. Philippians 3:20–21).

The precious Holy Spirit is a gift to each and every believer (John 16:7; Acts 2:17, 38). It is our pleasure to have fellowship with Him (2 Corinthians 13:14). It is our joy to worship Him! We should be continually conscious of Him and of His work in our life. We should call on Him and depend on Him for strength, wisdom, and spiritual power as we endeavor to live the life of a Christian.

One Hope – Christ's Return, the Resurrection of Believers, and the Coming Kingdom

Christian hope is not wishful hope. It is not a dream or a gamble. It is not pie in the sky. It is a confident anticipation of ultimate victory and enormous blessings. It is "the sense of well-being and security which results from having something or someone in whom to place confidence resulting in inner peace and absence of fear." It is a confident expectation that is a product of a person's faith in "God's sovereign control of man's destiny and God's total dependability" (Quoted phrases are from the *Dictionary of New Testament Theology*, Volume 2; Colin Brown, Editor).

Christian hope was clearly a powerful conviction and motivating factor in the lives of believers in the apostolic era. Their hope was based on the physical resurrection of Jesus Christ from the dead (1 Peter 1:3), and the promise of eternal life and immortality (Titus 1:2). Suffering poverty and persecution and facing the real possibility of martyrdom, the early Christians were focused on the hope and reward beyond this world and this present life.

Christian hope is set in contrast against the bleak background of sin and death. Even the creation itself groans and travails in hope of deliverance from the awful curse and consequences of sin. The creation eagerly awaits deliverance (Romans 8:22), and so do believers who understand the hope that is theirs in Christ for eternal glory and joy (Romans 8:23).

The hope of the Christian is one of the three great essentials of Christian experience: "Now these three remain: faith, hope, and love" (1 Corinthians 13:13). Hope is a powerful motive toward personal purity in the life of the believer. "And everyone who has this hope in Him purifies himself just as He is pure" (1 John 3:3).

The Christian's hope consists of three wonderful future realities:

1. A Heavenly Home - Living in God's Presence

Jesus made the promise to His disciples that He was going away to prepare a place for them and that one day they would be with Him in His Father's house (John 14:1–6). The author of Hebrews speaks of the anticipation and desire for a heavenly home in Hebrews 11:14–16 when he says: "Now those who say such things make it clear that they are seeking a homeland. If they had been remembering that land they came from, they would have had opportunity to return. But they now aspire to a better land – a heavenly one."

The Bible tells us that to be absent from the body is to be present with the Lord. And since the Lord Jesus is presently present in heaven, then to be absent from the body would be to be in heaven with the Lord (2 Corinthians 5:1, 6–8). When Paul spoke of the possibility of his death, he said "to depart and be with Christ is far better" (Philippians 1:22–23).

2. The Return of Christ and the Resurrection of Believers

The Believer's Blessed Hope

The believer is admonished to watch, wait, work, and to be pure and ready for Christ's coming, which is called our "blessed hope" (Titus 2:13; 1 Thessalonians 1:10). Scripture declares in Hebrews 9:28: "so also the Messiah, having been offered once to bear the sins of many, will appear a second time, not to bear sin, but to bring salvation to those who are waiting for Him." And 1 Corinthians 15:51–52 says, "We will not all fall asleep (die), but we will all be changed, in a moment, in the twinkling of an eye at the last trumpet. For the trumpet will sound and the dead will be raised incorruptible, and we will be changed."

This great event and future hope is also dramatically described in even more vivid detail in Philippians 3:20–21 and especially in 1 Thessalonians 4:13–18:

> We do not want you to be uninformed, brothers, concerning those who are asleep, so that you will not grieve like the rest, who have no *hope*. Since we believe that Jesus died and rose again, in the same way God will bring with Him those who have fallen asleep through Jesus. For we say this to you by a revelation from the Lord: We who are still alive at the Lord's coming will certainly have no advantage over those who have fallen asleep. For the Lord Himself will descend from heaven with a shout,

> with the archangel's voice, and with the trumpet of God,
> and *the dead in Christ will rise first* (emphasis added).

Sleep is a gentle metaphor that replaces the harsh reality of death by referring to how the body appears when death has occurred. It does not indicate that the soul is sleeping, for the believer has left the body and is present with Christ. That soul-sleep is not scriptural is clear from Ecclesiastes 12:7 and 2 Corinthians 5:1-8. Ecclesiastes 12:7 vividly describes exactly what occurs at death: "And the dust returns to the earth as it once was, and the spirit returns to God who gave it." And in 2 Corinthians Paul declares: "Therefore, being always of good courage, and knowing that while we are at home in the body we are absent from the Lord -- for we walk by faith, not by sight-- we are of good courage, I say, and prefer rather to be absent from the body and to be at home with the Lord (2 Corinthians 5:6-8).

3.   The Kingdom - Reigning with Christ

A third aspect of the believer's hope is the honor of reigning with Christ. This includes the rewards that will be bestowed on each individual Christian for eternity and an eternal earthly kingdom (2 Timothy 2:12; Revelation 5:10; 20:4, 6; 22:5).

So the believer's hope is an essential truth to Christian faith and is a wonderful and amazing future prospect for all true believers in Christ.

One Lord - Jesus Christ

The Importance of the Lordship of Jesus

"The lordship of Jesus Christ is the keystone of Christianity! 'Jesus is Lord' is probably the earliest of the Christian confessions and worked its way into the various acts of Christian worship" (*Evangelical Dictionary of Theology*, p. 647). It was the strongest truth emphasized by the early, apostolic church. Dr. G. Campbell Morgan called the lordship of Christ "the central verity of the Church," and Dr. A. T. Robertson, a Greek

New Testament scholar, stated that it is "the touchstone of our faith." Jesus Christ is called Savior twenty-four times in the New Testament, but He is called Lord four hundred and thirty-three times!

The lordship of Jesus Christ was the keystone of the apostolic church. According to F. F. Bruce, the lordship of Christ was an important part of primitive Christology. He states: "Even more important, however, than these 'christologies' in themselves was the acknowledgment of Jesus as Lord in a sense which implied universal sovereignty" (F. F. Bruce in *Paul – Apostle of the Heart Set Free*, p. 66).

Three Great Truths Concerning the Lordship of Jesus Christ

1. The Lordship of Jesus Is the Initial Confession of the Christian

> If you confess with your mouth, *"Jesus is Lord,"* and believe in your heart that God raised Him from the dead, you will be saved (Romans 10:9; emphasis added).

We observe that the lordship of Jesus demonstrates that He is divine and that He is sovereign. However, here in Romans 10:9–10 His lordship is stated to be based on His resurrection, demonstrating the accomplishment of His death and His power, authority and victory over sin and its consequent penalty, death. He has mastered sin and death, and therefore has the right to all authority in heaven and on earth. The emphasis in this particular passage is not on deity but on sovereignty. In the same context, Paul says, "for the same Lord is Lord of all." The phrase "Lord of all" is emphasizing once again His sovereign authority and power in its universal realm.

2. The Lordship of Jesus Is the Authentic Confession of the Christian

> And no one can say *"Jesus is Lord,"* except by the Holy Spirit (1 Corinthians 12:3b; emphasis added).

The MacArthur Study Bible says this about this verse: "What a person believes and says about Jesus Christ is the test of whether he speaks from the Holy Spirit. He always leads people to Christ's Lordship (cf. 2:8–14; John 15:26; 1 John 5:6–8)." It would appear that both His deity and His sovereignty are in view in this confession. "Jesus is Lord" on our lips continues to authenticate our faith in Him and our discipleship throughout our lives on earth.

3. The Lordship of Jesus Will Be the Cosmic Confession of the Universe

> For this reason God also highly exalted Him and gave Him the name that is above every name, so that at the name of Jesus every knee should bow—of those who are in heaven and on earth and under the earth—and every tongue should confess that *Jesus Christ is Lord*, to the glory of God the Father (Philippians 2:9–11; emphasis added).

The lordship of Jesus is of cosmic significance since it will be the ultimate confession of all of creation. Once again we observe that His lordship is based on the merits of His redemptive accomplishment. Here, the words "for this reason" stand out to make the case for His lordship. The confession of His lordship is in tandem with the bowing of every knee. There is no room for doubt that the bowing of the knee is an act of recognition of His lordship as well as submission to Him as Lord of the universe.

His lordship implicitly demands submission and obedience. Anything short of a heartfelt attitude and practical action of submission and obedience is not acceptable. Through our continuing faith we must grow in our understanding of who Jesus was and is, what He has accomplished in His victorious death and resurrection, and the authority He possesses due to His exaltation. "The life of the community, of disciples, is lived under Jesus's Lordship (Romans 14:8)" (*Evangelical Dictionary of Theology*, p. 647).

The Meaning of Christ's Lordship

What does the word "Lord" mean as it relates to Jesus Christ? As a noun, the Greek word "kurios" means "lord, ruler; one who has control over people and things" (*The New International Dictionary of New Testament Theology*, Volume 2, Colin Brown, Editor). The Greek word "kurios" is used in the Septuagint, or LXX, six thousand, eight hundred, and fourteen times to translate the personal name of God, Yahweh or Jehovah.

In Psalm 110:1, David prophetically spoke of Christ saying: "The LORD says to my Lord: 'Sit at My right hand until I make Your enemies a footstool for Your feet.'" Here, the Messiah is placed prophetically in a position of sovereignty with the anticipation of the ultimate and total defeat of His enemies.

After Jesus's death and resurrection, He ascended to the Father's right hand and is seated in authority above all authorities having been given all authority in heaven and on earth (Ephesians 1:19–22; Matthew 28:18). For the early Christians or disciples, this exaltation due to His victorious death and resurrection is what commanded their submission and allegiance to Jesus's lordship (Philippians 2:9–11). Furthermore, when John the Baptist announced the coming of the Messiah, he heralded the news as follows:

> As it is written in Isaiah the prophet, Look, I am sending My messenger ahead of You, who will prepare Your way: A voice of one crying out in the wilderness: "Prepare the way for *the Lord*; make His paths straight" (Mark 1:2–3; emphasis added).

In ancient times, a messenger would go before a king to announce the king's coming so people would prepare to receive and honor the king. That custom emphasized the submission of subjects to the sovereignty and authority of a king, or of one of great authority. The authority of Christ as Lord is inherent in this prophetic proclamation regarding Messiah's coming.

The implications and associations are unmistakable. The Messiah would be Yahweh, or Jehovah, and He would possess divine sovereignty. Though fully human, Jesus demonstrated His deity and sovereign authority throughout His earthly ministry.

He is Lord Over Creation

Jesus stated that as the Son of man He was Lord of the Sabbath. The Sabbath was the sacred symbol of God's rest over creation. By making this statement, Jesus was declaring His sovereignty as the Creator over creation. Scripture states: "Through him all things were made; without him nothing was made that has been made" (John 1:3 NIV); and "the world was made through him" (John 1:10 NIV); and "For by him all things were created: things in heaven and on earth, visible and invisible, whether thrones or powers or rulers or authorities; all things were created by him and for him" (Colossians 1:16).

Jesus's sovereignty as the creator was remarkably demonstrated many times during His life. He cursed the fig tree and it died. He calmed the storm. He summoned fish to be caught. Jesus restored physical bodies that had been ravaged by disease. He transformed water into wine. He walked on water on the Sea of Galilee. He had the power to give life to the dead.

He Is Lord over the Angels

Angels ministered to Him. He had, and still has, authority over the angels. He could have called twelve legions of angels, that is, seventy-two thousand angels, to rescue Him from the cross (Matthew 26:53). All the angels are to worship Him (Hebrews 1:6).

He Is Lord over the Demons

They feared Him and obeyed Him. He could cast them out and send them wherever He desired (Mark 5:1–18; Luke 8:28–38; Matthew 8:28–34).

He Is Lord over the Church

Ephesians 1:22 says: "And He put all things in subjection under His feet, and gave Him as head over all things to the church."

He Is Destined To Be Lord over the Earth

He will reign as King of kings and Lord of lords as the book of Revelation teaches (Revelation 11:15; 17:14; 19:6).

What Jesus Said about His Lordship

Jesus Himself made the implications of His lordship clear when He spoke of it: "Why do you call me 'Lord, Lord,' and don't do the things I say" (Luke 6:46)?

"Not everyone who says to Me, 'Lord, Lord!' will enter the kingdom of heaven, but only the one who does the will of My Father in heaven" (Matthew 7:21).

Meaning and Application of His Lordship

Jesus's lordship as it relates to the gospel is most clearly explained by Peter in his sermons to the Jews in Acts chapter 2 and to the Gentiles in Acts chapter 10.

> For it was not David who ascended into the heavens, but he himself says: The Lord said to my Lord, "Sit at My right hand until I make Your enemies your footstool." Therefore let all the house of Israel know with certainty that *God has made this Jesus, whom you crucified, both Lord and Messiah* (Acts 2:34–36; emphasis added)!

This passage clearly emphasizes several things that focus on the sovereignty of Jesus Christ in relation to His lordship. First, the concept of "throne" implies sovereign rule. It is in this exalted position of sovereignty that He is declared to be "Lord." As if this were not clear enough, the New Testament makes the emphasis on the sovereignty due to His lordship plain in another passage:

> He demonstrated this power in the Messiah by raising Him from the dead and seating Him at His right hand in the heavens—far above every ruler and authority, power and dominion, and every title given, not only in this age but also in the one to come. And He put everything under His feet (Ephesians 1:20–22a).

Christ's exaltation to the Father's right hand is to the position of sovereign lordship. It is a position that is "far above all rule and authority and power and dominion." Furthermore, God the Father has "put all things in subjection under His feet." On the basis of this lordship, Jesus told His disciples, "All authority has been given to me in heaven and on earth" (Matthew 28:18).

According to Ursinus, Christ has the right to claim lordship over our lives for four reasons:

1. By right of creation – He made us
2. By right of redemption – He saved us
3. By right of preservation – He keeps us
4. By right of ordination or appointment – He is head over the Church

Jesus's Lordship and the Lord's Supper

According to *The Dictionary of New Testament Theology*, a significant number of expressions regarding the Lord's Supper connect it with the lordship of Jesus:

- The table of *the Lord* (1 Corinthians 10:21)
- The death of *the Lord* (1 Corinthians 11:26)
- The cup of *the Lord* (1 Corinthians 10:21; 11:27)
- The *Lord's* Supper (1 Corinthians 11:20)

- Be judged by *the Lord* (1 Corinthians 11:32)

In mentioning that the supper was a proclamation of the death of the Lord until He comes, Paul is referencing what scholars say was a closing hope and prayer by the early Christians after the supper: "Maranatha—*our Lord* come!"

This expression found in 1 Corinthians 16:22 is Aramaic language. That clearly indicates that it was a very early expression of primitive Christianity.

The lordship of Jesus Christ is a major principle of the gospel and was a major principle of the apostolic church. How therefore, can we separate His lordship from what it means to be a Christian or disciple of Jesus? When we arbitrarily separate the two, we diminish the effect of the call of Christ to separate ourselves from the world and to follow Him. When we fail to preach His lordship, we also separate the freeness of grace from the loving and loyal obligation we owe to Christ–His claims upon the lives of those who have been bought by His blood. These are inseparable, but many churches and pastors today attempt to divide them. They emphasize a cheap gospel of grace with no further obligation to live in obedience.

The essence of sin is that each human has "turned to his own way" (Isaiah 53:6). This is rebellion. The essence of true salvation results in submission to God and His way. A model for this submission can be seen in the saving work and the lordship of Christ. He submitted voluntarily, even when He had other choices. This is the straight and narrow road. This is the road each of us must walk as we pick up our cross to follow Him.

Without question, we must never compromise the truth that salvation does not result from any of our works. It is solely provided by the infinite and wonderful grace of God. Once we are saved, we become a new creation that is created by God for good works, and it becomes our privilege and joy to serve Him by doing good works. Good works are, therefore, the proof of our salvation, not its cause.

When sharing the gospel, we must present Christ and the gospel to those who would trust Him as their Lord and Savior in such a way that they will be captivated by who He is and the significance of what He did for them. They may not understand all of the implications of Christ's lordship, but they need to surrender their hearts, to love Him, and to want to follow Him. If nothing changes following our profession of faith and we still follow our own path, how can we say that we have true saving faith? How can we say that we have become new creations in Christ, and that all things have become new (2 Corinthians 5:17)? If there is no growing love and obedience, we are not Christians and have no claim to salvation through Christ.

The Relationship of Jesus's Lordship and Deity

We have examined the lordship of Christ with regard to His sovereignty, but Christ's deity is a substantial reality of His lordship as well. The term Lord, i.e. "Adonai," in the Hebrew Old Testament is used as a title for God. Therefore the use of this title for Jesus in the New Testament also implies His deity. Based on the contexts themselves and on the number of passages where this happens, the implication becomes an overwhelming statement of the fact of Christ's divinity or deity – that Jesus was God. The deity of Christ can be seen in numerous ways in the New Testament:

1. He Possesses the Attributes of Deity

    Omnipotence (All-Powerful)
    John 1:3 (cf. Hebrews 1:10–12); Colossians 1:16–17; Hebrews 1:3

    Sovereignty
    Matthew 28:18; Revelation 1:8

    Omniscience (All-Knowing)
    Matthew 11:27; John 2:24–25 & 16:30

    Omnipresence (All-Present—everywhere)
    Matthew 18:20 & 28:20; John 3:13

Sinlessness
John 7:18 & 8:46; 2 Corinthians 5:21; Hebrews 4:15 & 9:11–14; 1 Peter 2:22

Divine Fullness
John 8:12; 1 Corinthians 1:30–31; Ephesians 1:2–3; Colossians 2:3, 9

Eternality & Immutability (Unchangeableness)
Isaiah 9:6; Micah 5:2; John 1:1–3 & 8:58 & 17:5, 24; Hebrews 13:8; 1 John 1:1; Revelation 1:11

2. Divine Offices and Prerogatives Belong to Him

He Is Savior
Isaiah 43:11; Matthew 1:21; John 3:17; John 4:42; Acts 15:11; 1 Timothy 1:15 & 4:10; Hebrews 7:25

- He forgives sin: Matthew 9:2, 6; Mark 2:7; Luke 7:47–48; Acts 13:38–39
- Through Him sin is purged: John 1:29; Hebrews 9:14 & 10:10, 12, 14

He Is Mediator between God and Man
John 14:6; 1 Timothy 2:5

He Was and Is To Be Worshiped
John 5:23; Philippians 2:9–11; Hebrews 1:6

He Is the Judge of All of Mankind
Psalm 7:8 &,9:8, & 96:10, 13 & 110:6 (some of these passages are Messianic, that is, directly concerning Christ); Isaiah 66:16; John 5:22; Acts 17:31; Hebrews 1:8

He Is the Life and the Giver of Eternal Life
John 1:4 & 5:21, 26 & 14:6; John 10:27–28 & 17:1–2; Acts 3:15

He Is the Resurrection (the One who resurrects)
John 5:28 & 11:25

He Is To Be Believed in Just As God the Father Is Believed in
John 1:12; 6:35, 47; 14:1; Acts 16:31

Prayer Is Answered in His Name
John 15:16 & 16:23

3. He Claimed To Be God
    John 5:18; 8:58–59; 10:30, 33, 38; 14:10–11; 17:21; Matthew 26:64–65

In John chapters 8 and 10, and in Matthew chapter 26, the Jewish leaders all clearly recognized that He was claiming to be God, and because of that they accused Him of blasphemy. They wanted to kill Him for claiming to be God!

4. Those Who Observed His Life Most Closely Believed He Was God

Thomas forthrightly announced his faith in Jesus as God saying: "My Lord and my God" (John 20:28). For a Jew to acknowledge one who had been a normal human and who still remained in a resurrected human body to be God was huge!

On what has been called the Mount of Transfiguration, Peter, James, and John saw Jesus transfigured. His divine glory was put on display for them to see. Concerning that event, Peter proclaims that they were "eyewitnesses of His majesty" (2 Peter 1:16–17). John declared: "we observed His glory, the glory as the One and Only Son from the Father" (John 1:14). What they saw was the majesty or glory that is the characteristic of God–the Shekinah or divine glory!

5. There Are Direct Statements in the Word of God Affirming His Deity

Isaiah 7:14 declares: "Therefore, the Lord Himself will give you a sign: The virgin will conceive, have a son and name him *Immanuel*" (emphasis added).

Compare this to Matthew 1:21–23:

"She will give birth to a son, and you are to name Him Jesus, because He will save His people from their sins. Now all this took place to fulfill what was spoken by the Lord through the prophet: See, the virgin will become pregnant and give birth to a son, and they will name Him *Immanuel*" (emphasis added).

The name Immanuel is the Hebrew word that means "God with us."

There are several other verses stating that He is God, including Isaiah 9:6: "For a child will be born for us, a son will be given to us, and the government will be on His shoulders. He will be named Wonderful Counselor, *Mighty God*, Eternal Father, Prince of Peace" (emphasis added).

Isaiah chapter 40 is an extraordinary chapter indicating the deity of the Messiah, of Christ. It is clearly prophetic concerning the future coming of the Messiah. Isaiah 40:3 says:

> A voice of one crying out: *"Prepare the way of the LORD*
> in the wilderness; make a straight highway *for our God*
> in the desert"* (emphasis added; cf. Matthew 3:1–3;
> Mark 1:1–2; and Luke 3:4–6 – Luke's account is the
> most complete).

Verse three identifies the coming one as "the LORD" saying "prepare the way of the LORD." Whenever either the word "Lord" or the word "God" is in capitals such as "LORD" or "GOD," it indicates that the Hebrew word used in the text is the personal name for God. The personal names often used for God are transliterated as Yahweh or Jehovah. Since John the Baptist was the forerunner of Jesus going ahead of Him to announce the arrival of "the LORD," this was telling the world that Jesus was Yahweh, "the LORD!" John was like a herald in that day that would go ahead of an important person or king and loudly proclaim his coming. This was to prepare people so they would be ready to show honor to this important person. It also calls the one who is coming and that the people should be prepared to welcome and honor, "our God," a notable declaration of His deity.

Then Isaiah 40:5 announces: "And *the glory of the LORD will appear, and all humanity will see it together, for the mouth of the LORD has spoken*" (emphasis added; see also John 1:14 & 2:11; Matthew 17:2; Hebrews 1:1–2; 2 Peter 1:16–17). Jesus Christ was "the glory of the LORD!" In this verse, Isaiah explains that "the glory of the LORD will appear and all humanity will see it." In its essential meaning, the glory of the LORD is the radiance or outshining of the sum total of all of God's glorious attributes, of His character. In the physical manifestation of the glory of the LORD, the brilliant radiance of His being is a blinding light. It is the physical manifestation and radiance of the perfections of God's being–of all that God is.

The first appearance of this glory of God was in the journey of Israel after leaving Egypt. It appeared as a brilliant, luminous glory-cloud by day and as a massive and tall pillar of fire by night (Exodus 13:21; Exodus 16:7, 10). The glory of the LORD appeared on Mount Sinai for six days during the time of the giving of the Ten Commandments (Exodus 24:16–17). The glory appeared in the Tabernacle in the wilderness (Exodus 40:34–35). Then the glory of the LORD appeared later to Isaiah in the Temple (Isaiah chapter 6) and to Ezekiel (Ezekiel chapter 1).

The existence of the glory in the Tabernacle pictures God with mankind and especially with His people. The Tabernacle was located in the very center of Israel's camp, showing God's presence in the midst of His people. It is wonderfully associated with John 1:14 where the Scripture says, "The Word became flesh (a graphic way of describing His humanity) and took up residence (Greek, literally "tabernacled" or "tented") among us. We observed His glory, the glory as the One and Only Son from the Father, full of grace and truth." The Tabernacle was a large tent used in the wilderness wanderings since it could be taken down and moved from place to place. God's glorious presence was in the Tabernacle in the midst of His people during their wilderness wandering, and later God's glory or glorious presence was among His people in the person of Jesus, His Son, who was the glory of God – full of grace and truth (John 1:14)! But before He came to earth He was the radiance of God's glory (John 17:5 & Hebrews 1:3).

Later in this great 40th chapter of Isaiah, the deity of the Messiah, of Christ, is again declared! Isaiah 40:9–11 proclaims: "Zion, herald of good news, go up on a high mountain. Jerusalem, herald of good news, raise your voice loudly. Raise it, do not be afraid! Say to the cities of Judah, *'Here is your God!'* See, *the Lord God comes* with strength, and His power establishes His rule. His reward is with Him, and His gifts accompany Him. He protects His flock like a shepherd; He gathers the lambs in His arms and carries them in the fold of His garment. He gently leads those that are nursing" (emphasis added).

Throughout Isaiah chapter 40, a herald is raising his voice to announce to Jerusalem and the nation of Judah the coming of their king. The announcement is: "Here is your God" (v. 9)! Explanation comes immediately in verse 10: "See, *the Lord God* (the personal name of Yahweh) comes with strength" (emphasis added). He is then described as "a shepherd" of His people or flock (v. 11).

Following this, His strength and power is then proven by His creative work (vs. 11–26). This theme of His strength is exalted in verse 28 and then applied to Him giving strength to His own people in verses 29–31. Could this possibly be what Paul was referring to when he said: "I can do all things through Christ who strengthens me" (Philippians 4:13 NKJV)?

There are a number of verses in the New Testament that dogmatically declare the deity of Christ. John 1:1 is one of those: "In the beginning was the Word, and the Word was with God, and *the Word was God*" (emphasis added). In Greek it literally states "God was the Word." Logically, and literally, this passage says: "God was the Word" (v. 1).

And then the passage goes on to state: "And the Word became flesh and lived among us" (v. 14). Therefore, the Word was and is God!

Another verse unequivocally asserting the deity of Christ is Romans 9:5: "The forefathers are theirs, and from them, by physical descent, came the Messiah, *who is God over all*, blessed forever. Amen" (emphasis added). This is possibly the clearest, strongest and most direct statement in all of the New Testament that declares that Jesus Christ was God in the flesh. And Colossians 2:9 is almost as strong a statement of His deity: "For in Him (Jesus Christ) the entire fullness of God's nature dwells bodily."

Then there is the marvelous apostolic creed found in 1 Timothy 3:16: "And most certainly the mystery of godliness is great: He (He is contextually 'God') was manifested in the flesh, justified in the Spirit, seen by angels, preached among the Gentiles, believed on in the world, taken up in glory." This profession is believed by Bible scholars to have been a universal creed among the Christians of the first century.

Equally impressive is the declaration of Hebrews 1:3: "He (the Son, vs. 1–2) is the radiance of His ('God's', v. 1) glory, the exact expression of His nature, and He sustains all things by His powerful word. After making purification for sins, He sat down at the right hand of the Majesty on high." In his book *Systematic Theology,* Wayne Grudem comments on Hebrews 1:3: "Jesus is the exact duplicate of the 'nature' (or being, Greek is *hypostasis*) of God, making Him exactly equal to God in every attribute."

Summary Regarding Jesus's Lordship

To the first disciples, and to all true disciples thereafter, Jesus Christ is recognized as their Lord! This is the heart of our faith. Submission to someone else is not a very popular concept in today's culture. It may not be a popular message, but faithfulness to Jesus Christ demands that we submit to His lordship each day. It further requires that we share this essential core of the message as we tell others of the good news. They too must submit to His lordship to be counted as His true disciples. The following song portrays the lordship of Jesus in a marvelous way.

Name of All Majesty
Timothy Dudley-Smith

Name of all majesty, fathomless mystery,
King of the ages by angels adored;
Pow'r and authority, splendor and dignity,
Bow to His mastery – Jesus is Lord!

Child of our destiny, God from eternity,
Love of the Father on sinners outpoured;
See now what God has done sending His only Son,
Christ the beloved One – Jesus is Lord!

Savior of Calvary, costliest victory,
Darkness defeated and Eden restored;
Born as a man to die, nailed to a cross on high,
Cold in the grave to lie – Jesus is Lord!

Source of all sovereignty, light, immortality,
Life everlasting and heaven assured;
So with the ransomed, we praise Him eternally,
Christ in His majesty – Jesus is Lord!

© Hope Publishing Co. – Used by permission

One Faith - The Gospel

It is both shocking and alarming to realize that the gospel of Jesus Christ is not receiving priority in many evangelical churches today. In some cases, it is not being preached at all. Dr. Erwin Lutzer, pastor of Moody Memorial Church in Chicago, Illinois, lamented this fact on a national radio broadcast. Many churches today are more interested in "feel-good" and "self-help" messages. Others promote a prosperity gospel. Still others seek to grow their numbers through entertainment and soft-petal the gospel if they give it at all.

Matt Chandler addresses this deficiency of gospel proclamation in his book, *The Explicit Gospel.* The flyleaf of the cover of his book states: "Here is a call to true Christianity, to know the gospel explicitly, and to unite the church on the amazing grounds of the good news of Jesus!" Commenting on Chandler's book, D. A. Carson said: "That the gospel is not clearly taught in classic liberalism is disheartening but not surprising. That frequently the gospel is not taught in evangelical congregations is both disquieting and surprising. Evangelicals will not deny the gospel, but they may assume it while talking about everything else - and that is tragic. He (Chandler) issues a robust call to make the gospel an explicit and central part of our preaching and takes pains to show what that looks like. Amen and Amen."

In *The Good News We Almost Forgot*, Kevin DeYoung declares: "The chief theological task now facing the Western church is not to reinvent or to be relevant but to remember. We must remember the old, old story. We must remember the faith once delivered to the saints." DeYoung is speaking about the gospel of Jesus Christ.

The Definition of "One Faith"

Is the term "one faith" referring to subjective faith, which has to do with personal conviction concerning the truth? Or does it refer to objective faith, the body of truth, the content of the teaching itself? In reality, the subjective and objective cannot and should not be separated. The faith of Christians is one that is personal. It is held with conviction in the heart (Romans 10:10). However, the faith of Christians is one that has an object of faith, Jesus Christ and His redemptive work (Acts 16:31 & 20:21).

There are four specific reasons why the term "one faith" refers specifically and technically to the gospel.

First, notice the context in which "one faith" occurs. It is in a triad preceded by "one Lord" and followed by "one baptism." What logically goes between "one Lord" and "one baptism" if it is not faith in the gospel? While one might be prone to take the word faith, in "one faith," as meaning subjective faith only, other evidence makes it clear that "the faith" or "one faith" is a technical reference to the gospel. It is good news with content. It refers objectively to the truth of God's plan as executed through the life, death, and resurrection of His Son, Jesus Christ.

Some biblical expositors interpret "one faith" broadly as the comprehensive body of Christian truth. This interpretation would not be in harmony, however, with the context. If the term means the entire body of Christian truth, then "one faith" would no longer be on an equal and complementary plane with the other doctrines in the passage. If it is interpreted to mean the entire body of Christian truth, then "one faith" is redundant and meaningless since some doctrines have already been stated.

In addition, the term "one faith" is also undoubtedly synonymous with the term "the faith" as seen in most contexts of both terms in the New Testament. They both refer to the gospel, the redemptive work of Christ in its historic character as well as in all of its implications and applications. Let's look at several examples.

"So the preaching about God flourished, the number of the disciples in Jerusalem multiplied greatly, and a large group of priests became obedient to *the faith*" (Acts 6:7; emphasis added). The priests already believed other Old Testament truths that would be included in the comprehensive body of Christian belief. Their response in the context of the passage, however, was referring to believing the gospel. The gospel is the heart and distinctive tenet of the "Christian faith." Therefore, "the faith" in this context is equivalent to the objective gospel.

"But Elymas, the sorcerer, which is how his name is translated, opposed them and tried to turn the proconsul away from *the faith*" (Acts 13:8; emphasis added). Obviously the preaching and acceptance of the gospel are in view in this context as distinguished from various other Old Testament concepts.

"By whom we have received grace and apostleship, for obedience to *the faith* among all nations, for his name" (Romans 1:5 NASB; emphasis added). The term "among all nations" is associated with Paul's following the Great Commission and his spreading of the good news of the gospel with all people. Therefore, it is apparent that "the faith" in this context refers to the gospel.

The apostle Paul had come to faith in Christ and in the gospel. This resulted in an incredible change in him. In commenting on this total turnaround, the scripture says: "they simply kept hearing: 'He who formerly persecuted us now preaches *the faith* he once tried to destroy'" (Galatians 1:23; emphasis added).

"Just one thing: live your life in a manner worthy of *the gospel of Christ*. Then, whether I come and see you or am absent, I will hear about you that you are standing firm in one spirit, with one mind, working side by side for *the faith of the gospel*" (Philippians 1:27; emphasis added). Nothing could be clearer in the context of this verse and the context of the entire first chapter of Philippians than that the term "the faith" is referring to the gospel, to our redemption through Christ's death and resurrection.

"If indeed you remain grounded and steadfast in *the faith*, and are not shifted away from the hope of *the gospel* that you heard. *This gospel* has been proclaimed in all creation under heaven, and I, Paul, have become a minister of it" (Colossians 1:23; emphasis added). In this context, "the faith" and "the gospel" appear to be used interchangeably.

In Jude 3, "the common salvation" means the same as "the faith which was once for all delivered to the saints." Again, the term "the faith" is related to the gospel.

Other Scriptures that also use the term, "the faith," are Acts 24:24; 2 Corinthians 13:5; Colossians 2:6–7; and Revelation 14:12. These agree with the premise above that the term refers to the gospel and not some broader compilation of Christian teachings.

A final reason that the term "one faith" is evidently speaking of the gospel is that many translators and interpreters have taken the words "the faith" to mean the gospel. An example is the *New Living Translation* that translates Jude 3 "urging you to defend the truth of *the Good News*" (emphasis added). "Good News" is a synonym for the gospel. In Robert Letham's outstanding work, *The Holy Trinity – In Scripture, History, Theology and Worship,* he comments on Ephesians 4:5, saying: "One Lord means Jesus Christ, the Son who is the cornerstone of the church (2:20). One faith in turn points to the unity of the content of the Christian gospel" (*The Holy Trinity*, p. 84).

Although Martin Luther was not commenting on these particular verses or this particular idea, in expressing the core of his beliefs about faith and salvation he mingles the terms in such a way as to make the conclusion clear. "For faith grounds us on the works of Christ, without our own works, and transfers us from the exile of our sins into the kingdom of His righteousness. *This is faith; this is the gospel; this is Christ*" (*What Luther Says, An Anthology*, Volume 2 Page 922; Concordia; emphasis added).

"One faith" therefore speaks of the gospel both simply and comprehensively. "One faith," simply put, is Christ's redemptive work. But "one faith" also comprehensively includes a broad sweep of important and precious truths:

The Comprehensive Meaning of the Gospel

The gospel in its origin: *the Gospel of God*
The gospel in its historical reality: *the death, burial and resurrection of Christ*
The gospel in its resident efficacy or power: *Christ alone*
The gospel in its essential nature: *grace alone*
The gospel in its reception: *faith alone*

Each of these concepts must be carefully considered for us to clearly and completely understand the gospel.

The Gospel in Its Origin – the Gospel of God

In 2 Corinthians 11:7, we are introduced to the concept that the gospel was God's original idea and was performed solely by His initiative. Several passages prove this, including Acts 2:23. The plan of salvation, or the gospel, was originated before the creation of the universe as explained by Ephesians 1:4, 2 Timothy 1:9, 1 Peter 1:19-20, and Revelation 13:8. The gospel was, therefore, not only God's plan, but obviously it was also God's initiative, since at that time He was the only one in existence.

The Gospel in Its Historical Reality

1 Corinthians 15:1–4 states:

> Now brothers, I want to clarify for you the gospel I
> proclaimed to you; you received it and have taken your
> stand on it. You are also saved by it, if you hold to the
> message I proclaimed to you—unless you believed to no
> purpose. For I passed on to you as most important what
> I also received: that Christ died for our sins according to
> the Scriptures, that He was buried, that He was raised
> on the third day according to the Scriptures.

The apostle Paul continues in that chapter by citing the eyewitnesses
to the resurrection of Christ, those who saw Him after He was raised
from the dead.

Christianity is unique in regard to its historical foundation as far as
the origin of religions is concerned with the exception of Old Testament
Judaism. Christianity is founded on verifiable, public, historical events
as witnessed by numerous people. The miracles of Christ and His
death and resurrection were the primary events multitudes of people
witnessed.

Other religions are based on:

- One individual's dream
- Some claimed revelation to one individual
- A private encounter by an angel to one individual
- A private idea of one individual

Those individuals then told other people about the revelation, dream,
or idea. There is a world of difference in the origin of Christianity when
compared to the origin of all other religions. There is no comparison!

Because of the substantial historical evidence for Christ, His
ministry and miracles, and His death and resurrection, many skeptics

such as Lee Strobel, with a Yale Law School law degree and a degree in journalism, and a practicing investigative journalist, have come to place their faith in Jesus Christ. His book, *The Case for Christ*, is a powerful examination of this evidence.

The Gospel in Its Resident Power – Christ Alone

The gospel is both literally and symbolically embodied in Jesus Christ. He alone as Savior has the power to save us from our sin. Obviously that is the reason the gospel is also called "the gospel of Christ" (2 Corinthians 2:12 & 9:13).

Furthermore, 1 John 2:2 says, "He himself (Jesus Christ) *is* the propitiation for our sins" (emphasis added). It does not say that He Himself *was* the propitiation for our sins, but that He *is* presently the propitiation for our sins! Propitiation is the satisfaction of God's wrath against our sin that makes it possible for God to have mercy on us. The word "propitiation" is biblically related to the Mercy Seat, which was located in the sanctuary. The sanctuary was known as "the Holy of holies." In the Old Testament, the Mercy Seat was the cover for the Ark of the Covenant. It was the symbol of God's response to atonement or payment for human sin. This is still true, except today we know that the payment for our sin comes only from Christ, the one and only true Mercy Seat. The text therefore means that Jesus is presently at the Father's right hand as our advocate and is the very embodiment of the satisfaction of God's wrath against our sins. He is the very basis of divine mercy toward us. No wonder we are invited: "let us draw near with confidence to the throne of grace, (the presence of God in the Holy of holies), so that we may receive mercy" (Hebrews 4:16 NASB). Forgiveness and mercy are in Christ alone (Acts 13:38-39; Ephesians 1:7).

The Gospel in Its Essence - Grace alone

> But none of these things move me, neither count I my life dear unto myself, so that I might finish my course

with joy, and the ministry, which I have received of the Lord Jesus, to testify *the gospel of the grace of God* (Acts 20:24 - KJV; emphasis added).

We can only be made "right" with God through His pure grace apart from works and apart from keeping the law. The apostle Paul champions this truth in two of his epistles, Romans and Galatians. Paul marshals this truth over and over in Romans. In Romans 3:2 he states, "They are justified *freely* by His *grace* through the redemption that is in Christ Jesus" (emphasis added). Then in Romans 4:16 he notes, "This is why the promise is by faith, so that it may be according to *grace*, to guarantee it to all the descendants—not only to those who are of the law, but also to those who are of Abraham's faith. He is the father of us all" (emphasis added). In Romans 5:15, 17 he declares, "But the gift is not like the trespass. For if by the one man's trespass the many died, how much more have *the grace of God and the gift* overflowed to the many by the *grace* of the one man, Jesus Christ. Since by the one man's trespass, death reigned through that one man, how much more will those who receive the overflow of *grace* and *the gift of righteousness* reign in life through the one man, Jesus Christ" (emphasis added). And finally in Romans 11:6 he observes, "Now if by *grace*, then it is not by works; otherwise *grace* ceases to be *grace*" (emphasis added).

Grace is unmerited, undeserved, unearned favor. The word itself, with its companion word, gift, δορα - dora, emphasizes the freeness or gratuity of that which is given. The word "gift" as it relates to the freeness and grace of salvation is stated in several Scriptures. Romans 6:23 says, "*the free gift of God* is eternal life" (NASB; emphasis added). Ephesians 2:7–9 is a key passage concerning God's grace and the free gift of salvation apart from works. It is a wonderful expression of the grace and gift of salvation in Christ. Paul exudes with delight when he declares:

So that in the coming ages He might display the immeasurable riches of His *grace* in His kindness to us in Christ Jesus. For by *grace* you are saved through faith, and this is not from yourselves; it is *God's gift— not from works*, so that no one can boast (Ephesians 2:7-9, emphasis added; cf. 2 Timothy 1:9 and Romans 5:1).

The contrast between grace and works is made clear many times in Paul's writings. In Titus 3:5 he says, "Not by works of righteousness which we have done, but according to his mercy he saved us" (NKJV; emphasis added). In Galatians 2:16 he declares, "nevertheless knowing that a man is *not justified by the works* of the Law but through faith in Christ Jesus, even we have believed in Christ Jesus, so that we may be justified by faith in Christ and *not by the works of the Law*; since by the works of the Law no flesh will be justified (NASB; emphasis added).

It is immensely helpful to understand the relationship between the law, the Old Testament Mosaic law including the Ten Commandments, and how we can be right with God. First, because God is the Creator, He is the authority over the universe, and over all human beings. He has spoken to us in His Word and in it has given us His law that is to govern our lives. His law is absolute and is the authoritative standard of righteousness. Most importantly, the law of God is a reflection of God's character. God is perfect righteousness or justice. Deuteronomy 32:4 NKJV says:

> He is the Rock, His work is perfect; For all His ways are justice. A God of truth and without injustice; Righteous and upright is He (See also Psalm 97:2; Mark 10:18; Psalm 71:19; Psalm 119:37 & 142; and Psalm 145:17).

Righteousness is the principles and practices of that which is right. Righteousness is expressed by the practice of righteousness. God's law is the bedrock of all true righteousness. The law is foundational and is unchangeable justice, morals, and ethics.

The law is God's standard of judgment in eternity. Because God is just, He will punish all sin and evil that has not been already forgiven through Christ's sacrifice for sin. Because God is just, He will punish the wicked according to the quality and quantity of their wickedness and will reward the righteous, those who are saved by faith in Christ, according to the quality and quantity of their good works. Because God is just, He will balance the books when in eternity He judges all of humanity. He will make up for injustices and suffering of the righteous. He will lessen the severity of punishment of the unrighteous in eternity when they too have suffered unjustly on earth. The Bible assures us with encouraging statements that all inequities and all miscarriages of justice will be made right in the eternal state. Only God who is all-knowing and infinitely wise will be able to judge and make His decision with perfect justice.

The truth about judgment in eternity is clearly and repeatedly declared in the Bible. A few brief quotations will emphasize this truth for us. Ecclesiastes 12:14 NKJV is one of the clear statements: "God will bring every work into judgment, with every secret thing, whether it is good or whether it is evil." Another is Acts 17:31 NKJV: "God has appointed a day when He will judge the world in righteousness by that man that He has ordained."

The Bible declares to us that no human being is capable of measuring up to God's standard of perfect righteousness. "There is no one righteous, not even one" (Romans 3:10 NKJV). And Ecclesiastes 7:20 NKJV states: "There is not a just (righteous) person on the earth who does good and does not sin." The powerful point God makes regarding the righteousness required by the law is: "For all have sinned, and come short of the glory of God" (Romans 3:23 KJV). The glory of God is the radiance of all of God's perfections, His perfect righteousness. But the conclusive declaration is: "Now we know that whatever the law says, it says to those who are under the law, that every mouth may be stopped, and all the world may become guilty before God" (Romans 3:19; NKJV).

The law, therefore, became our tutor or teacher to bring us to Christ. "Therefore the law was our tutor to bring us to Christ, that we might be justified by faith" (Galatians 3:24 NKJV). The law teaches us that we cannot be righteous and right with God by our own works or efforts, or by keeping the law. The result is, we need for God to do something to make us righteous and right with Him.

That is where God stepped in and provided a perfect righteousness for all of mankind, for all of us who are unrighteous. This is beautifully expressed in Romans 3:21 NIV 1984:

> But now, *a righteousness from God, apart from law*, has been made known, to which the Law and the Prophets testify. *This righteousness from God comes through faith in Jesus Christ* to all who believe (emphasis added).

The next verse explains that this righteousness provided by God has been made possible by the redemption that is in Christ. That is, Jesus lived the perfect life of righteousness that we cannot live. This righteousness provided by God apart from the law is called *the gift of righteousness* (Romans 5:17 NKJV).

However, in ignorance and blindness, some people still attempt to earn or merit their own righteousness by keeping the law or by religious and charitable works. They disregard God's provision of righteousness through His son and attempt to establish their own righteousness. That's why Romans 10:3–4 NIV states:

> Because they disregarded the righteousness from God and attempted to establish their own righteousness, they have not submitted themselves to God's righteousness. For Christ is the end of the law for righteousness to everyone who believes.

Jesus Christ is the "end" or the fulfillment, the fullness, the goal of the law! He is the perfect epitome of the law, the living essence, the sum and substance of the law. And His perfect righteousness becomes a gift of righteousness to all who receive it by faith. But remember, a gift, though offered and made available, is not ours until we personally accept it.

God managed to provide this righteousness required by the law to make it possible for people to be made acceptable to God without violating His own standard or requirement for justice or righteousness. Leander Keyser, a Lutheran theologian, explains this well in *The Philosophy of Christianity*: "Here, too, we see the profundity and fundamental character of the Christian religion. Had God forgiven men's sins directly and saved them by a mere fiat, an eternal ethical principle, namely justice, would have been brushed aside by mere sentimental love. But the divine love is holy love, righteous love, and therefore it will not rudely trample upon the ethical principle of justice, which is an eternal principle with God, and pertains to the very structure of a moral universe."

The fact or truth that *salvation is a gift of pure grace* makes authentic Christianity unique among all the religions and religious systems of the world. Every other religion and religious system is based, either in part or in full, on works and human achievement. They teach that to be made right with God you have to do something. Authentic Christianity is the only religion on the face of the earth that teaches a salvation of pure grace, that is, salvation as a gift totally apart from works or human merit. All other religions and religious systems are alike and similar in their demand for works and human merit in order to be accepted by their god or to acquire Nirvana, heaven, or a place in the Kingdom of God on earth.

So abundant and lavish are the declarations and descriptions in the New Testament of God's grace in regard to salvation that one writer comments: "Everywhere in the earlier epistles we found the doctrine of God's grace exhibited abundantly. It is like the star-studded vault of heaven, which continually flashes myriads of bright diamonds, and like tiny drops of sparking early morning dew scattered over a great meadow" (*What Christians Believe*, p. 299).

In summary, Christ took the guilt and punishment of our sin, and He provided us with His perfect righteousness, in order to make us totally and perfectly righteous before God. 2 Corinthians 5:21 states this clearly: "He made the One who did not know sin (Christ) to be sin for us, so that we might become the righteousness of God in Him." Jesus took our sin and gave us His righteousness. He paid for our sin and provided us with His righteousness.

The Universal Character of the Gospel

Another truth regarding the gospel is that it is universal in what it offers and promises. Romans 1:16 states,

For I am not ashamed of the gospel, because it is God's power for salvation to everyone who believes, first to the Jew, and also to the Greek (Gentile).

These two terms include all of humanity. No one is left out.

John's Gospel makes the universal character of the gospel vividly clear. The following verses illustrate this truth:

> The true light, who gives light to everyone, was *coming into the world.* He was *in the world,* and *the world* was created through Him, yet *the world did not recognize Him.* He came to His own, and His own people did not receive Him. But to all who did receive Him, He gave them the right to be children of God, to those who believe in His name (John 1:9–12; emphasis added).

The theme of "the world" runs throughout the Gospel of John. In fact, the word "world" is used seventy-seven times in John's Gospel and two or three times in his first epistle. In his Gospel it is always speaking of the world of humanity - the whole world of humanity. The true light, Jesus, created the world of humanity and then later came "into" the world of humanity. His coming into the world of humanity is vividly described in John 1:14, "the Word became flesh and took up residence among us." This passage states that when He came, the world, humanity, did not recognize Him for who He was. Even more amazing, His own people, the Jews, did not widely receive Him although He was one of them and came to them.

In John 1:29 the announcement of John the Baptist declares, "Behold the Lamb of God that takes away the sin of *the world.*" (NKJV – emphasis added) Furthermore, John 3:16–19 states:

> For God so loved *the world,* that He gave His only begotten Son, that whoever believes in Him shall not perish, but have eternal life. For God did not send the

Son into *the world* to judge *the world,* but that *the world* might be saved through Him. He who believes in Him is not judged; he who does not believe has been judged already, because he has not believed in the name of the only begotten Son of God. This is the judgment, that *the Light has come into the world,* and men loved the darkness rather than the Light, for their deeds were evil (NASB – emphasis added).

In these verses we find the theme of "the world" continued. God loved the world. God did not send His Son into the world or the realm of humanity in order to judge the world. God sent His Son into the world so that the world of humanity might be saved through Him. The Light has come into the world of humanity, but men did not choose Him because they loved darkness - sin, unrighteousness, wickedness, evil - rather than the Light - goodness or love, truth, and righteousness.

The universal character of the gospel is reiterated again and again in John's writings! To see the many references to the world in John's Gospel, and the majority of them are relevant to the universal nature of the gospel, take a look at the following verses: John 4:42; 6:14, 33, 51; 8:12; 9:5, 39; 10:36; 12:46–47; 16:8, 28.

These verses in John's Gospel and in his first letter or epistle (the book of 1 John) about "the world" fit into three main themes:

1. The Great Invasion – the Son of God coming into the world
2. The Great Salvation – the Son of God providing salvation for the world
3. The Great Commission – the Son of God sending His disciples into the world

All three of these themes stress the universal nature and character of the gospel. It is for everyone.

The gospel of Jesus Christ is intended for all races, languages and ethnic groups of mankind (Revelation 5:9). Furthermore, the gospel embraces all human beings regardless of class distinctions or gender

(Galatians 3:28). And finally, the provision of salvation itself, as the effect or power of the gospel, is universal (1 Timothy 2:4–5 & 4:10; Hebrews 2:9; 1 John 2:2 & 4:9–10, 14).

Lewis Sperry Chafer, in his eight-volume *Systematic Theology* observes: "There are three major aspects of truth set forth in New Testament doctrine relative to the unmeasured benefits which are provided for the unsaved through the death of Christ. Each of these aspects of truth is in turn expressed by one word." Those three are presented below in "The Gospel in Its Universal Applications." Observe that the biblical term "world" is used in the scriptures for propitiation and reconciliation and that 1 Timothy 2 that uses an equivalent term "all humans or people" in verses 1, 4, and 6, speaking in the context of the passage of God's desire and provision for all to be saved.

The Gospel in Its Universal Applications

Observe the gospel in its universal applications as God provides it for the human race, making salvation possible and available to all:

> *Redemption (1 Timothy 2:4, 6)*
> The payment of sin's ransom price to free men from sin's slavery and tyranny
>
> *Propitiation (1 John 2:2)*
> The satisfaction of God's justice against sin making it possible for God to be merciful and forgiving
>
> *Reconciliation (2 Corinthians 5:19)*
> The making of peace between God and mankind, thus clearing the way for man's restoration to fellowship with God

Each of these is available to the whole human race, making salvation and reconciliation to God possible for every human ever born. Our responsibility is simply to accept the gift with a heart of repentance and faith.

After stating the three universal aspects of the gospel, Dr. Chafer notes: "There are at least four other great words, *forgiveness, regeneration, justification, and sanctification*, which represent spiritual blessings secured by the death of Christ; but these are to be distinguished from the three already mentioned in one important particular, namely, that these four words refer to aspects of truth which belong only to those who are saved."

The Gospel in Its Limited Applications

As mentioned, certain promises in the gospel are made specifically and only for those who repent and believe the gospel by placing their trust in Christ and His redemptive work on the cross for their salvation. These include:

Forgiveness (Ephesians 1:7)
The glorious blessing of having our sins pardoned, forgiven, and forgotten as if they never occurred

Regeneration (John 3:3, 6; Titus 3:5; 1 Peter 1:3)
The miraculous imparting of spiritual (eternal) life through a spiritual birth

Justification (Romans 5:1)
The forensic or legal declaration by God that a sinner is made righteous through the shed blood and righteousness of His Son

Sanctification (Hebrews 10:10, 14)
Initially setting the believer in Christ apart for holy purposes and then God's grace working progressively and practically in his life to produce holy living

These benefits, uniquely given to true believers in the gospel, are the only provision for any person's salvation.

The gospel in its various aspects is the subject of much of the New Testament:

The Gospel in relation to faith	the book of Romans
The Gospel in relation to grace	the book of Galatians
The Gospel in relation to the Church	the book of Ephesians
The Gospel in relation to Christ	the book of Colossians
The Gospel in relation to godliness	the book of Titus
The Gospel in relation to purpose in life	the book of Philippians
The Gospel in relation to suffering	the book of 1 Peter
The Gospel in relation to the Old Covenant	the book of Hebrews
The Gospel in relation to destiny and eternity	the book of Revelation

The Powerful Nature of the Gospel

The Gospel and the Necessity of the New Birth

Regeneration or spiritual birth is an essential aspect of the gospel. John's Gospel illustrates vividly its real nature. Jesus told Nicodemus in John chapter 3 about a spiritual birth or being "born again." He explained that just as man has experienced a physical birth to enter into this world, he needs a spiritual birth to enter into the Kingdom of God. (John 3:3–6) This statement clearly excludes other means of being made right with God. A spiritual birth is required. Jesus said, "You must be born again" (John 3:7). The new birth is not optional. It is essential and necessary.

Jesus further taught us that this spiritual birth is a work performed by the Holy Spirit (John 3:6–8) and that faith is the key requirement for spiritual birth (John 3:15-18, 36). Jesus later illustrated this same truth to the Samaritan woman in John chapter 4. It is living water that satisfies and gives eternal life. Eternal life is spiritual life in its present and continuous form for time and eternity. As the biblical text tells us, this dear woman had many broken relationships, deep disappointments and emotional pain. But when this woman's heart was transformed by new, fresh life and overflowing joy, she thrillingly testified to her entire town that Jesus was the long expected Messiah and that what He had given her had satisfied the deepest longings and needs of her heart. The result was that many of the Samaritans believed in Him because of her testimony (John 3:39). She had experienced a spiritual birth!

One of the primary points Jesus presents to her is that she must "ask" for that water. Faith is a choice to receive the water of life, salvation. It is an act of the will just like the faith Jesus required of Nicodemus. This too excludes all methods of salvation that do not require a heart of faith.

A birth implies that a life that follows. Later, John's Gospel reveals the evidence of the type of life produced by the spiritual birth will result in spiritual fruitfulness. Fruit is produced by the life of the tree or vine. A lack of evidence of spiritual life in those who profess to be Christians is the primary reason that many outside the church are repulsed by the hypocrisy they see. Those who have been spiritually born and possess spiritual life will naturally live their faith so that others will be drawn to Christ and the gospel.

The Gospel in Its Acceptance: Faith Alone

The references to the requirement of faith in John's Gospel appear to pour out of John's inkwell. It seems that every time John dips his pen in, it comes out dripping the word "believe" onto the parchment! The following verses herald the message in his Gospel of believing for salvation: John 1:7, 12; John 3:14, 15, 16, 18, 36; John 4:42; John 5:24; John 6:29, 35, 40, 47, 68–69; John 8:24; John 11:25–27; John 12:36, 46; John 14:1, 6; and John 20:29–31.

The following is a sampling of these verses in order to grasp their truth about believing:

> But to all who did receive Him, He gave them the right
> to be children of God, to those who *believe* in His name
> (John 1:12; emphasis added).

For God loved the world in this way: He gave His One and Only Son, so that everyone who *believes* in Him will not perish but have eternal life (John 3:16; emphasis added).

I assure you: Anyone who hears My word and *believes* Him who sent Me has eternal life and will not come under judgment but has passed from death to life (John 5:24; emphasis added).

For this is the will of My Father that everyone who sees the Son and *believes* in Him may have eternal life (John 6:40; emphasis added).

Jesus said, "Because you have seen Me, you have *believed*. Those who *believe* without seeing are blessed." Jesus performed many other signs in the presence of His disciples that are not written in this book. But these are written so that you may *believe* Jesus is the Messiah, the Son of God, and by *believing* you may have life in His name (John 20:29–31).

John's Gospel is not by any means the only book that explains the gospel in relation to faith as opposed to works, although it does focus on it quite extensively. In Acts 13:38–39 Paul says, "Therefore, let it be known to you, brothers, that through this man (Jesus Christ) forgiveness of sins is being proclaimed to you, and everyone who *believes* in Him is justified from everything, which you could not be justified from through the law of Moses" (emphasis added). Paul answers the question of the Philippian jailor, "What must I do to be saved?" in Acts 16:31: "So they said, '*Believe* on the Lord Jesus, and you will be saved – you and your household'" (emphasis added).

Paul taught authoritatively that faith is the means of salvation. As we examine his teaching regarding this, it is important to note that "believe," the Greek word "pisteuo," and faith, the Greek word "pistis," come from the same stem or root word, "pist."

The great apostle emphasized faith as the means of being saved in his two great books, Romans and Galatians. Romans 1:16–17 announces the theme of the book of Romans in grand style. Paul says that he is not ashamed of the gospel of Christ. The gospel, he says, "is God's power for salvation to everyone who *believes*"(emphasis added).

In the very next verse, verse 17, where he quotes Habakkuk 2:4, he declares that a righteousness from God is revealed in the gospel. Romans 1:17:

> For in the gospel a righteousness from God is revealed,
> a righteousness that is by *faith* from first to last, just as
> it is written: The righteous will live by *faith* (NIV 1984;
> emphasis added).

Immediately after Paul talks about "a righteousness of God apart from law," he lays great stress on faith in 3:22, 25–26: "This righteousness from God comes through *faith* in Jesus Christ to all who believe.... God presented him as a sacrifice of atonement, through *faith* in his blood . . . he did it to demonstrate his justice at the present time, so as to be just and the one who justifies those who have *faith* in Jesus" (NIV 1984; emphasis added). Paul mentions the word "faith" in that short passage three times! Twice faith is "faith in Jesus" or "faith in Jesus Christ." Once it is "faith in His blood." In addition, the righteousness provided by God is "to all who *believe*, since there is no distinction (between Jew and Gentile)" (emphasis added).

Paul was not finished declaring the relationship of faith to the reception of the gospel as the one and only means of salvation. Chapter 4 of Romans is dedicated to proving that truth. "Faith" or "believe" are used no less than sixteen times in chapter 4! Romans 4:5 assures: "But to the one who does not work, but *believes* on Him who declares righteous the ungodly, his *faith* is credited for righteousness" (emphasis added).

This theme appears to climax in Romans 5:1–2 with two more references to faith. Romans 5:1 is the conclusion of perhaps the entire section that begins in Romans 1:16–17 when 5:1 declares: "Therefore, since we have been declared righteous by *faith*, we have peace with God through our Lord Jesus Christ" (emphasis added). Then in chapter 10 he comes to the powerful conclusion, "For Christ is the end of the law for righteousness to everyone who *believes*" (Romans 10:4 NASB; emphasis added).

In Galatians, Paul again heralds the truth of "sola fide" – "faith alone." In 2:16 he says: "We know that no one is justified by the works of the law but by *faith* in Jesus Christ. And we have *believed* in Christ Jesus, so that we might be justified by *faith* in Christ and not by the works of the law, because by the works of the law no human being will be justified" (emphasis added). Notice his emphasis on faith in this verse. This is exciting – that we can be declared righteous or justified apart from any religious works and merit of our own!

Paul is not done yet. In Galatians 3:6–7 he again uses the words "faith" and "believe" twice in two short verses: "Just as Abraham *believed* God, and it was credited to him for righteousness, so understand that those who have *faith* are Abraham's sons (emphasis added). Then in 3:11 he quotes Habakkuk 2:4 just as he did in Romans 1:17, assuring his readers that "the righteous will live *by faith*" (emphasis added). Then in 3:14 he states: "so that we could receive the promise of the Spirit through *faith*" (emphasis added).

Finally in Galatians 3:24–26 he stresses faith by another use of the word in triplicate. There he speaks of being "justified by faith," and of faith superseding the law, and concludes by saying, "for you are all sons of God through *faith* in Christ Jesus" (emphasis added).

Paul's teaching about faith in reference to salvation does not end with his two books about the gospel, Romans and Galatians. It continues throughout a number of his epistles. In Ephesians he states, "in Him (Jesus Christ, the Messiah) when you *believed* – were sealed with the promised Holy Spirit (1:13; emphasis added). In 2:8 he says "you are saved through *faith*" (emphasis added).

In Philippians 3:9 Paul reiterates his great theme of "the righteousness of God based on faith." It asserts: "And be found in Him (Christ Jesus my Lord) not having a righteousness of my own from the law, but one that is through *faith* in Christ – the righteousness from God based on *faith* (emphasis added).

Finally, the author of Hebrews exalts faith as the medium of securing salvation. In Hebrews 10:38 he also refers to Habakkuk 2:4: "But My righteous one will live by *faith.*" On the heels of that statement he shows in chapter 11, "the Faith Chapter" of the Bible, that true faith is comprehensive and pervasive. Faith believes in God as the Creator of the universe (11:3). Faith believes in the sinfulness of man and the necessity of sacrifice for sin (11:4). Faith is walking through life with God and sharing our lives with Him in fellowship (11:5). Faith is fearing God or reverencing Him and His Word so that we act on His Word in obedience (11:7). Faith believes in a future life and eternal home and reward (11:8–10).

Many other truths about the nature of faith are illustrated in the remainder of Hebrews chapter 11, "the Faith Chapter," but these are sufficient to illustrate the nature of faith. Our faith in the sacrifice of Christ and its sufficiency for our forgiveness must be this deep, life-filling type of faith (Hebrews 10:10–14). It is much, much more than simple intellectual assent.

In conclusion, "one faith," the gospel, is not a creed, but a dynamic doctrine. Standing between "one Lord" and "one baptism" it is the very core of conviction, the driving force of our Christian faith. It is the apex of God's revelation to man. It is the precious treasure of God, "the faith that was delivered to the saints once for all" (Jude 3). As characterized by the apostle Paul in 2 Timothy, it is a sacred and precious deposit to be guarded, defended, confirmed, and proclaimed. The gospel is the power of God to give us salvation, and it is powerful enough to save all of mankind (Romans 1:16).

When the great apostle Paul was approaching the time of his death, he wrote the book of 2 Timothy. To Timothy, a young missionary pastor he gave his dying words of bequeath.

> Timothy, I have fought a good fight in proclaiming, defending and promoting the gospel. I have finished my race and now I am passing the torch to you. Timothy,

> I have kept the faith (the gospel), I have fulfilled my
> responsibility in guarding the sacred trust, the glorious
> gospel. Now I am passing the torch to you! I am
> handing off the baton for you to run the next leg of the
> race. The grave responsibility of guarding, defending
> and proclaiming the gospel is now in your hands (2
> Timothy 4:6–7 paraphrased in context of the book of
> 2 Timothy)!

Any religious system that rejects the true nature and applications of the gospel is not "Christian" regardless of its claims to be Christian and regardless of its heritage and tradition. If a church or religious group rejects the gospel of the grace of God, rejecting salvation by grace alone through faith alone in Christ alone, then that church or group is not truly Christian. A denomination or group may confess every other essential doctrine, but if it does not confess and believe the true, authentic gospel of Jesus Christ that is the very heart of the Christian faith, then it is a false and deceptive religious system. Those who believe the gospel should avoid such a church and separate themselves from it. They should join themselves to a church that preaches the true gospel of Jesus Christ.

> I am amazed that you are so quickly turning away
> from Him who called you by the grace of Christ, and
> are turning to a different gospel— not that there is
> another gospel, but there are some who are troubling
> you and want to change the gospel of Christ. But
> even if we or an angel from heaven should preach
> to you a gospel other than what we have preached
> to you, a curse be on him! As we have said before,
> I now say again: if anyone preaches to you a gospel
> contrary to what you received, a curse be on him
> (Galatians 1:6-9)!

One Baptism–Confession and Commitment

Baptism is one of the seven major doctrines of the Christian faith. Yet in contemporary times its importance and significance have been minimized.

"One baptism" is water baptism; however, it is not simply the act but also the significance or meaning of the act that is monumentally important. Baptism is a doctrine or teaching that is of supreme importance to the Christian faith.

First of all, baptism is important because it is the personal declaration of faith of the believer in the person and saving work of Christ. It is a declaration of faith in Christ and in the gospel. Baptism pictures the death, burial, and resurrection of Christ. The believer is united with Christ in His death, burial, and resurrection. Therefore, baptism also pictures the believer's death to his old life, burial of his old life, and resurrection to a new life– (Romans 6:1–4). It is a public declaration to the world of where one stands in relation to Christ and the gospel.

> Therefore we were buried with Him by baptism into death, in order that, just as Christ was raised from the dead by the glory of the Father, so we too may walk in a new way of life. (Romans 6:4)

However baptism is not only a confession of faith, but it is also a commitment of the one being baptized to be a disciple of Jesus Christ. It is the initiation ceremony for a new disciple, and thus the beginning of his development and life as a disciple (Matthew 28:19). This means that baptism is the visible and public turning point in the life of the new believer.

Baptism Is Associated with Our Acceptance of Jesus Christ as Savior

In Acts 2:38 baptism is seen as a reflection of our repentance and faith in Christ. After believing and repenting, almost three thousand were baptized as a testimony of their faith in Christ and their commitment to Him. In Acts 8:36–37 the Ethiopian eunuch was baptized by Philip once he became satisfied with the eunuch's faith in Jesus Christ. When Peter preached Christ to the Gentiles at the home of Cornelius and they had believed and received the Holy Spirit, baptism was the next consideration and was immediately put into action (Acts 10:43-48). When Paul and Silas preached Christ to the Philippian jailor and his household, and told them that they had to believe on Christ to be saved, they believed. Paul and Silas baptized them later that same evening (Acts 16:30–34). When relating the story of his own salvation, Paul stated that Ananias said to him, "Arise, and be baptized, and wash away your sins 'calling on the name of the Lord'" (Acts 22:16). Once again, baptism has to do with repentance of sin and faith in Jesus Christ.

Baptism Is a Confession of our Faith in Christ

Baptism bears witness to our faith and trust in Christ, trust in His person and in His work of redemption (Acts 2:41; 8:12, 13). Confession of Christ is an intimate part of baptism. To be baptized in "the name of the Lord Jesus," as Acts 8:16 indicates, is to publicly acknowledge Jesus Christ as Lord. "Calling on His name," as in Acts 22:16, is a phrase that throughout the Bible means worshipping God in public confession and declaration of faith whether by an individual or a fellowship of believers. In Acts 22:16 it is more specifically worshipping Christ in the act of baptism. As to "calling on the name of the Lord" being an act of worship, two prime examples would be Genesis 4:26b: "At that time people began to call on the name of the LORD," and Romans 10:13 "whoever calls on the name of the Lord" (see the significant context, Romans 10:9–10). This act of worship in the heart includes acknowledging publicly that Jesus Christ has been raised from the dead and that He is Lord!

Baptism Is a Natural Act of Obedience to Christ

Baptism should be expected as evidence of faith in and allegiance to Jesus Christ. Anyone who says that he trusts Jesus Christ as his Lord and Savior but refuses to be baptized is refusing to publicly confess Him as his Savior and Lord and is refusing to commit himself to be His disciple. The refusal of baptism is, therefore, tantamount to a denial of faith in Jesus Christ and allegiance to Him.

The early church did not recognize anyone as a Christian unless they had made public their confession of faith and commitment to discipleship by baptism. Because of this, they only allowed those who had been baptized to partake of the Lord's Supper. *The Didache* ("The Teaching") was written between 50 and 80 A.D. and was universally used by the early church as a pre-baptismal catechetical manual. *The Didache* 9:5 states: "And let no one eat or drink from your eucharist (the Lord's Supper) except those baptized in the name of the Lord."

The importance of baptism as a statement of faith in Christ and a believer's testimony to the world of his commitment to Christ is clearly communicated and explicitly commanded by the following verses: Mark 16:16 where it declares, "He who has believed and has been baptized shall be saved; but he who has disbelieved shall be condemned." Note that this verse presumes that all who are saved will be obedient in baptism. By itself, baptism has no power to remove sin. However, baptism is a profoundly important and necessary act of obedience although not essential for salvation. The thief on the cross would be with Jesus in heaven even though he was unable to be baptized.

It is the obedient, public proclamation of our repentance and faith and our public commitment to follow Christ as His disciple that gives baptism its significance and power. Acts 2:41 says, "So then, those who had received his word were *baptized*; and that day there were added about three thousand souls" (emphasis added). Luke records in Acts 8:12-13, "But *when they believed* Philip preaching *the good news* about the kingdom of God and the name of Jesus Christ, *they were being baptized*, men and women alike. Even *Simon himself believed; and after being baptized*, he continued on with Philip" (emphasis added). And Luke poignantly portrays Paul's testimony of his baptism in Acts 22:16: "Now why do you delay? Get up and *be baptized*, and wash away your sins, *calling on His name*" (emphasis added). These are examples of people being baptized when they trusted in Christ and committed their lives to Him. The examples should speak volumes to us.

Baptism Symbolizes Repentance, Forgiveness, and Cleansing of Sin

John's baptism was a prelude to Christian baptism, and elements of its meaning carry over into Christian baptism. Thus baptism, in light of the redemptive work of Christ and the believer's faith in Christ and His redemptive work, also addresses sin. The believer is confessing repentance of sin, confidence in Christ's power to grant forgiveness of sin and cleansing of sin. Physical water cannot of itself cleanse the sin of man's heart. It only illustrates and symbolizes the cleansing that comes because of faith in Christ and His blood that actually cleanses us from all sin (1 John 1:7).

A number of Scriptures about baptism speak of confessing sins, forgiveness of sins, and cleansing of sins. One of these regarding the baptism practiced by John the Baptist, Matthew 3:6, asserts, "and they were being baptized by him in the Jordan River, as they *confessed their sins*" (emphasis added). Then also concerning John's baptism Mark 1:14 states: John the Baptist appeared in the wilderness preaching a baptism of repentance *for the forgiveness of sins*" (emphasis added). Peter gave this admonition as he concluded the first Christian sermon, the first gospel sermon: "Peter said to them, '*Repent*, and each of you be baptized in the name of Jesus Christ for *the forgiveness of your sins*; and you will receive the gift of the Holy Spirit'" (Acts 2:38; emphasis added).

Baptism Symbolizes the Gospel and Our Union with Christ

Our physical baptism is a picture of our spiritual baptism. It is a picture of our union with Christ. It first pictures that union as the believer being placed into or baptized into the body of Christ so that he is spiritually united to Christ. 1 Corinthians 12:13 makes that statement. It declares that it is the Holy Spirit who spiritually places the believer into union with Christ by baptizing the believer into Christ's (spiritual) body. In Luke 3:16 and also in Acts 1:5 we are told that the one who baptizes us is the Holy Spirit. The key passage, however, is 1 Corinthians 12:13. It declares:

> For by one Spirit we were all baptized into one body, whether Jews or Greeks, whether slaves or free, and we were all made to drink of one Spirit.

As a result of being united with Christ we are made to share with Him in His death and resurrection (Romans 6:3–4). His death has become our death and His resurrection our resurrection. We have died to our old life by His death. We have been buried with Him. The old person we were no longer exists. We have been raised together with Christ to a new life. So baptism portrays the believer's experience of the saving power of the gospel of Jesus Christ.

While spiritual baptism takes place the moment one receives Jesus Christ as his Lord and Savior by repentance and faith, it is then publicly pictured by the believer's baptism. The believer's baptism therefore pictures first the death, burial, and resurrection of Christ. Then it pictures the believer's death with Christ to sin, the burial of his old life, and his resurrection to a new life in Christ.

Baptism is, for the reasons mentioned above, a monumental declaration of the gospel itself and also a wonderful expression of the believer's personal experience of the saving power of the gospel! It is no wonder that baptism is given such a prominent place as being one of the seven foundational doctrines of our faith.

Baptism Is a Commitment to Be a Disciple of Christ

Jesus Christ commanded everyone who believes on Him, and therefore wants to be His disciple, to be baptized. Baptism is the initial step of declaring one's discipleship. It is our initiation into the community of disciples. Becoming a disciple then continues throughout the rest of one's life.

Baptism is associated with discipleship in the New Testament a number of times. This was true from the earliest New Testament testimony. John 4:1–2 indicates this when it notes: "Therefore when the Lord knew that the Pharisees had heard that Jesus was making and baptizing more disciples than John." And Jesus Himself associated baptism with discipleship in Matthew 28:19, "Go therefore and make disciples of all nations, baptizing them."

Baptism Unites the New Believer with the Local Visible Church

Spiritual baptism unites us not only with Christ but also places us in union with His Body, the Church. It joins the new believer both with Christ and with other believers (1 Corinthians 13:14; John 14:20; 1 Corinthians 10:16–17; Ephesians 4:4). Therefore, water baptism, which pictures spiritual baptism, is correspondingly the entrance into the local church. It joins the new believer into the body of other disciples, the local church.

The joining of believers together in a community of disciples is pictured by what occurred on the day of Pentecost at the birth of the Church. The ones who heard and believed Peter's preaching of the gospel and were baptized were "added" to the other believers. Phillip Schaff in Volume 1 of *History of the Christian Church* states: "It (baptism) incorporates the penitent sinner in the visible church, and entitles him to all the privileges, and binds him to all the duties of this communion (fellowship of believers)."

To put it another way, baptism is the visible joining of a person to the company of Christ's disciples (Acts 2:38, 41; cf. 5:13–14). The commitment to discipleship, therefore, was a commitment both to Christ and to the community of disciples. This commitment to the Church is due to the spiritual relation of the Church to Christ. It is His Body, and He is its head. As G. R. Beasely-Murray points out in his signal work, *Baptism in the New Testament*, "Baptism to Christ is baptism to the Church; it cannot be otherwise, for the Church is the Body of Christ."

The joining of believers to Christ and to one another is illustrated in the Old Testament, according to the apostle Paul. He gives a vivid vision of this truth in 1 Corinthians 10:1–4 (NASB):

> For I do not want you to be unaware, brethren, that our fathers were all under the cloud and all passed through the sea; and all were baptized into Moses in the cloud and in the sea; and all ate the same spiritual food and all drank the same spiritual drink, for they were drinking from a spiritual rock which followed them; and the rock was Christ.

In this passage it is obvious that Moses is a type of Christ and Israel a type of the Church. Passing through the sea was a symbol of baptism. In that momentous experience the people of Israel were joined to Moses as their head and leader and they were bonded to one another. They subsequently shared in essentials common to all of them. They shared the same spiritual food and drink. The same truth is pictured by Christian baptism. Christ and His people are joined or bonded together by baptism. And Christians all spiritually share Christ's body as our spiritual food and His blood as our spiritual drink.

One God and Father of All - the Father Who Unites All

The divine person of the Father is the focal point of the triune being we call God. The Father is the unifying source and power over all beings that worship Him, submit to Him, and come under His care. He is the sovereign and providential overseer of all things. The Father provides and protects. Far more than just the practical values extended to all under His all-knowing care is the loving relationship that exists between the Father and those who are His children.

Strangely, while there are almost an incalculable number of books written about Jesus Christ the Son, and a considerable number of books written about the Holy Spirit, I am aware of only one single book written about God the Father. That book is *Knowing God the Father Through the Old Testament* by Christopher J. H. Wright. Given the lack of commentary regarding God the Father, it is especially important to look at what the Bible says about Him.

As I began to think about God the Father only a few Scriptures about Him came to mind. This led to my erroneous conclusion that the Word of God has little to say about Him. However, when I performed a search in Power Bible, a Bible search engine, it revealed that there are hundreds of references. The search engine would not allow all of them to be brought up at once. When just the four Gospels were selected, once again the search engine would not allow those to be brought up because they were so numerous. Power Bible asked if there was a desire to view just the first two hundred references in the Gospels!

How astounding! Scripture does say a lot about the Father. On further investigation I discovered that this subject is actually more complex and enigmatic than the other two persons of the Godhead, the Son and the Holy Spirit. For whatever reason, it seems that we read over Scriptures about God the Father without being aware of their presence and significance.

Research reveals that there are four aspects to the Fatherhood of God the Father.

1. The Universal Fatherhood of God

There is a sense in Scripture in which the Father is the father over all creation and over all of humankind in terms of His provision and care (Psalm chapter 104). There is benevolence, kindness, a profusion of goodness that streams from God the Father to His creation and to all of His creatures. He sends the rain on the righteous and the unrighteous because of His innate generosity and because of the goodness of His heart. The fatherhood of God over creation is one of measureless bounty!

In Hebrews 12:9 He is called "the Father of spirits." When this verse is viewed in light of Ecclesiastes 12:7 that says: "then the dust will return to the earth as it was, and the spirit will return to God who gave it," we understand that every human soul or spirit is a special creation of God and that He has exercised loving care in creating us and providing for us.

The author of Hebrews references this in part in Hebrews 12:22–23

> But you have come to Mount Zion and to the city of the living God, the heavenly Jerusalem, and to myriads of angels, to the general assembly and church of the firstborn who are enrolled in heaven, and to God, the Judge of all, and to *the spirits of the righteous made perfect* (emphasis added).

There is a universal, creation sense, in which all humans are God's children, His offspring. Paul alludes to this when preaching to the erudite, educated crowd on Mars Hill in Acts 17:29, "Being then the children of God, we ought not to think that the Divine Nature is like gold or silver or stone, an image formed by the art and thought of man."

The angels are called "sons of God." They are His special creation as well. They also, in some respect, are like His children. In James 1:17 He is designated as "the Father of lights." It portrays Him as the father, creator and sovereign, over the planets and stars. In that fatherly role He sends down every blessing to His children on earth because of His infinite goodness. Matthew 5:45 says: "so that you may be sons of your Father who is in heaven; for He causes His sun to rise on the evil and the good, and sends rain on the righteous and the unrighteous."

2. The Fatherhood of God to Israel

We who are Christians gain valuable insights into our relationship to God as our Father by observing God's fatherly relationship with

Israel. There are parallels and similarities between God's relationship to Israel and the relationship of God the Father to us. Exodus 4:22 says: "Then you shall say to Pharaoh, 'Thus says the LORD, Israel is My son, My firstborn'"(Also see Deuteronomy 32:6; Jeremiah 31:9; Hosea 11:1).

Like a father, God was the protector and provider for Israel. He nurtured them, guided them, and loved them like a father loves his children. He watched over them, and disciplined them as needed and best for them. In spite of this, the Jewish people largely missed seeing the kind of relationship God sustained with them. To them, expressing God's tender love and patience was more of a figure of speech than a reality of His fatherhood. Yet God's prophets declare, "Don't all of us have one Father? Didn't one God create us? Why then do we act treacherously against one another, profaning the covenant of our fathers" (Malachi 2:10)?

The Jews' reverence for God was such that they could not think of Him as having any real similarities to them. This prevented them from thinking of God as their father or calling Him "father." Yet David, because of his close personal relationship with God, understood the special reality of God's relationship as Father. He refers to this nature of God and His tenderness and mercy toward Israel in Psalm 103:13: "Just as a father has compassion on his children, so the LORD has compassion on those who fear Him."

3. God the Father and His Son

Jesus speaks of God as "my Father" in such a natural way that His disciples, observing His miracles and hearing His wisdom did not question His claim. But the Pharisees, scribes and Sadducees understood precisely what He was claiming. They charged him with blasphemy for calling God His father! That's why John 5:18 says, "But He answered them, 'My Father is working until now, and I Myself am working.' For this reason therefore the Jews were seeking all the more to kill Him, because He not only was breaking the Sabbath, but also was calling God His own Father, making Himself equal with God."

Jesus tenderly speaks numerous times about "my Father" to those He is teaching. The warm intimacy of the relationship between the Father and the Son is tenderly expressed again and again. In John 3:35 He says, "*The Father loves the Son* and has given all things into His hand" (emphasis added). Then in John 5:20 He declares, "For *the Father loves the Son*, and shows Him all things that He Himself is doing; and the Father will show Him greater works than these, so that you will marvel" (emphasis added). Jesus told His disciples, "All things have been handed over to Me by *My Father*; and no one knows the Son except the Father; nor does anyone know the Father except the Son, and anyone to whom the Son wills to reveal Him" (Matthew 11:27; emphasis added). Thus Jesus revealed the unique and special relationship between the Father and Himself.

Jesus also explained to His disciples the reverent position the Father held in His eyes when in Matthew 10:32-33 He stated, "Therefore everyone who confesses Me before men, I will also confess him before *My Father* who is in heaven. But whoever denies Me before men, I will also deny him before *My Father* who is in heaven" (emphasis added). And our Lord added that our relationship to Him is dependent on our reverence and obedience toward the Father in Matthew 12:50, "For whoever does the will of *My Father* who is in heaven, he is My brother and sister and mother" (emphasis added).

There was and is complete union between the Father and the Son - oneness. In John 10:30 the Lord Jesus proclaims, "I and the Father are one." As we look at what the Scriptures say about the relationship between the Father and the Son several important principles emerge.

The Father toward the Son

Two things are shown at Jesus's baptism and His transfiguration. The first is the Father's love for Jesus. Matthew 3:17 observes: "And suddenly a voice came from heaven, saying, 'This is *My beloved Son*, in whom I am well pleased'" (emphasis added). And in Matthew 17:5: "While he was still speaking, behold, a bright cloud overshadowed them; and suddenly a voice came out of the cloud, saying, 'This is My beloved Son, *in whom I am well pleased.* Hear Him'" (emphasis added)! The other thing we see is that the Father was pleased with, or proud of, His Son.

There are three principles demonstrated in the Father's relationship to His Son that illustrate the relationship every father should have with each of his children. Those three principles are: (1) Identity, (2) Love, and (3) Approval. The three most powerful things any father can do to impact the lives of his children are these three. A father should make it clear and should verbalize it to his children and in front of others, "You are (or this is) my son" or "You are (or this is) my daughter." That identity does something powerful in the soul or psyche of a child. A second thing that needs to be verbalized and demonstrated by a father toward his children is, "I love you." The heart of the father toward the child should say: "You are the apple of my eye, very precious to me." Again, this gives strength to a child like nothing else can. And finally, children need to hear their father say, "I am proud of you!" Children need the approval of their father more than the approval of any other human being. This also does something powerful to a child's spirit or soul.

Another wonderful aspect of the Father's relationship with His Son is the Father rewarding the Son for the Son's obedience. In John 6:37 Jesus states: "All that the Father gives Me will come to Me, and the one who comes to Me I will certainly not cast out." Believers are a gift from the Father to the Son. The author of Hebrews makes this clear in Hebrews 2:13 when he says: "And again: 'I will put My trust in Him.' And again: 'Here am I and the children whom God has given Me.'" In John 10:29 Jesus declares: "My Father, who has given them to Me, is greater than all; and no one is able to snatch them out of the Father's hand."

The Son toward the Father

John's Gospel reveals several things to us about the Son's relationship to the Father. The first is that the Son's purpose is to glorify the Father. This is evident from several passages. In John 12:28 we discover that it was Jesus's passion to glorify the Father, as He spoke this desire in view of His imminent crucifixion. "'Father, glorify Your name.' Then a voice came out of heaven: 'I have both glorified it, and will glorify it again'"

(NASB). Then in John 14:13 Jesus said, "Whatever you ask in My name, that will I do, so that the Father may be glorified in the Son" (NASB). And again Jesus expressed His ultimate passion in John 17:1, "Jesus spoke these things; and lifting up His eyes to heaven, He said, 'Father, the hour has come; glorify Your Son, that the Son may glorify You'" (NASB).

The second principle is the Son's commitment to do the will of the Father because He loves Him and wants to please Him. Hebrews 10:4–10 tells us that Jesus giving His very life on the cross was the purpose of Him becoming human and of coming into this world. This offering of His life as a sacrifice was the supreme act of obedience in doing the Father's will. Even though this was His most dramatic act of obedience, everything else in His life that preceded it was also the result of His obedience to the Father's will.

Hebrews 10:4–10 (NKJV) declares:

> For it is not possible that the blood of bulls and goats could take away sins. Therefore, when He came into the world, He said: "Sacrifice and offering You did not desire, But *a body You have prepared for Me*. In burnt offerings and sacrifices for sin You had no pleasure." Then I said, *"Behold, I have come*--In the volume of the book it is written of Me *--To do Your will, O God."* Previously saying, "Sacrifice and offering, burnt offerings, and offerings for sin You did not desire, nor had pleasure in them" (which are offered according to the law), then He said, *"Behold, I have come to do Your will, O God."* He takes away the first that He may establish the second. *By that will we have been sanctified through the offering of the body of Jesus Christ* once for all (emphasis added).

Another principle is the Son's willing dependence on the Father to show Him what He wanted Him to do. This is explained in John 8:28: "So Jesus said, 'When you lift up the Son of Man, then you will know that I am He, and I do nothing on My own initiative, but I speak these things as the Father taught Me.'" Throughout His ministry, we are told repeatedly of Jesus's frequent and extended times spent praying to His Father. The purpose of much of this was undoubtedly to learn the Father's will so He could carry it out. Think of how in the Garden of Gethsemane He prayed for the cup to be removed from Him. "Not My will but Yours, Father" was His request, even when faced with the ultimate horror of bearing all the sin of mankind.

God the Father and His Children or Sons

We have seen that there is a universal sense of God's fatherhood over all of mankind and toward all of His creatures. There is, however, a limited, specific, and special sense in which the Father is the father of His household of faith, the Father of Christians only. They alone are His children, spiritually born into His family, named after Him, loved uniquely by Him, and provided and protected in a special way by Him. He provides for His own by blessing us in special ways spiritually. Ephesians 1:3 tells us "Praise be to the God and Father of our Lord Jesus Christ, who has bestowed on us in Christ every spiritual blessing in the heavenly realms." His love for His children is exceptional: "Look at how great a love the Father has given us, that we should be called God's children" (1 John 3:1).

The relationship God has with those of us who are His children is pictured by the relationship He had and has with His Son. This is implied by Jesus in John 20:17: Jesus said to her, "'Stop clinging to Me, for I have not yet ascended to the Father; but go to My brethren and say to them, 'I ascend to My Father and your Father.'" Although God's love for His one and only Son is unique and supreme in degree, there are similar though lesser expressions of that relationship toward all of His children who are also called "the sons of God."

The fatherhood of the Father is observed in His loving relationship with His Son. There is deep mutual affection. The Son reveres and honors the Father, and the Father loves and adores His Son, delights in Him, and honors Him before all. The Father seeks what is ultimately best for His Son. Passages, particularly in John's Gospel, express and explain this special relationship (See John 5:19–20, 30, 36–37; John 6:37–40; John 8:28–29, 54–55; John 10:14–15, 25, 28–30, 38; John 14:7–11, 20, 28–31; John 16:27–28, 32; John 17:4–5, 20–21.) This relationship of unity that exists between the Father and the Son is extended to all who abide in the Son. They are becoming unified in similarity to the oneness of the Father and the Son. John 14:20, 23 states:

> In that day you will know that I am in My Father, and you in Me, and I in you. If anyone loves Me, he will keep My word; and My Father will love him, and We will come to him and make Our abode with him (NASB).

This same truth is reiterated in 1 John 1:3:

> What we have seen and heard we proclaim to you also, so that you too may have fellowship with us; and indeed our fellowship is with the Father and with His Son Jesus Christ (NASB).

This intimate fellowship and union between the Father and the Son is therefore expanded in some fashion to include fellowship and union with all true believers.

Jesus taught His disciples to pray to the Father and explained how He cares about us and our needs (Matthew 6:9, 32). In effect Jesus was showing us that the relationship we have with the Father is similar to the relationship He had with the Father. So now we are children of God by faith in His Son, Jesus Christ! Our hearts therefore cry, "Abba, Father." Romans 8:15 states: "For you have not received a spirit of slavery leading to fear again, but you have received a spirit of adoption as sons by which we cry out, 'Abba! Father'" (NASB)! And Galatians 4:6 declares: "Because you are sons, God has sent forth the Spirit of His Son into our hearts, crying, 'Abba! Father'" (NASB)!

This is very touching and expresses the intimacy of our relationship. "Abba," the ancient Aramaic word, was probably the first word spoken by babies in Jesus's day, much as babies today are first taught to say "Dada." Paul repeated it using the Greek word for "father," indicating that Jews, Aramaic, and also Gentiles, Greek, can call on God as their Father through faith in Christ. It is spoken tenderly, like the word "Daddy," with warmest affection and deepest respect.

"Our Father in heaven, may Your name be revered." As we think of this reverence for God's name, we need to remember that in biblical times, the name of someone expressed their full character. We must hold the justice, compassion, goodness and love of God in highest respect as we contemplate Him and come before Him in prayer.

In this relationship with our Heavenly Father, we who are His children are blessed in many wonderful ways:

Loving Intimacy - John 14:23 says: Jesus answered and said to him, "If anyone loves Me, he will keep My word; and My Father will love him, and We will come to him and make Our abode with him" (NASB).

Guiding and Teaching - Matthew 16:17 states: "And Jesus said to him, 'Blessed are you, Simon Barjona, because flesh and blood did not reveal this to you, but My Father who is in heaven'" (NASB).

Reward - Matthew 6:6 records: "But you, when you pray, go into your inner room, close your door and pray to your Father who is in secret, and your Father who sees what is done in secret will reward you" (NASB).

Inheritance - Romans 8:16–17 and Revelation 21:7 declare: "The Spirit Himself testifies with our spirit that we are children of God, and if children, heirs also, heirs of God and fellow heirs with Christ." And "He who overcomes shall inherit all things, and I will be his God and he shall be My son" (NASB).

Protection and Security - John 10:29 says: "My Father, who has given them to Me, is greater than all; and no one is able to snatch them out of the Father's hand"(NASB).

Goodness and Providing - Matthew 6:32 states: "For the Gentiles eagerly seek all these things; for your heavenly Father knows that you need all these things" (NASB). The Father loves His children and is generous and kind toward them as Matthew 7:11 notes: "If you then, being evil, know how to give good gifts to your children, how much more will your Father who is in heaven give what is good to those who ask Him" (NASB)!

Chastening - Hebrews 12:5–7 reminds us: "And you have forgotten the exhortation which speaks to you as to sons: 'My son, do not despise the chastening of the LORD, Nor be discouraged when you are rebuked by Him; For whom the LORD loves He chastens, And scourges every son whom He receives.' If you endure chastening, God deals with you as with sons; for what son is there whom a father does not chasten" (NKJV)?

Likeness of Character - The Father is the one from whom our character comes as mentioned in Matthew 5:44–45, 48: "But I say to you, love your enemies and pray for those who persecute you, so that you may be sons of your Father who is in heaven; for He causes His sun to rise on the evil and the good, and sends rain on the righteous and the unrighteous ... Therefore you are to be perfect, as your heavenly Father is perfect" (NASB).

The Father Is Our Teacher - John 6:45 says: "It is written in the prophets, 'And they shall all be taught by God.' Therefore everyone who has heard and learned from the Father comes to Me" (NKJV).

The Father Is Ours to Love and Worship according to John 4:23: "But an hour is coming, and now is, when the true worshipers will worship the Father in spirit and truth; for such people the Father seeks to be His worshipers " (NASB).

In conclusion of these glorious truths, we hear warmest affection and deepest adoration in the two following verses. 1 Corinthians 8:6

reminds us, "yet for us there is but one God, the Father, from whom are all things and we exist for Him; and one Lord, Jesus Christ, by whom are all things, and we exist through Him" (NASB). And our humble and grateful response is: "For this reason I bow my knees before the Father" (Ephesians 3:14 NASB).

The Overarching Truth - Who is above all, and through all and in all

In terms of the relationships within the Holy Trinity and in their relation to creation and to the grand work of redeeming mankind, the Father is above all (Ephesians 4:6; 1 Corinthians 11:3). All flows from Him, through His Son, and is accomplished by the Spirit. The Father sent the Son and the Father and the Son sent the Holy Spirit. In the Trinitarian relationship the Father is both preeminent and prominent. In the works of creation and redemption the Son is preeminent. In the era of Israel and in the birth and on-going ministry of the Church the Holy Spirit is preeminent.

The Father's preeminence in relation to the Son is seen in numerous ways. Some of those include the fact that the Father sent the Son into the world (John 10:36). Jesus then stated that He was going to ascend to His Father (John 20:17). The greatest indication of the Father's prominence, however, is that all thanks and gratitude are to be directed to the Father. Jesus directed thanks to the Father in Matthew 11:25. In Colossians 1:12 & 3:17 we are instructed to give thanks to the Father.

Ephesians 4:4–6 records the seven essential doctrines of the Christian faith. As you observe them: "one body, one Spirit, and one hope of your calling, one Lord, one faith, and one baptism and one God and Father – who is above all, and through all, and in all," notice that the triune being of God permeates or encompasses the whole body of doctrine or truth. In the passage we observe the one Spirit, and then one Lord, the Lord Jesus Christ, and then the one Father. It is as if the triune being of God is dispersed among the other doctrines. All Christian truth is living truth and is animated by God, by our triune God. God is at work in a dynamic fashion in the operation of the essential truths or doctrines of the Christian faith. He is their author and animator and they are His acclamation!

This short passage about the unifying truths and realities of the Christian faith that concludes the passage wraps it all together with God Himself – Father, Son, and Holy Spirit. It concludes with the Father *who is above all* – the Son who is *through all* – and the Holy Spirit who is *in all*. This places the emphasis of the whole passage where it ought to be - on our glorious God who provides and performs everything necessary for our salvation.

God is at the heart of all that is essential truth. All is His sovereign plan and work! The triune being of God is the most important truth about who God is and what He is like. In *The Forgotten Trinity,* James White says, "the Trinity is the highest revelation God has made of Himself to His people. It is the capstone, the summit, the brightest star in the firmament of divine truths." In another declaration he says, "The doctrine of the Trinity is the most immense of all the doctrines of religion. It is the foundation of theology. Christianity, in the last analysis, is Trinitarianism. Take out of the New Testament the person of the Father, the Son, and the Holy Spirit, and there is no God left."

While the word "trinity" is not found in Scripture, the doctrine of the Trinity is clearly and explicitly found in the Scriptures. The question is, "When did God reveal Himself as Father, Son, and Holy Spirit or as a triune being?" The late Presbyterian biblical scholar B. B. Warfield stated that the Trinity is not revealed in either the Old Testament or the New Testament. He declares that the triune being of God was revealed *between* the two testaments in historic events: the Incarnation, revealing the Son of God, and in the outpouring of the Holy Spirit on the day of the Feast of Pentecost. He also states that in the New Testament the triune being of God appears over and over, but as assumed, not as a revelation. My conclusion of the matter is this: we might say that the Trinity was *anticipated* in the Old Testament, was *announced* historically between the Testaments by the incarnation of Christ and outpouring of the Holy Spirit at Pentecost, and is *assumed* in the New Testament.

The first mention of God in the Scriptures, Genesis 1:1, uses the word Elohim for God. Elohim is plural. We would translate it "gods" but it is used in conjunction with a singular verb form. While this is not conclusive proof of the Trinity, it may be considered suggestive. The Bible presents to us progressive revelation – one truth after another, each built on the one before. In that way God has continually revealed more and more about His being and nature as well as His purposes and plans. Though we will never comprehend God fully, Christians will have eternity to increase our understanding of His awesome grandeur.

The Importance of the Trinity

The Trinity or triune being of God is a mystery, as John Calvin said, "more to be adored than investigated." However, contemplation of the Trinity is, as Augustine also noted, "supremely rewarding, for this is our God, who has truly made himself known to us to the limits of what we are able to understand, giving himself to us, and thus by the Spirit granting through the Son access to the Father in the unity of his undivided being."

Orthodox Definitions of the Trinity

Philip Schaff, the classic church historian, states: "Our idea of God is more true and deep than our terminology, and the essence and character of God far transcends our highest ideas." Nevertheless, it is a worthwhile endeavor to define and describe the being of God even with our limited vocabulary and understanding.

The three persons of the Trinity share identical divine substance, indwelling one another, and are both together and separately the whole God. There is only one divine essence or substance. Father, Son and Spirit are one in essence, or as theologians would say, "consubstantial." The Athanasian Creed states concerning the Trinity: "Now this is the catholic (universal) faith: That we worship one God in trinity and trinity in unity, neither blending their persons, nor dividing their essence. For the person of the Father is a distinct person, the person of the Son is another, and

153

that of the Holy Spirit, still another. But the divinity of the Father, Son and Holy Spirit is one, their glory equal, their majesty coeternal."

In *The Good News We Almost Forgot*, Kevin DeYoung explains the Trinity with seven salient statements: (1) There is only one God. (2) The Father is God. (3) The Son is God. (4) The Holy Spirit is God. (5) The Father is not the Son. (6) The Son is not the Holy Spirit. (7) The Holy Spirit is not the Father.

The image below represents the triune being of God:

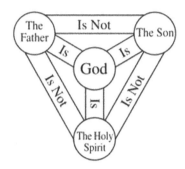

It is important to note that the members of the Trinity indwell one another and to understand to some extent what that means. Turning again to the great church historian, Philip Schaff, we read: "The divine persons are in one another, mutually penetrate, and form a perpetual intercommunication and motion within the divine essence; as the Lord says: 'I am in the Father, and the Father in me;' and 'the Father that dwelleth in me, he doeth the works.'" (*History of the Christian Church;* Volume III, pp. 679–680)

The idea of God being both one and three may seem to some like a contradiction. However, Lutheran theologian Leander S. Keyser wrote in *The Philosophy of Christianity*, "By these tokens we conclude that God is one in one respect and three in another respect: one in substance and Godhood; three in centers of self-consciousness, persons, or Egos. And since He is not one and three in the same respect, but in different respects, there is no contradiction in holding that He is both one and three."

There is what has been called "an immanent Trinity" that speaks of the persons of the Godhead being of the same substance or essence.

There is also what has been termed "an economic Trinity" that clarifies the fact that the Father, Son, and Holy Spirit have willingly assumed different roles in relation to the work of salvation, in their relation to one another and in their relation to mankind. That is why there is a willing subordination within the Trinity without reducing the equality of the members of the Trinity.

Each of the three members of the Trinity delights in the good of the others. This is distinctive from the sinful nature that seeks its own interest rather than the interests of others. This is the true nature and expression of all that love is, for God is love (1 John 4:8). Inherent in the very nature of God is seeking the interest of others. This is also the type of relationship God wants us to have in all the various kinds of relationships we have: family, friends, co-workers, neighbors and the world of humanity at large. The three persons of the Godhead are coeternal and coequal in power and glory. There is love for one another within the being of God and between the three persons of the Godhead.

God is not a monad. A monad is an indivisible, impenetrable unit of substance. God is love, and in order for love to exist, there must be more than one. There is a perfect love-relationship between the Father, Son, and Holy Spirit. This allows God to be love in His essence and to be independent without needing any person's or any creature's love. God could therefore exist alone without any other being existing and He would still be love because to love requires someone to love. In His own being as three persons, that love existed and continues to exist.

With God there can be no jealousy or competition, for each member of the Godhead desires the best and the most for the others. Furthermore, each member of the triune being of God is fully and totally God apart from the others. All of this is truly a mystery and must be accepted by faith. And may I add this – that as a young boy at age 11 my Sunday School teacher, Edward Brownhill, taught our class about the Trinity. While I didn't understand it, I accepted it with simple, child-like faith, and was wonderfully blessed by that truth even then. Ever since I've been immensely grateful to Mr. Brownhill who moved to Georgia from the Bronx in New York where he had grown up.

When humans create "god" in their imaginations the tendency is to think of God within the limits of human understanding and what seems rational to the human mind. It is, therefore, easy to understand a god who is singular and simple. The true and living God, as revealed in the Bible, however, is an intriguingly complex being. We should expect Him to be complex and beyond our limited, finite understanding. To accept God for who He is, and for what He is like, requires faith and stretches man's understanding beyond its limits. Even then we still come up infinitely short in our understanding of God. We utterly fail to fully understand and appreciate God, the Infinite One.

Old Testament Suggestions of the Trinity

The Trinity and the Creation of the Universe

In Genesis 1:1 the word "God" is the Hebrew word "Elohim." Elohim is a plural noun that could be translated "gods;" however as already mentioned, it is used with a singular verb for the word "created." Genesis 1:2 speaks of the Spirit of God and His involvement in the work of creation (see also Job 26:13). In Genesis chapter 1 God speaks words of creative power ten specific times in performing His work of creation. "And God said, 'Let there be light'" and etc. In the first chapter of John's Gospel, Jesus Christ is called "the Word of God (John 1:1–4). John goes on to state that Jesus is the Word of God through whom the universe was created!

The Trinity and the Creation of Man

Genesis 1:26–27 says, "Then God said, 'Let *Us* make man in *Our* image, according to *Our* likeness'" (emphasis added). There is apparent deliberation and determination made within the being of God Himself. To avoid this apparent fact, some have postulated that God was deliberating with the angels. God would not have said to the angels, "Let *Us* make man in *Our* image." Man or mankind is an entirely different being than the angels. Furthermore it is only of man that it is said that they are made in the image of God.

When analyzing Genesis 1:26–27, Jewish rabbinical commentators were often perplexed by this apparent plurality. This was also true for them when they attempted to interpret other passages that seem to suggest a plurality within God, such as Genesis 3:22; 11:7; and Isaiah 6:8.

In the creation of mankind in God's image, God is revealed as having relationship within His own being. We have already observed that there is deliberation between the members of the Trinity or Godhead. This indicates the existence of relationships between the members. This being the case, communion and communication are inherent in the very nature and being of God. Man has received his relational and social nature and our communicative ability because God has these characteristics and we are made in His image.

Also, the form of this statement clearly indicates the equality of the persons within the Godhead. The words, "Let us" and "in our image" appear to assure us of the equality of the distinctive persons within the being whom we know as God.

In Genesis 3:22 we discover another strong suggestion of the plurality and equality of the three within the Godhead. It says, "The LORD God said, 'Since man has become like one of *Us*, knowing good and evil'" (emphasis added). Similarly, Genesis 11:7, "Come, let *Us* go down there and confuse their language" (emphasis added) demonstrates once again this plurality and equality. You cannot have an "us" without there being more than one person.

The Trinity Pictured In Theophanies

A theophany is an appearance of God in the form of a human being. In addition to the Scriptures explained above, the plurality and equality within the Godhead are suggested in the theophanies of the Old Testament.

An interesting theophany occurs in Genesis chapters 18 and 19. In 18:1–2 it says:

> Then the LORD appeared to Abraham at the oaks of Mamre while he was sitting in the entrance of his tent during the heat of the day. He looked up, and he saw

three men standing near him. When he saw them, he ran from the entrance of the tent to meet them and bowed to the ground."

It is possible that this passage is suggestive of the triune being of God, or the Trinity. In 18:20–21 the LORD, as if speaking to Himself, Says, "'I will go down (to Sodom) and see.' Then the men turned away from there and went toward Sodom while Abraham was still standing before the LORD" (NASB).

What we have in this passage is the three who had been called an appearance of the LORD now splitting up. One stays with Abraham, and the other two go to Sodom. Notice that the text says that the LORD went down to Sodom but also says that the LORD stayed and stood before Abraham! Once again this is suggestive of the plurality of God's being and perhaps suggestive of God's triune being. God speaks wonderfully through His Word to illustrate to us what He is like!

The Shema Supports the Possibility of the Trinity

Shema means "Hear!" or "Listen!" Deuteronomy 6:4–5 is called the Shema by the Jews:

> Listen, Israel: The LORD our God, *the LORD is one.* Love the LORD your God with all your heart, with all your soul, and with all your strength" (emphasis added).

The primary meaning of the text above is that Yahweh or Jehovah is God alone. It is His uniqueness that is primarily in view. He is the one and only Sovereign One.

But the text not only indicates Yahweh's uniqueness, but also His unity. This is true according to commentaries by Peter C. Craigie, John MacArthur, and others. The Hebrew word "one" is echad. There are two different Hebrew words that are translated "one." Echad is a word that means "a unity of plurality." "Heis" is the other word for "one" and is a primary numeral indicating strict singularity. The author of Scripture would probably have used this word, "heis," instead of "echad" if he had not intended to give the sense of a unity of plurality. "Heis" is never used with the potential meaning of unity of several things into one.

The word chosen by the Holy Spirit and written by Moses here in the Shema, "echad," may very well express the plural being of the one and only true God. The *Theological Wordbook of the Old Testament* by R. Laird Harris, Gleason L. Archer, Jr., and Bruce K. Walke, states that echad is closely related to the Hebrew word yahad "to be united" and "recognizes diversity within that oneness." It also states: "some scholars have felt that, though one, echad, is singular, the usage of the word allows for the doctrine of the Trinity."

To illustrate the meaning of echad we can look at its use in a couple of passages where the general concept is made clearer. These examples are parallels of kind or similarity that may serve to enlighten us about what God is like. The first Biblical use of "echad" is in Genesis 2:24 where the Scripture says that the man and woman, when they are married, become echad, "one" flesh. Obviously, there are still two distinct entities, but they have become one in unity. Another clear illustration is found in Genesis 11:1. There the LORD says, regarding the people building the tower of Babel, "the people are one," (echad).

So the LORD is one or "echad" – a unity of plurality. There is only one God, but He exists in a plurality of distinct persons even as the two examples above may illustrate. Two people become one in the union of marriage. Their oneness is oneness of love, commitment to each other, caring for each other, and giving themselves to each other. May that also be true of the members of the Trinity? Might there be an infinite love for each other and an unbreakable and immutable commitment to each other? Then in Genesis chapter 11, many people are galvanized into one, in solidarity, in view of their plan, will, and purpose. Could that picture the solidarity, strong unity of purpose and will of the three members of the Godhead? How helpful these principles might be in instructing us regarding the relationship of the persons of the Trinity.

Rather than understanding and recognizing the plural meaning of the word "echad," the Jewish people focused their attention on the unity part – that there is only one God. This belief in one God, monotheism, was a notable distinction compared to the nations surrounding them. All of the other nations believed in many gods and practiced polytheism. It is perhaps because of the Jews' firm commitment to maintain the distinction of there being only one God that they failed to remain open to the mystery of the plurality of God's being. In reaction to the polytheism of the nations around them, the Jews therefore developed a rigorous and tenacious monotheism that refused to consider a plurality of personalities within the Godhead. By the time of Jesus and the apostolic era, this dogmatic monotheism was firmly embedded in the Jewish psyche. It was the soul of the nation. It is no wonder that many Jews reacted to Jesus's claims of divinity by accusing Him of blasphemy and wanted to stone Him to death!

What is most amazing is, with the exception of one man, all the writers of the New Testament were Jews with this conviction staunchly fixed in their minds and hearts. And yet, they were able, with the help of the Holy Spirit, to perceive the plurality of God's being as Father, Son, and Holy Spirit. This, in itself, certainly makes a persuasive statement about how convinced the writers of the New Testament were in regard to the triune being of God. It required them to form an entirely new paradigm about the most important religious idea ingrained in them by the power of thousands of years of entrenched tradition.

Passages Expressing the Distinctions within the Trinity

In Psalm 45:6–7 we discover the Psalmist saying that God anointed God!

> Your throne, God, is forever and ever; the scepter of Your kingdom is a scepter of justice. You love righteousness and hate wickedness; therefore God, your God, has anointed you, more than your companions, with the oil of joy.

The meaning of this verse is clear. One is God whose throne is forever and ever and whose scepter is a scepter of justice. But then speaking of that One who is God, the Scripture says, "Therefore, God, your God, has anointed you." Here is God anointing God.

Ecclesiastes 12:1 commands, "So remember your Creator in the days of your youth: Before the days of adversity come, and the years approach when you will say, 'I have no delight in them.'" The Hebrew text here literally says, "Remember now your *Creators*" (emphasis added). The pronoun *"them"* also obviously refers to the Creators in the text and is also plural. This is another suggestion of the plurality of the Godhead.

One of the most intriguing Old Testament passages appearing to indicate a plurality within the Godhead is Isaiah 6:1–3, 8:

> In the year that King Uzziah died, I saw the Lord seated on a high and lofty throne, and His robe filled the Temple. Seraphim (believed to be a special class of angels) were standing above Him; each one had six wings: with two He covered His face, with two He covered His feet, and with two He flew. And one called to another: "Holy, holy, holy is the LORD of Hosts; His glory fills the whole earth." Then I heard the voice of the Lord saying: "Who should I send? Who will go for *Us*?" I said: "Here I am. Send me" (emphasis added).

In the passage there is first of all the cry of the Seraphim, "Holy, holy, holy is the LORD of hosts." The three-fold cry of "holy" could possibly suggest the triune being of God. Even more telling is the question that gives the genuine appearance of God talking with Himself and saying, "Who will go for *Us*?"

There is a strong suggestion of the plurality of the being of God in this question. Notice the amazing use of the pronouns in this verse. The first pronoun is singular and thus God is speaking in the unity of His being; however, the second pronoun is plural indicating a plurality within God's being.

Perhaps the most compelling passage indicating the plurality of God in the entire Old Testament is Isaiah 48:12, 16–17:

161

> Listen to Me, Jacob, and Israel, the one called by Me: I
> am He; I am the first, I am also the last . . . Approach Me
> and listen to this. From the beginning I have not spoken
> in secret; from the time anything existed, I was there.
> And now the Lord GOD has sent me and His Spirit.

In the context of this chapter, what we are actually seeing in this portion are three divine beings. The quotation begins in verse 12 where the One speaking says, "I am the first, I am also the last. My own hand founded the earth, and My right hand spread out the heavens." The quote continues on until in verse 16 He says, "And now the Lord GOD has sent me and His Spirit."

The beginning of his quotation states that He is "the first and the last," unquestionably a divine title (See also Isaiah 44:6 & 48:12; Revelation 1:8). Remember that this divine title, "I am the first and the last," also applies to Jesus Christ (Revelation 2:8; Revelation 22:13). The obvious conclusion is that Jesus Christ is Yahweh or God!

In this passage this is Yahweh (Jehovah) speaking as Jesus! But then he says, "And now *the Lord GOD* (God in all capitals is Yahweh or Jehovah) has sent *me* and *His Spirit.*" Jesus as Yahweh says that Yahweh has sent Him and His (Yahweh's) Spirit. It would appear that all three members of the Holy Trinity are clearly identified in this passage!

God the Father and God the Son in the Old Testament

God is mentioned as Father just over twenty times in the Old Testament. This fits with the three-fold mention of God in the New Testament as Father, and leaves open the possibility of the other members of the Trinity – the Son, and the Holy Spirit.

Psalm 2:7 & 12 are accepted as Messianic, and make a remarkable statement:

> I will declare the LORD's decree: He said to Me, "You are
> My Son; today I have become Your Father." Pay homage
> to the Son, or He will be angry, and you will perish in

your rebellion, for His anger may ignite at any moment. All those who take refuge in Him are happy.

Who is this who is the Son of the LORD? At Jesus's baptism, God clearly answers this question. "Kiss the Son" (KJV) means we are to pay homage to and worship the Son (*Theological Wordbook of the Old Testament,* pp. 1435 & 1436). In the realm of eternity there is no time. Therefore "today" speaks of eternity, time immemorial from the infinite past into the present and throughout future eons. It is a fact in every moment of eternity as well as in every moment of time.

A passage that may suggest that God has a son, but is not dogmatic, is Proverbs 30:4:

> Who has gone up to heaven and come down? Who has gathered the wind in His hands? Who has bound up the waters in a cloak? Who has established all the ends of the earth? What is His name, and *what is the name of His Son,* if you know? (emphasis added)

Since the question of this passage is a rhetorical one, the fact of a Son is not conclusive, but the passage might suggest the idea that God has a Son.

The Divine Designations of the Messiah in the Old Testament

Prophetic passages in the Old Testament regarding the Messiah (Hebrew = "Messiah"; Greek equivalent is "Christ") vividly vindicate the deity of Christ, that is, that He was God:

Isaiah 7:14 - "God with us"
Isaiah 9:6 - "mighty God"
Micah 5:2 - "whose origin is from of old, from everlasting"
Daniel 7:14 - eternal sovereignty

The Spirit of God in the Old Testament

The Holy Spirit or Spirit of God is mentioned nearly four hundred times in the Old Testament. It is also clear that Yahweh acts through the Spirit. The Spirit is also linked with the Messiah in three passages showing how He supports and empowers the ministry of the Messiah as well as how He will empower Messiah's future universal kingdom reign (Isaiah 11:1–2; 42:1; 61:1).

The Spirit is anticipated to come as a future gift to all God's people (Joel 2:28; Ezekiel 11:19; 36:26; 37:12; Zechariah 12:10). The fulfillment of this gift being bestowed on God's people is abundantly attested to throughout the New Testament.

New Testament Proofs of the Trinity

The Spirit in the New Testament

Scriptures are so much deeper than the capacity of man's mind. Concerning the divine author of the Scriptures, it is said: "the Spirit searches everything, even the deep things of God. For who among men knows the concerns of a man except the spirit of the man that is in him? In the same way, no one knows the concerns of God except the Spirit of God" (1 Corinthians 2:10b–11). The Holy Spirit was "sent" by the Father and the Son. (John 14:16–17; 16:5–11). A significant number of passages regarding the Holy Spirit in the New Testament are also cited in this chapter under the heading "One Spirit."

Key New Testament Passages Mentioning
All Three Members of the Trinity

One key New Testament passage that mentions all three members of the Trinity is Matthew 3:16–17:

> After *Jesus* was baptized, He went up immediately from
> the water. The heavens suddenly opened for Him, and

> He saw *the Spirit of God* descending like a dove and coming down on Him. And there came *a voice from heaven: This is My beloved Son.* I take delight in Him (emphasis added)!

All three members of the Trinity are pictured in the baptism of Jesus. *Jesus, the Son of God*, was in the water being baptized. He witnessed *the Holy Spirit* coming down from the heavenly realm. And then a voice was heard coming from heaven. Clearly, this voice was *the Father speaking* to His Son. He spoke words of affirmation and commendation, saying just how proud He was of Jesus. Here, in this single tableau, we can see the distinction between the persons of the Holy Trinity and their interaction with one another.

Another passage in the New Testament that is of major importance regarding the three persons of the Trinity is Matthew 28:19:

> Go, therefore, and make disciples of all nations, baptizing them in the name of *the Father* and of *the Son* and of *the Holy Spirit* (emphasis added).

In this text we see all three members of the Trinity specifically mentioned. One of the more interesting features of the text, however, is that newly made disciples are to be baptized in the *name* (singular) of the Father, Son, and Holy Spirit. There is *one* God who is three distinctive persons. "In the name of" speaks of the authority of all three members of the Godhead.

There are several passages indicating that the Son and the Spirit were creators of the universe. John 1:1–3 states:

> In the beginning was the Word, and the Word was with God, and the Word was God. He was with God in the beginning. All things were created through Him, and apart from Him not one thing was created that has been created.

Christ and the Holy Spirit are also spoken of as agents of creation in other Scriptures: Job 26:13 (ASV, KJV, & NKJV); Colossians 1:15–20; Hebrews 1:3 & 11:3.

Another verse that speaks of all three members of the Godhead says:

> Paul, a slave of *Christ Jesus*, called as an apostle and singled out for *God's* good news— which He promised long ago through His prophets in the Holy Scriptures— concerning *His Son, Jesus Christ our Lord*, who was a descendant of David according to the flesh and was established as the powerful *Son of God* by the resurrection from the dead according to *the Spirit of holiness* (Romans 1:1–4; emphasis added).

Without mentioning specifically the word "Father," the apostle Paul speaks of God, "whose Son is Jesus Christ our Lord." Here we have a clear delineation of both the Father and the Son. Paul goes on to speak of the Spirit of holiness, who had a part in the resurrection of Christ.

Romans 5:1, 5 is another passage that references all three persons of the Godhead when it declares: "Therefore, since we have been declared righteous by faith, we have peace with *God* through *our Lord Jesus Christ*. This hope does not disappoint, because God's love has been poured out in our hearts through *the Holy Spirit* who was given to us." Verse 1 of this passage references God, the Father, and our Lord Jesus Christ. Then verse 5 notes the giving of the Holy Spirit to believers. Once again all three members of the Trinity or Godhead are presented to us.

Yet another passage bearing witness to the Trinity is Romans 7:4–6: "Therefore, my brothers, you also were put to death in relation to the law through the crucified body of *the Messiah*, so that you may belong to another—to Him who was raised from the dead—that we may bear fruit for *God*. For when we were in the flesh, the sinful passions operated through the law in every part of us and bore fruit for death. But now we have been released from the law, since we have died to what held us, so that we may serve in the new way of *the Spirit* and not in the old letter of the law" (emphasis added). Here, in this brief passage, we have yet another mention of all members of the Trinity. The presence of each is also highlighted in such a way as to help us understand how God has chosen to interact with us through each of the persons of His being.

We are beginning to see that the New Testament is replete with references to the triune being of God, and specifically to the members of the Trinity. Romans 8:1–3a affirms:

> Therefore, no condemnation now exists for those in *Christ Jesus*, because *the Spirit's* law of life in Christ Jesus has set you free from the law of sin and of death. What the law could not do since it was limited by the flesh, *God* did. He condemned sin in the flesh by *sending His own Son* in flesh like ours under sin's domain, and as a sin offering (emphasis added).

Here again, all three persons of the being of the Godhead are discussed.

Over and over, in a natural and consistent manner, we find the members of the Trinity intertwined throughout the New Testament as in Romans 8:11, "And if *the Spirit* of Him who raised *Jesus* from the dead lives in you, then He who raised Christ from the dead will also bring your mortal bodies to life through His *Spirit* who lives in you" (emphasis added). Here careful observation makes it clear that "Him who raised Jesus" is obviously speaking of God the Father. "The Spirit who lives in you" is speaking of the Holy Spirit. And of course "Jesus" is referencing the Son of God.

Another simple and clear mention of the members of the Trinity is found in Romans 15:30: "Now I implore you, brothers, through *the Lord Jesus Christ* and through the love of *the Spirit*, to agonize together with me in your prayers to *God* on my behalf" (emphasis added). It is through the Lord Jesus and through the love of the Spirit that prayers are offered by believers to God the Father.

Explaining the cooperative work and ministry of the members of the Trinity, 1 Corinthians 12:4–6 states: "Now there are different gifts, but the same *Spirit*. There are different ministries, but the same *Lord*.

And there are different activities, but the same *God* is active in everyone and everything" (emphasis added).

What is known as the Apostolic Benediction is found in 2 Corinthians 13:14 and speaks eloquently of the Trinity: "The grace of *the Lord Jesus Christ*, and the love of *God*, and the fellowship of *the Holy Spirit* be with all of you" (emphasis added). This verse highlights all three persons of the triune being of God while also pointing out one primary characteristic of each. Notice what each brings to us: love from the Father, grace from the Son, and fellowship with God from the Holy Spirit. What an amazing set of gifts! And all of these come from our mysterious, amazingly incredible God!

The New Testament is hardly finished yet in extolling the triune being of our God. Another testimony to that wonderful truth is Galatians 4:4–6: "But when the completion of the time came, *God* sent *His Son*, born of a woman, born under the law, to redeem those under the law, so that we might receive adoption as sons. And because you are sons, God has sent *the Spirit* of His Son into our hearts, crying, 'Abba, Father'" (emphasis added)!

And then there is Ephesians 2:18: "For through *Him* (the Messiah, Christ Jesus) we both have access by one *Spirit* to *the Father*" (emphasis added). And there is Ephesians 4:4–6, which we have previously explained. Permeating the great and cardinal convictions of our faith are one Spirit, and one Lord, and one God and Father. These three, the distinct persons of the triune being of God, in divine concert are the one God who works our salvation! The Father is above all, the Son through all, and the Spirit in all! How glorious is the work of our salvation wrought by the entire being of the Godhead!

When it comes to passages referencing all the members of the Godhead or Trinity, we aren't done yet. See even more of them like 2 Thessalonians 2:13–14: "But we must always thank *God* for you, brothers loved by the Lord, because from the beginning *God* has chosen you for salvation through sanctification by *the Spirit* and through belief in the truth. He called you to this through our gospel, so that you might obtain the glory of *our Lord Jesus Christ*" (emphasis added).

Then there is Hebrews 9:14: "How much more will the blood of *the Messiah*, who through *the eternal Spirit* offered Himself without blemish to *God*, cleanse our consciences from dead works to serve the living God" (emphasis added)? And there is 1 Peter 1:2: "According to the foreknowledge of *God the Father* and set apart by *the Spirit* for obedience and (for the) sprinkling with the blood of *Jesus Christ*" (emphasis added).

In Jude 20–21 the persons of the Trinity are referenced again: "But you, dear friends, building yourselves up in your most holy faith and praying in *the Holy Spirit*, keep yourselves in the love of *God*, expecting the mercy of our *Lord Jesus Christ* for eternal life" (emphasis added).

And there is one final, superb example mentioning the three persons of the triune being of God:

> John: To the seven churches in the province of Asia. Grace and peace to you from *the One who is, who was, and who is coming*; from *the seven spirits* (or the seven-fold Spirit) before His throne; and from *Jesus Christ*, the faithful witness, the firstborn from the dead and the ruler of the kings of the earth (Revelation 1:4–5; emphasis added).

This salutation in the final and climactic book of the Word of God is a magnificent tribute to the glorious triune being of God. John describes the Father in His eternal being as the one who inhabits eternity, transcending time, and who is projected into the future. This all speaks of His supremacy and sovereignty.

Then in a wondrous word picture, John shows us the person of the Holy Spirit as the perfect and multi-faceted One who is present with the Father before the throne. The Spirit's multi-faceted nature is acknowledged by several human authors of Scripture. Isaiah calls Him "the Spirit of wisdom and understanding, the Spirit of counsel and strength, and the Spirit of knowledge and of the fear of the LORD" (Isaiah 11:2). Jesus calls Him "the Spirit of truth" (John 15:26 & 16:13). Paul identifies Him as "the Spirit of holiness" (Romans 1:4).

Finally, in verses that both explain and exalt God the Son, John proclaims Jesus Christ and announces several of His numerous descriptive titles. He is "the faithful witness" who has given testimony to us about God by His prophetic office and ministry on earth. He is the "firstborn from the dead." His resurrection has made Him the exalted One who is destined to inherit the earth. The firstborn is a title of honor and prominence. Under Jewish tradition, the firstborn son always received a double inheritance, indicating the richness of the inheritance God has planned for Him. His last title is "ruler of the kings of the earth" in anticipation of His coming universal kingdom. When He rules, He will rule over all. There will be no other powers equal to His. What a spectacular salutation!

Equality in the Trinity

The pattern in which the members of the Trinity are named, as we have already seen, is not always Father, Son, and Holy Spirit. From our salvation perspective it is the Spirit through the Son to the Father (Ephesians 2:18). In 2 Corinthians 13:14 it is the Son, the Father, and the Spirit. T. F. Torrance in *The Christian Doctrine of God: One Being, Three Persons*, states that the fact that there is no one settled pattern shows, in Torrance's words, that there is "an implicit belief in the equality of the three divine persons." When introducing people of importance, the universal pattern is to name the most important first, and then to name the others in descending order of importance. This same pattern is used when seating guests at a banquet. The most important are seated at the head of the table. The farther away one is seated from the one giving the banquet, the lower the status. No pattern in naming or referencing the three members of the Trinity exists, therefore, implying equal importance.

In John's Gospel in particular we are told that the Father, Son, and Holy Spirit indwell one another. Their union is as important as their distinction. Jesus said, "I and the Father are one." He said that He was in the Father and the Father was in Him. Paul speaks of Christ being in or indwelling the believer. Christ indwelling the believer is, in fact, the indwelling of the believer by the Holy Spirit. That can only be true since the Son and the Spirit obviously indwell one another as well. Indeed, this is a glorious mystery that is beyond human understanding. Nevertheless, we should expect nothing less when we consider the truth of God being an infinite and incomprehensively complex being.

The Trinity Is Involved in Our Salvation

In the light of the Cross, the resurrection, and the coming of the Holy Spirit, we can see that God is inherently triune.

Ephesians chapter 1, more than any other passage of Scripture, develops the work of the Trinity in our salvation. In his seminal work, *The Holy Trinity – in Scripture, History, Theology, and Worship*, Robert Letham states: "Thus in the light of the Cross, the Resurrection, and the sending of the Holy Spirit at Pentecost, we can see that God is inherently triune." Letham further states: "Underlying all God's blessings described here (in Ephesians chapter 1) is the action of the Trinity." He then goes on to point out the following:

- Paul presents the Father as the source of all God's grace.
- Eternal election is the first work of the Father to be distinguished.
- Foreordination to adoption as sons is also a work of the Father.
- In Christ, the Son, we have redemption through his blood (v. 7).
- In the Son, the Father's cosmic purpose will be realized, whereby He is made the head of all created things (v. 10).
- The Holy Spirit seals us (v. 13).
- The Holy Spirit is the guarantor of our future inheritance (v. 14).

Letham observes, "Thus the whole panorama is a sweeping movement of God's grace toward us: from the Father, in or through the Son, and by the Holy Spirit."

In Ephesians 4:4–6, the work of the Trinity is seen to be involved in the work of salvation. In these verses, God pervades the entire scope of Christian truths. There is *one Spirit* who unites all believers into one body and who secures and will perform in power the one hope of the resurrection and immortality. There is *one Lord* who performs and provides the one faith or gospel and the one baptism that proclaims that faith with the historic performance of His death, burial, and resurrection; and finally, *one God and Father* who is the originator and administrator of it all.

Since God is the focus as the planner, provider, and performer who is above all, and through all, and in all, we therefore live in a God-centered, God-permeated universe. Also, for those who truly worship Him as supreme and sovereign, they will live God-centered lives. God has intentionally and purposefully revealed Himself through all things to mankind. He desires that we know what He is like and that we, in fact, know Him in a loving and personal relationship. Just as two people become acquainted through conversation and learning about each other, so it is with our relationship with God. We know Him by spending time talking together with Him in prayer. We spend time with Him in meditation in the Scriptures where He teaches us His thoughts and reveals Himself to us.

The Intimate Relationship of Members of the Trinity to One Another

The intimacy within the being of God is especially apparent in John chapters 14 through 16. In John 14:10 Jesus said: "Don't you believe that I am in the Father and the Father is in Me?" Then in the very next verse, he says: "Believe Me that I am in the Father and the Father is in Me." Jesus was telling that the natural and spontaneous works He did on earth were truly being done by the Father also. The statement is indicative of such oneness that what one did the other also did. Jesus continues to plainly express this reality in verse 20: "In that day you will know that I am in My Father, you are in Me, and I am in you." Here there is a sense in that believers share intimately in the fellowship of the Father and the Son (cf. 1 John 1:3). The more we grow spiritually, the more intimate this sharing becomes.

What Is God Like?

This leads us to a most important question. Other than God being a triune being, what is He like? Creation reveals that He is a being of infinite power and wisdom. The Bible reveals characteristics of God through His names, His declarations, His responses to people's actions, His involvement with and relationship to people, and through His works. When we see how God is revealed in the person of his Son, we can observe God's love, humility, compassion, mercy, grace, and generous self-giving nature as well as His truth, righteousness and justice.

Certainly there are declarations as to what God is like. He is holy and glorious (Isaiah 6:3). He is a God of truth (faithfulness in His character and to His Word), without iniquity, and just and righteous (His character includes absolute justice) (Deuteronomy 32:4). His character is pervaded with love (1 John 4:16), He is merciful (Psalm 86:15), good (Psalm 100:5) and kind (Titus 3:4).

There is one other interesting revelation of God's nature that is particularly enlightening and helpful as we seek to comprehend and know Him. Man is made in God's image. We are a finite likeness of God. Because of this, as we understand man's being we understand some very important things about God. Both God and man are creative. Both delight in making beautiful things including music, architecture and art. Both are creative in making mechanical devices and functional systems. Both God and man are social beings who seek relationships. Both are intelligent beings who are capable of abstract thought. They both are communicative beings who delight in expressing their thoughts and emotions to others. They are emotional beings capable of a wide range of feelings. And both God and humans are volitional beings having the free exercise of will and purpose. Take those attributes and extend them from their finite and sinfully marred form in man to their infinite and perfect expressions in God and we may begin to have an inkling of what God is like.

Do you spend much time with God? Are you aware that God desires your love and wants you to get to know Him better? He is so interested in you that He knows everything including every minute detail about you (Psalm 139)! Is He the most important person in your life? Is He an intimate part of your life? Do you think specifically and individually of the Father, and of the Son, and of the Holy Spirit? Do you worship each of them, but worship them together as the one true and living God? Do you contemplate God as worthy of your love, worship, praise, and adoration? Do your daily actions demonstrate your reverence and love for Him? Do you believe with conviction that He is worthy of being proclaimed by you as the God of the universe and Lord of all creation? Are you grateful for His infinite love and mercy lavished on you through His Son on the cross? Is God the most important one in your life? If these things are not true in our lives, then we need to re-examine our purpose in life as well as our priorities.

One of the most powerful spiritual experiences of my life has been at Promise Keepers when the Saturday morning sessions are opened with thousands of men singing acapella the great hymn, "Holy, Holy, Holy." For your benefit and blessing may I suggest that you contemplate the words of this marvelous hymn:

Holy, Holy, Holy
Reginald Heber

Holy, holy, holy, Lord God Almighty!
Early in the morning our song shall rise to Thee.
Holy, holy, holy, merciful and mighty:
God in three persons – blessed Trinity!

Holy, holy, holy, all the saints adore Thee,
Casting down their golden crowns around the glassy sea;
Cherubim and seraphim falling down before Thee,
Who wert, and art, and evermore shall be.

Holy, holy, holy, though the darkness hide Thee,
Though the eye of sinful man Thy glory may not see;
Only Thou art holy; there is none beside Thee,
Perfect in power, in love and purity.

Holy, holy, holy, Lord God Almighty!
All Thy works shall praise Thy name in earth and sky and sea.
Holy, holy, holy, merciful and mighty!
God in three persons – blessed Trinity!

Chapter 4

The Disciplines of Authentic Christianity

The Four Fundamental Practices of Authentic Christianity

Devoted to the apostles' teaching

Devoted to fellowship

Devoted to "the" breaking of bread (the Lord's Supper)

Devoted to (corporate) prayers

The Disciplines of an Authentic Church

The disciplines of an authentic church are found in the Church's prototype, the very first church. The early or primitive church of the book of Acts is the apostolic expression of what a Christian church is intended to be. It is what the Church was in its originality and its early potency. A major part of that pattern is placed clearly before us by the divine author of the Scriptures, the Holy Spirit. This pattern is found in Acts 2:41–42:

> So those who accepted his message were baptized, and that day about 3,000 people were added to them. And they devoted themselves to the apostles' teaching, to fellowship, to the breaking of bread, and to prayers.

The early Church practiced four disciplines. These were a regular and consistent part of the Church's life. The statement of their discipline in this regard is strong: "They devoted themselves to . . . ." The four disciplines are:

1. They devoted themselves to *the apostles' teaching.*
   (The apostles' teaching is the contents of the New Testament.)
2. They devoted themselves to *fellowship.*
3. They devoted themselves to *"the" breaking of bread* (the Lord's Supper).
4. They devoted themselves to *prayers.*

The statement of their practice of these disciplines is vigorous. The word "devoted" denotes intense and persevering effort in an activity. This is no simple observation of activities. It is a declaration of dynamic and determined practice of high-priority disciplines. For them, they were the central elements of church life. The priority of these disciplines exceeded every other activity in the life of the church. Sadly, today's church has become a Sunday morning afterthought for many. It does not drive everything else in the lives of its members.

Devoted to the Apostles' Teaching

So, what is "the apostles' teaching" that true disciples devote themselves to? The apostles taught the truths of the gospel and truths that are fruits or extensions of the gospel. They also taught the applications of the gospel to life and living. These applications covered such things as morals, ethics, values, worship, witness, and service.

In John 16:12–15, Jesus revealed where "the apostles' teachings" would come from. There He explained to His apostles that in the future they would receive special insight and guidance into all truth. This would happen after His death, resurrection, and ascension to heaven. He would send the Holy Spirit, the Spirit of Truth, and the Spirit would guide the apostles into the knowledge of all truth. These truths of the good news, its implications and applications, became the writings of the New Testament. It is in these books of the New Testament that we find "the apostles' teachings."

For this reason, the New Testament must receive substantial time in teaching doctrines and in teaching practical daily living for Christian believers as well as instruction for the function of Christian churches. The New Testament emphasizes the gospel and fleshes out the results of the gospel. The results of the gospel include the creation of the Church, the power and demand for holy living, the centrality of Christ in God's plan, and the mission of the Church in the world. The New Testament also gives clear and specific instruction to believers as to how we are supposed to live our lives.

It is important that a believer teach himself by studying God's Word. It is also vitally important that a believer be taught God's Word from spiritually mature pastors and teachers in the church. The teaching of a spiritually mature pastor or teacher who teaches the Bible accurately, and does not distort it falsely, will protect and rapidly grow the believer who is young in faith. The sound teaching of the New Testament, combined with diligent personal Bible study, will protect young believers from falling prey to their own misunderstanding of the Bible and to the teachings of false teachers and cults.

Most Americans have grown up hearing about Christianity all of their lives. One problem is that much of what they believe is culturally derived from movies, books, or TV shows. Much of what is taught about Christianity by these sources is distorted at best and false at worst. Real study and a willingness to learn from a more mature Christian is often necessary to restore truth to what the new Christian thinks he knows about the Christian faith.

A disciple should find and follow a pastor and church that is committed to the exposition and teaching of the Bible. It should not be teaching based on human opinions and fanciful interpretations, but teaching that earnestly endeavors to explain the literal and genuine meaning and application of the Holy Scriptures.

Devoted to Fellowship

Another discipline that a disciple should faithfully pursue is fellowship. In simplest terms, fellowship is sharing and partnering. It demands spending time with other believers. Essential to fellowship is being involved together in extending the gospel of Christ to the community and to the world (Philippians 1:5; 4:14–16).

In the context of Acts chapter 2, fellowship means "fellowship in worship" and "denotes the unanimity and unity brought about by the Spirit." "The individual was completely upheld by the community. It expresses a oneness of love and of devotion to Jesus Christ and to one another that results in regular and faithful attendance to worship together and spiritually and materially supporting one another" (*New International Dictionary of New Testament Theology; Volume 1*).

Fellowship also included eating meals together as a means of sharing one another's lives (*Acts: New Testament Commentary;* Simon J. Kistemaker). Scripture states that eating together was a frequent and continual practice of the early Church (Acts 2:46). Sharing a meal has historically been one of humanity's most important social interactions. When strangers showed up at Abraham's home, his first reaction was to invite them to dinner. When the prodigal son returned home, his father prepared a big dinner party for him. When people come to our homes today to socialize, it usually involves sharing food in some way. It was no different in the early church. Fellowship, however, is more than mere socializing. It is centered on the Lord and involves conversation about spiritual matters. The spirit of genuine fellowship in this regard is expressed in Malachi 3:16:

> Then those who feared the LORD spoke to one another, And the LORD listened and heard them; So a book of remembrance was written before Him For those who fear the LORD And who meditate on His name (NKJV).

Another aspect of the fellowship of believers appears to have been the partnership of promoting the gospel together (Philippians 1:5, 27). Paul certainly expressed the strong sense of love and joy between him and those in the Philippian church, their mutual fellowship, when he mentioned in chapter 4 their faithful financial support of his missionary ministry (Philippians 4:15–17). They were his partners in spreading the gospel of Christ. That partnership produced a real and tender bond between Paul and the Philippian believers. It was, in essence, fellowship.

Fellowship includes stimulating one another to love and good works. Specifically this includes the *"one anothers"* of the New Testament. Below emphasis is added to each biblical citation to bring attention to this. Believers are to:

> Be kindly affectionate to *one another* with brotherly love (Romans 12:10)

> Be of the same mind toward *one another* (Romans 12:16 & 15:5)

> Love *one another* (Romans 13:8; 1 Thessalonians 4:9; 1 Peter 1:22)

> Encourage and build up *one another* (Romans 14:19; 1 Thessalonians 5:11)

Receive *one another* (Romans 15:7)

Admonish *one another* (Romans 15:14; Hebrews 3:13)

Greet *one another* (Romans 16:16)

Serve *one another* (Galatians 5:13; 1 Peter 4:10)

Be patient and forgiving with *one another* in love (Ephesians 4:3; Colossians 3:13)

Speak truth to *one another* (Ephesians 4:25)

Be kind to *one another*, tenderhearted, forgiving one another (Ephesians 4:32)

Submit to *one another* (Ephesians 5:21; 1 Peter 5:5)

Esteem *one another* (Philippians 2:3)

Teaching and admonishing *one another* in singing (Colossians 3:16)

Comfort *one another* (1 Thessalonians 4:18 & 5:11)

Be hospitable to *one another* (1 Peter 4:9)

As we can see, fellowship is a rich and multi-faceted atmosphere of sharing our lives with one another as believers in the Lord Jesus Christ.

Devoted to the Breaking of Bread (Sharing the Lord's Supper)

A third discipline that the early Christians were devoted to was the observation of the Lord's Supper, also called Communion or the Eucharist. In the early apostolic church, this took place every Lord's Day, that is, every Sunday. The teaching of the Scriptures, singing hymns and spiritual songs, and the Lord's Supper were the primary features of worship for the early church. Jesus Himself did not command that we observe the Lord's Supper every week, but said, "As often as you drink this cup, do so in remembrance of me." The principle appears to be that it should be observed frequently as a way of recalling the importance of what Jesus did for us.

The Lord's Supper was an event that the community of disciples celebrated together. This celebration was a corporate act. Communion is not only fellowship of the believer with the Lord, but also the believers in fellowship with one another. It is a covenant meal, and, in fact, it was introduced by the Lord Jesus during another covenant meal, the Passover meal, the evening before His crucifixion. 1 Corinthians 10:16–17 says:

> Is not the cup of blessing which we bless a sharing in the blood of Christ? Is not the bread which we break a sharing in the body of Christ? Since there is one bread, we who are many are one body; for we all partake of the one bread.

Here Paul the apostle makes it clear that the Lord's Supper represents not only the death of Christ, but also our union with Him and with one another. If it represents our union with one another, then it should be observed together as an act of worship. Communion is our collective worship and joint proclamation of the sufferings and death of our Lord and Savior.

The Seven Primary Truths of the Lord's Supper

There are seven primary truths expressed by the Lord's Supper. The first three of these are pictured by the giving of His body. The second three are portrayed by the pouring out of His blood. The final one is a thrilling anticipation.

1. Sacrifice

The Lord said, "This is my body given for you." The first truth shown by His body is sacrifice. Hebrews 10:5–7, 10, 12, state that it was His body that was prepared for and offered as a sacrifice. And what a magnificent image it gives us! In 1 Corinthians 5:7, we are told that "Christ our Passover (Lamb) has been sacrificed for us." The same image of this sacrifice is painted for us in Isaiah chapter 53. There His body, like a lamb, was wounded (Hebrew = pierced) and bruised (Hebrew = crushed) for our sins and transgressions. It is by His stripes we are healed. Our sin was laid on Him! His body was sacrificed for us.

2. Substitution

The second truth His body teaches us is substitution. While Isaiah 53 expresses the idea that Christ died in our place as our substitute, other scriptures also declare it plainly. Passages like 2 Corinthians 5:21. Also 1 Peter 2:24: "He Himself bore our sins in His own body on the tree." The Passover meal itself pictures the substitution of the Lamb for the firstborn of every family.

3. Suffering

"He suffered for our sins, the righteous for the unrighteous," says 1 Peter 3:18. Isaiah says that "He was wounded for our transgressions and was bruised for our iniquities" (Isaiah 53:5). The psalmist prophetically and descriptively states that they pierced His hands and His feet (Psalm 22). And Peter speaks of the sufferings of Christ and the glories that would follow His sufferings (1 Peter 1:11). So much more could be said about our Lord's suffering. The Lord's Supper is a remembrance of His suffering on our behalf and should provoke a sense of deep gratitude in those of us He has saved by His suffering.

4. Remission (forgiveness) and Reconciliation

The fourth truth of the Supper is remission and reconcilie. It is the forgiveness of sin and the consequent restoration to fellowship with God. Jesus said, "This is my blood that is shed for many for the forgiveness of sins." It is this forgiveness that makes possible the restoration to fellowship and entering into a covenant relationship with God. The partaking of the Supper is itself an experience of fellowship with God. It is like the covenant meals of the Old Testament when the priests and the people ate certain sacrifices together in thanksgiving and celebration of the forgiveness provided by the sacrifice. This truth is highlighted by drinking the fruit of the vine that symbolizes Jesus's blood.

> In Him we have redemption through His blood, *the forgiveness of sins*, according to the riches of His grace (Ephesians 1:7 NKJV – emphasis added).

5. Redemption

Another important truth reflected by the blood as pictured in the Supper is redemption. Of course the Passover during which the Lord introduced His Supper was the celebration of the redemption of the nation of Israel, when the lambs were slain and the blood was put on the doorposts of the Jewish homes. The Passover "cup of blessing" mentioned by Paul was specifically the third in a series of four cups of grape juice or wine taken during the Supper, and it was "the cup of redemption" that was a part of the Passover meal. Jesus used it to picture His redemptive work in the shedding of His blood as the Lamb of God. Redemption sets us free and purchases our lives for God. It purchases us to be His people. In Ephesians 1:7, we read that in Christ "we have redemption through His blood." 1 Peter 1:18–19 explains that we have been "redeemed by the blood of Christ as of a lamb (a sacrificial lamb) without blemish and without spot."

6. Relationship (covenant)

"This is the blood of the new covenant," Jesus said. The Jewish nation had a special relationship with God. It was a contractual, not an unconditional, covenant relationship. God had joined them to Himself as a covenant nation. As such, they had a special relationship with God (Exodus 19:5–6). A similar relationship is established between Christ and His Church, according to 1 Peter 2:9–10. The Church, composed of Jews and Gentiles as one body, are in a covenant relationship with Christ. The covenant relationship provides blessings and requires responsibilities. It joins two parties to one another in a sacred bond and establishes a special, permanent commitment by each toward the other.

7. Anticipation

Paul says, "For as often as you eat this bread and drink the cup, you proclaim the Lord's death until He comes" (1 Corinthians 11:26). Surprisingly, the Passover meal that Jesus ate with His disciples was an unfinished meal. When He took the third cup of the four cups of the Passover He said that He would not drink again of that fruit of the vine until He would drink it new with them in the Kingdom (Mark 14:25). The four cups of the Supper were based on the covenant God made with Israel in Exodus 6:6-8. The third cup had to do with God's oath or vow to redeem them as a nation. The fourth cup in the Supper represented the kingdom of God. This is the conclusion because of the language of verse 8 when compared with Revelation 21:3 and 22:3–5. So He did not finish the Supper. He left it with an anticipation of finishing it with us in the coming Kingdom.

When we partake of the Lord's Supper, we should end it with the anticipation of finishing that covenant meal with Jesus one day in heaven! Some scholars believe that the anticipatory prayer found in 1 Corinthians 16:22, "Maranatha — Our Lord come!" was the spoken prayer that early Christians prayed at the conclusion of the Lord's Supper in anticipation of His coming.

Devoted to Prayers

In 2007 Lifeway.com published the results of a massive survey of more than 1,300 ministry leaders from Europe, North America, and elsewhere entitled, "The Top Ten Issues Facing Today's Church." It analyzes 3,700 issues and the results were the 20 most frequently submitted challenges. Taking those the survey respondents were asked to choose the top ten most critical to them. The result was:

1. Prayer
2. Discipleship
3. Leadership
4. Evangelism
5. Doctrine / Worldview
6. Apathy
7. Marriage
8. Relevance
9. Homosexuality
10. Abortion

Are you surprised that prayer was the number one most critical issue facing the church according to this significant survey?

The late, great British preacher Charles Haddon Spurgeon said, "Prayer is the breath of faith. Prayer meetings are the lungs of the church." Armin Gesswin declares: "The Early Church didn't have a prayer meeting. The Early Church *was* the prayer meeting. In the Early Church every Christian was a prayer-meeting Christian" (*Everything By Prayer*, p. 12). In *Prayer – Its Deeper Dimensions*, J. Edwin Orr observes as a result of his research on revivals, "No great spiritual awakening has begun anywhere in the world apart from united prayer."

The areas of the world where Christianity is making marked progress are areas or nations where Christians are engaged together in much prayer: Korea, China, Africa, South America, and India. Areas where prayer has been neglected, North America, Europe, and Australia, Christianity has suffered continuing decline. Unfortunately we do not feel our need of prayer and dependence on God like Christians in poorer countries do. And we have our programs and strategies that appear to succeed in drawing crowds of people. But the question is, "Where is the spiritual power that transforms lives and powerfully impacts the culture around us?"

A quick survey of the apostolic church in the book of Acts reveals that the early church was a church in constant prayer. Acts 2:42 says that the early disciples devoted themselves to praying. Again, the word "devoted" means intense and persevering application to a thing, or unwearied effort in it. In Acts 1:13–14 and 2:1, the first disciples, approximately 120, met for ten consecutive days in prayer just before the Holy Spirit came on the day of Pentecost. Someone said they prayed for *ten days* and preached for *ten minutes* and revival broke out!

In Acts 3:1, Peter and John were seen going up together to the for the hour of prayer. It appears that they habitually went there to lead a group of disciples in prayer. After being threatened by the Sanhedrin, demanding that Peter and John preach no more in the name of Jesus, the church of Jerusalem met for a prayer meeting and the place where they prayed was shaken (Acts 4:23–31). Later the church met to pray when Peter was imprisoned (Acts 12). The church of Antioch was praying and seeking to know God's will when God answered and told them to send out Paul and Barnabas to do the work He was calling them to do – and missions was born (Acts 13)! Paul and Silas were holding a prayer meeting when the Lord sent an earthquake that opened the doors of the jail and resulted in an entire household of people being saved (Acts 16). Paul met with disciples by the river where they were in the habit of gathering for prayer (Acts 20:36).

In the mind of the apostolic church, corporate prayer was one of the two most important ministries in church life. To them the ministry of prayer was of equal importance to the proclamation of the Word of God by the apostles. This is made clear in Acts chapter 6. It is in Acts 6:4 that we discover the importance of corporate prayer to the early church. As John Franklin points out in his outstanding book, *And the Place Was Shaken*, Acts 6:4 literally reads, "But we to the prayer and the ministry of the Word will steadfastly continue." These two ministries are elevated to a level of top priority. Franklin notes: "Frankly I know of nothing else in ministry anywhere in the Old or New Testament that is put on the same par as the proclamation of God's Word, except prayer!" The apostolic church was an excellent example of corporate prayer and illustrates the powerful results of corporate prayer.

Franklin also points out that thirty-seven verses can be identified with Jesus's teaching and practice of prayer. Of the thirty-seven verses or references to prayer, he says that thirty-three of them were addressed to a plural rather than singular audience. Franklin then concludes that Jesus's instruction decisively leaned toward praying with others, not just praying in private.

The Lord blessed me wonderfully in giving me the opportunity to serve as pastor of my first church in the small town of Hartwell, Georgia. It was a praying church! When first arriving there was some numerical growth as people came because of the new young pastor and wife. In time, however, our attendance dropped again to a level a little lower than when we had arrived. I desperately feared failure, both personal failure and failure for the church. Not knowing what to do, I began going to the church office early every Monday through Friday morning and spending two hours in prayer – not in prayer and study – just in prayer. It was prayer for revival – prayer for the Lord to revive me, to revive the people in our congregation, and to empower us to see people come to faith in Christ.

After nine months nothing had happened and things actually appeared to get a little worse. My wife was the only person who knew about my praying. I then challenged the congregation to come and join me in prayer anytime between 6:00 a.m. and 8:00 a.m. – just pop in and pray for revival. We did that for three or four months, and many of our dear people came and prayed, but still nothing happened.

Then in the fall of 1974 I told the congregation that the Lord had given me assurance that He was going to answer our prayers, and we could end our special time of prayer. Still, nothing happened for about two and a half months. Then it came. The first Sunday of 1975, I felt it as the service started. Service after service people began coming forward and praying at the altar with tears, getting things right with the Lord.

Attendance began to spontaneously grow. Testimony times turned into a time of wonderful refreshing as people spoke of how the Lord was working in their lives and rejoiced, giving Him the glory. Often tears trickled down their faces as they testified. We began to see people who were not Christians attend and receiving Christ as their savior. In the next year and a half our attendance more than tripled and our small church that began with an attendance of 40 saw about 50 baptisms during that year and outreach grew as our Vacation Bible Schools ran close to 200 per night! The church was alive and vibrant in every area of ministry. And what does it all mean? God answers the prayers of His people!

Prayer is a very powerful spiritual weapon. Someone once said that Satan laughs at our toil and mocks our wisdom, but that he trembles when we pray! There is no power on earth as great as the power of prayer. When we by faith seize the promises of God and call on the One who is all-powerful, He answers and demonstrates His power and His faithfulness to His Word. Someone said, "Faith honors God, and God honors faith!"

During my college years the Lord put in my path several books about prayer that convinced me of its importance. Two of those books were *The Power of Prayer* by R. A. Torrey, and *Why Revival Tarries* by Leonard Ravenhill. While involved in a ministry of sharing the gospel on the streets of Athens, Georgia, during my junior year of college, two other students from our Christian university and I went onto the campus of the University of Georgia to contact a student we had met on the streets. Not finding the student at his dorm, we were harassed and heckled by some UGA students. As we walked away one of my teammates reacted saying, "There is no hope for students on this campus." His statement evoked a deep concern in me, but I said nothing. The hour and half drive back to our university found me quiet in the back seat grieving in my heart for the University of Georgia students and crying out to the Lord for their salvation.

The Lord made it clear to me that He wanted me to reach UGA students with the gospel. During that week I found a designated prayer room in my dorm where I knelt several times daily and prayed my heart out asking God to do something great the next Saturday night. Claiming God's promise in Jeremiah 33:3 I determined to go back to that campus and to find a way to reach students there with the gospel.

Saturday night came, and a freshman student agreed to go with me to the campus. It was a dreary and dismal evening with drizzling rain – not very encouraging. We walked for about half a mile seeing only two or three students. UGA was known as a "suitcase campus" as many students went home on the weekends. No one knew about my burden and week of prayer. Then I stopped, and said, "We're going to pray!" And I prayed a loud prayer. Reminding the Lord of how His promise had been claimed, I asked Him to do something great and mighty right away. Walking another 50 yards we saw a student walking across a huge courtyard between dorm buildings. Making our courses intersect, he stopped and I handed him a gospel tract. He asked me what we were doing on UGA campus, and we told him. He introduced himself to us, Dan Coutcher, a forestry major.

Had God done anything great that night? Well, you tell me. It was the beginning of a weekly meeting that started in Dan's dorm room and led to a ministry on 20 college campuses within a few years and 14 years later there were 70 staff members serving on college campuses with that ministry! Dan met and married a wonderful Christian woman, Lois Howell, and they served in college ministry for over 30 years seeing the lives of scores, perhaps hundreds of college students transformed by Christ. Do you think God did great and mighty things that night?

Again the Lord revealed to me the power of prayer. When I was a pastor in Lawrence, Kansas, our church had purchased a building that the church that previously owned had outgrown. It was in a bad location, with very poor visibility and accessibility. Yet that church had been compelled by attendance to go to several services and eventually to have to buy property and build a larger building. The reason? I later found out through a very close friend of the pastor of that church that he was a man who prayed four hours a day. He was not a great or eloquent preacher, just a solid Bible teacher. But God grew that church because of prayer!

When Pastor Jim Cymbala accepted the call to his first pastorate he arrived at Brooklyn Tabernacle and found a once great, but now dilapidated building and only a handful of people. The community was riddled with drugs and crime. Feeling desperate he sought the Lord in prayer and led the people to cry out to God. As the Lord began to move in the lives of the people and in the community, the church was reborn in prayer. As they prayed they saw miracle after miracle in people's lives. This inspiring story of how Jim Cymbala's ministry and church were impassioned by prayer that impacted the community around them is found in his book, *Fresh Wind, Fresh Fire.*

In *Fresh Wind, Fresh Fire,* Cymbala declares: "Prayer cannot truly be taught by principles and seminars and symposiums. It has to be born out of a whole environment of felt need." Later he powerfully states: "What does it say about our churches today that God birthed the church in a prayer meeting, and prayer meetings today are almost extinct?" Then later he notes: "The neglect of prayer is the fearful token of dead spiritual desires." He also says: "We need the fresh wind of God to awaken us from our lethargy." And finally he emphatically remarks: "The work of God can only be carried on by the power of God."

The church in America today lives in an atmosphere of affluence with the Laodicean spirit of lethargy, neither cold or hot, but lukewarm and nauseous to God. We think we are doing great because we draw crowds with programs, entertaining music and marketing strategies. However, those produce little genuine transformation of lives and make little or no impact on the depraved culture around us. Yet we think that we are just fine, not needing God and His power because we are rich and have need of nothing. We already have everything we need to be "successful" with the ABCs of attendance, buildings and cash, as Cymbala would say. But Jesus tells us that we are clueless! He tells us that we are in fact poor, and wretched and miserable and blind!

In conclusion, prayer is distinguished as one of the four disciplines of the Church, and it deserves much more than casual practice in our churches today. Corporate prayer needs to be elevated to a place of preeminent importance in the life of every church. Will your church place an appropriately strong emphasis on prayer? Will leadership in your church preach on prayer and call the people of God to pray in faith and desperate dependence on God? Will your church plan for special seasons of prayer? Will your church set aside regular times of prayer?

The apostle Paul charges the Church:

> With every prayer and request, pray at all times in the Spirit, and stay alert in this, with all perseverance and intercession for all the saints (Ephesians 6:18).

Conclusion Regarding the Disciplines of the Church

The church of the book of Acts modeled the four disciplines as a pattern for all churches of all times. There is no authentic Christianity if they are not an important part of the life of the church. It is imperative that we pursue these disciplines with passionate tenacity. And that will happen only when we place them front and center in the church's ministry. We must be intentional. If we are, and if we develop these disciplines, they will produce flames of light and winds of life for our churches!

Chapter 5

The Deportment of Authentic Christianity

The Principles and Practices of Christian Character and Conduct

Christian Character
The Motive for Christian Character
The Example of Christian Character
The Power for Christian Character
The Characteristics of Christian Character

Christian Conduct
Renewal of the Mind
Living the Christian Virtues
Developing Proper Family Relationships
Practicing Right Relationships in the Local Church
Living a Christian Testimony Before Unbelievers
Manifesting a Right Attitude Toward Government
Maintaining an Alert Disposition

Authentic Christian Character and Conduct

The qualities and standards taught in the New Testament epistles:
Christian attitudes, character, and conduct

This chapter will consist of two sections: one on Christian character and the other on Christian conduct.

The section on Christian character will describe what Christian character is, what motivates Christian character, and what the resulting characteristics of Christian character are. These are all found repetitiously in the New Testament epistles or letters.

The section on Christian conduct will deal with a number of specific principles of conduct that are found repeatedly in the New Testament. These apparently are very important guides for us to follow as we live our lives.

Christian Character

The first chapter of the book of 2 Peter presents the stages of growth in Christian character. In the last verse of 2 Peter, the apostle admonishes us: "But grow in the grace and knowledge of our Lord and Savior, Jesus Christ" (NIV). The Greek text says, "But *you*" (emphasis added – *you* is singular), *you* personally or individually, grow spiritually. Let's put it plainly: Your spiritual growth is your own personal responsibility. You are the one who can, with God's grace, make it happen. And God has already provided His grace for that purpose as we will see.

The Motive for Christian Character

It is impossible to develop Christian character if we approach it simply as a duty, or the right thing to do. It is likewise impossible if we only attempt to mimic characteristics of Christian character because we think we are supposed to have certain Christian characteristics. Christian character is more than a veneer of actions we perform or impressions we create to present a Christian image or to impress others.

194

Christian character stems from the divine nature, God's nature, planted in us. There are desires that become a part of us due to the nature of God planted in us (1 John 3:9).

First, consider the principle of motivation. Because the nature or character of God has become a part of us through the spiritual birth, that nature now within us has natural impulses or tendencies to live out the character of God in our lives. Christian character, therefore, is rooted in God's character and develops according to that pattern. The innate spiritual desire to be godly or God-like is the motive that drives the development of Christian character.

Now consider the principle of imitation. A practical help in the development of Christian character is a clear focus on what God's character is like in order to imitate it. Each of us should study what God is like and grow a desire to be like Him (2 Corinthians 3:18). The goal is that Christian character will reflect what God is like in order to glorify Him as others see Him in our lives. Our goal as Christians should be that we are so much like Christ, who is the perfect human image of God, that others see Him in us as they watch us. And we need to be aware that there is always someone watching.

The Example of Christian Character

Jesus Christ is the perfect example and model of godliness or Christian character. He was the perfect ideal of all that God intended each human being to be. He becomes, therefore, our model and supreme example. His life and character is the pattern for us to follow.

We can develop a picture of what Christian character looks like by studying the characteristics of Jesus. In considering what Scripture says about God in the Old Testament and regarding Jesus Christ in the New Testament, certain major characteristics stand out as prominent. In the Old Testament, we see God's characteristics: faithfulness to His commitments and to His word; justice and righteousness; goodness, which includes generosity toward His creatures; as well as mercy and compassion. In studying the life of Jesus in the New Testament, the characteristics of grace, love, compassion, forgiveness, mercy, kindness, righteousness and truth stand out. These are accompanied by submissiveness to the will of God, serving God by selflessly and sacrificially serving others, and an attitude of meekness and humility.

You may want to pause here and make a list of these qualities and then use the list to pray for the Lord to grow these qualities in your life. If you ask for these in prayer consistently over a period of time, you will discover that your attitudes, spirit, and character will be transformed. You will become much more like Christ! And your life will glorify God more and more.

The fruit of the Spirit listed in Galatians 5:22–23 provides many characteristics of Christian character as do the virtues taught in 2 Peter 1:3–11. The fruit of the Spirit includes: love, joy, peace, patience, kindness, goodness, faith, gentleness, and self-control. However, a study of 2 Peter, chapter one, is perhaps the best starting point for the study of Christian character, and of how it is motivated, empowered, and developed. So we will begin there.

What Makes Christian Character Possible

God's Power for Christian Character

> For His divine *power* has given us everything required
> for life and godliness (2 Peter 1:3a; emphasis added).

Whatever spiritual sufficiency believers have is not because of any ability we possess in ourselves. It is God's power alone that enables us to develop godly character. It is the same power that raised Christ from the dead (Ephesians 1:19–20). It is a power that has made us alive with Christ (Ephesians 2:5–10). Peter certainly emphasizes this (1 Peter 1:3).

The grammar of the original language of the New Testament states that this divine power has been given to us in the past but with continuing or ongoing results in the present and into the future. God has permanently bestowed His power on believers. And the word "granted," or "given," is a word that always carries a regal sense, describing an act of great generosity usually exercised by a sovereign. God has permanently and generously granted His divine power to those who are believers so that we might have the strength and ability to develop Christian character.

God's Provision for Christian Character

When we became Christians, God gave us everything required for life and godliness! Without asking for anything more, we already have every spiritual resource needed to produce holiness and to persevere in holy living. Nothing is lacking or missing.

God's Power and Provision for Godliness

The Greek word for godliness used by Peter is "eusebeia." It encompasses both true reverent worship and, flowing out of that worship, active obedience in life as a whole. Another definition of godliness is that piety which, characterized by a God-ward attitude, does that which is well-pleasing to Him.

A faithful life and godliness are not native to the human heart. They are God's gifts freely granted through our union with Christ. The enablement for a faithful life and godliness are truly amazing gifts!

God's Calling Establishes His Purpose and Destiny for Our Lives

In 2 Peter 1:3b, we read: "Through the knowledge of Him who *called us* by His own glory and goodness" (emphasis added). The word used for knowledge here is *epignosis,* which refers to a knowledge that is deep and genuine. It is not merely intellectual, but knowledge that is the product of personal experience (Philippians 3:7–10).

Godliness flows out of our personal and genuine knowledge of God, and that comes through our experience of personal fellowship and interaction with Him. This includes our experience of Him in worship as well as His providential workings in our lives. An excellent book that explains how God interacts with us in our lives is Henry Blackaby's *Experiencing God.* That should be a "must-read" for every Christian.

197

Knowing Christ should result in our knowing His calling on our lives. He called us because of His own glory and goodness, not because of anything we did to deserve it. His glory speaks of His divine glory – a great motivation for obedience and holiness. His goodness, virtue, and moral excellence speak of Jesus's morally perfect earthly life. People are drawn to Jesus the Messiah because of His virtuous life and perfect humanity. Seeing His purity and excellence inspires us to follow Him, to live lives of virtue and beauty.

One effect of His divine power is that He provides everything required for a life of faithfulness and godliness. It is possible for each of us who are in Christ to become godly! That is a pretty amazing thought. Our calling is both an eternal one anticipating glory and a temporal one that calls for virtue or moral excellence as we live each day.

God's Promises Motivate and Encourage Christian Character

2 Peter 1:4a declares: "By these (Christ's glory and goodness) God has given (granted) us very great and precious promises." "Has given" is the same word as in verse 3 and is also in the perfect passive tense, indicating something already done but with ongoing results in the present and into the future. "Very great" translates "megistos," meaning magnificent or the very greatest. "Precious" is very highly valuable. They are "very great" (magnificent) and "precious" (highly valuable) promises! These promises certainly relate to salvation. They assure us of the reality and availability of the numerous gifts resulting from our salvation. These promises are given to us in the New Testament.

The Two Results of the Precious Promises

In 2 Peter 1:4b, we discover the first result of the precious promises God has made to us: "So that through them you may share in the divine nature."

As we embrace God's promises in His Word and believe them, and then act on them, God's nature becomes an active part of our lives resulting in the growth of Christian character (Hebrews 2:10). This statement is so important that you may want to reread it and stop to think about its meaning for you. The Word of God, and specifically His promises, plays a major role in producing Christian character. It is primarily His promises that motivate us because of the temporal and eternal rewards they secure for us. His promises not only give us hope and strength, but they also empower us to live godly lives.

The second result of God's great and precious promises is that they enable us to escape the corruption that is in the world. 2 Peter 1:4c states: "Escaping the corruption that is in the world because of evil desires."

Corruption is a word denoting a decomposing, rotting organism and its accompanying stench. To God, all sin is corruption. It stinks to high heaven! Evil desires of every kind include: greed, illicit sexual desires, prideful desire for power and prestige, desire for revenge, and other similar base desires. The word "escaping" depicts the successful flight from danger. This escape from the corruption of the world is part of the process of our restoration to the image of God.

Christian character requires the repudiation of all evil desires and fleeing from them. To make Christian character possible, a believer must, by God's grace, separate from the filthy attitudes, thoughts, and practices of the ungodly world system. We live in a fallen world, and our lives are constantly touched, tainted and tempted by it.

The Characteristics of Christian Character

We discover a list of the major characteristics of Christian character in 2 Peter 1:5. It says:

> For this very reason, make every effort to supplement your faith with goodness, goodness with knowledge, knowledge with self-control, self-control with endurance, endurance with godliness, godliness with brotherly affection, and brotherly affection with love.

This is a list of progressive steps to Christian maturity. *Faith* is the first step. The Greek word used here is in the present perfect tense, which means the beginning of faith that occurs and is established in the present with continuing results into the future. The kind of faith Peter is talking about is not just intellectual belief in God. This is made clear in the *Dictionary of New Testament Theology,* edited by Colin Brown, where it states, "True biblical faith in the believer is constituted by a loyalty and commitment to God and solidarity with him." This is where true Christian character begins. This is its origin, its bedrock! This faith is the very foundation of Christian character, and without it, there will never be growth in Christ-likeness.

Goodness is the second quality of Christian character Peter cites. The word "goodness" here is also translated as virtue or moral excellence in other translations. It is moral goodness. It is more than morality in just the physical sense, although that is included. It is goodness of one's entire moral character, and it includes sexual purity, truthfulness, kindness, generosity, and integrity.

That which should be added to goodness is *knowledge.* The Greek word for knowledge here means experiential knowledge, that is, knowledge that is based on personal experience. It is a spiritual knowledge that comes as a result of fellowship with God and walking on life's journey with Him. It is deep, personal knowledge of God. Knowledge means understanding Him and His will. It is more than head knowledge, although that is certainly included. It is heart knowledge. It is spiritual wisdom. Such knowledge becomes a vital part of one's character and a conscious part of one's daily life.

The Christian's development of Christian character is well underway with the qualities we have already considered, but more needs to be supplied. Next on Peter's list is *self-control*, also mentioned as one of the products of the fruit of the Spirit (Galatians 5:22–23). In Peter's day, self-control was used when speaking about athletes in regard to their personal self-discipline and self-restraint. In his commentary on 2 Peter, John MacArthur states: "Thus, a Christian is to control the flesh, the passions, and the bodily desires, rather than allowing himself to be controlled by them (1 Corinthians 9:27; Galatians 5:23)." A disciple is to be self-controlled when it comes to spending, eating, sexual desires, temper, responses to others, and speech. Self-control also includes the avoidance of addictive substances, bad attitudes, and unwholesome activities. An excellent picture of self-control is given to us in Proverbs 16:32: "He who is slow to anger is better than the mighty, and he who rules his spirit than he who takes a city" (NKJV).

Endurance or perseverance is another trait that is to be a part of our Christian character. It is patience or endurance in doing what is right. It is keeping on keeping on, even when it is very hard to. Endurance means that the believer remains steadfast through difficulties, trials, temptations, and all kinds of struggles. Life is full of all kinds of roadblocks. Unless we stay the course, we fail. This quality is a major part of the strength of one's character. The Christian life can be very difficult at times. It may sometimes even seem impossible. In Jesus's most difficult hour, a moment of indescribable pressure, this trait of endurance enabled him to bare great suffering and distress, as Hebrews 12:1b–2a says:

> Let us run with endurance the race that is set before us,
> fixing our eyes on Jesus, the author and perfecter of our
> faith, who for the joy set before Him *endured* the cross"
> (NASB; emphasis added).

Another very important aspect of Christian character is *godliness*. Quoting MacArthur again: "To be godly is to live reverently, loyally, and obediently toward God." To live a godly life is to live one filled with God's character. Godliness is a characteristic that distinguishes the believer from the ungodly world. To be godly is to have a different demeanor from that of the world. Godly demeanor is a reverent spirit as described by Peter in his first letter: "And if you call on the Father, who without partiality judges according to each one's work, conduct yourselves throughout the time of your stay here in fear (Greek: reverential fear)" (1 Peter 1:17 NKJV). This reverence holds God and the things of God in highest esteem and is repulsed by all that is contrary to God and the things of God. As this verse concludes Peter's explanation of godliness, consider the challenge of 1 Peter 1:13–16:

> Therefore, prepare your minds for action; be self-controlled; set your hope fully on the grace to be given you when Jesus Christ is revealed. As obedient children, do not conform to the evil desires you had when you lived in ignorance. But just as he who called you is holy, so be holy in all you do; for it is written: "Be holy because I am holy."

To godliness we are to add *brotherly affection*. This involves both attitudes and actions of affection. It is a family kind of love that willingly sacrifices for other members of the family, whether our spiritual family, or even the family of mankind (1 John 4:20). We are to have concern and affection for all people, but especially for those of the family of faith. Without such feelings, the unity so critical to Christ's body is impossible. It is very easy to allow ourselves to be annoyed with others.

Brotherly affection also includes forgiveness. To have this kind of high regard and respect for those around us, we must be willing to forgive their faults and quirks. It involves a humility that is so overwhelmed by the forgiveness we have received that we are compelled to forgive others. One reason forbearance and forgiveness are so important is that they provide a lubrication where relationships and working together in service are concerned.

The top step of this eight-step climb to Christian maturity and character is *love*, agape. Love is the crowning jewel of Christian character. When we can love all people in a selfless and sacrificial way like Christ, we have become spiritually mature. Paul says that this virtue or character trait is greater than faith or hope, and he describes the ways in which godly love demonstrates itself – see 1 Corinthians chapter 13. This chapter is often used in weddings to express how husbands and wives are to regard one another. In truth, however, it should describe our view and relationship with all people.

A selfless, sacrificial love for God and for our fellow man is supernaturally poured into our hearts by the Holy Spirit (Romans 5:5). We certainly can't achieve it apart from God bestowing it in our hearts and us receiving it freely while recognizing it as an amazing gift of grace. When we have experienced God's love on such a personal level, only then are we able to give it to others. This love as described in Romans 5:8 is powerful motivation for us to sacrificially meet the needs of others.

Agape, godly love, is evidenced by compassion, mercy, grace, forgiveness, acceptance, patience with people, and service to meet the needs of others. It is the same quality of love commanded of husbands in Ephesians chapter 5 and as demonstrated by Jesus Christ who loved His bride so much that He "gave Himself up for us." Ephesians says that husbands are to have sacrificial love for their wives. Jesus certainly demonstrated this for us.

All of these things taken together form Christian character. They are what God desires as we cooperate with the Holy Spirit in growing spiritually toward maturity in Christ. It is a process called sanctification. This process occurs over the course of our lives, setting us apart for God's service. It prepares us in some yet unknown fashion for our ultimate glorification, when we will be made perfectly holy and will serve God in eternity (Philippians 3:20–21; Revelation 22:3).

A fitting close to our consideration of Christian character is Jude 24–25 (NIV):

> To him who is able to keep you from falling and to present you before his glorious presence without fault and with great joy – to the only God our Savior be glory, majesty, power and authority through Jesus Christ our Lord, before all ages, now and forevermore! Amen.

Christian Conduct

One of the best ways to know if we possess Christian character is to observe our behavior or conduct. There are a number of principles and practices of Christian conduct that are addressed over and over in the New Testament letters. These form basic and foundational patterns for Christian disciples to live by.

Renewing the Mind

Renewing the mind is the first and basic principle of Christian conduct. It is the daily act of putting on Christ and renewing our mind (Romans 12:1–2 & 13:11–14; 2 Corinthians 10:4–5; Ephesians 4:22–24; and Colossians 3:10).

Renewing the mind refers to filling our minds with God's truth as a replacement for the carnal or worldly thoughts that bombard us constantly. This renewal requires transformation on a daily basis. In Romans 12:2 God makes the need for this renewal clear. If we do not renew our minds, then we will be pulled and sucked back into the world's way of thinking, and consequently, our thoughts and actions will start to conform to the world.

In this passage, Paul uses the Greek word "metamorphoo." From it we get our English word "metamorphosis." In science, this word is used for the transformation of a caterpillar in its cocoon into a beautiful butterfly. Clearly, Paul is stating that renewal of the mind and our thoughts results in real, dramatic transformation.

In 2 Corinthians 10:4-5, Paul states that the battle for the mind is spiritual warfare. He uses military terms like "weapons," "strongholds," and "taking every thought captive," the idea of capturing the enemy. He declares that ideas, opinions, and arguments that are against Christ must be demolished. In military speech, that means they must be blown up and obliterated!

The chapters of Ephesians 4 and Colossians 3 present the positive goal of this transformation. The process of renewal of the mind is aimed at restoring the individual, who was created in the image of God, into that perfect image once again. Sin has marred and distorted God's image within us, but the renewal of the mind through God's truth is powerful. It restores the individual so that we once again think like God and begin to act like God in righteousness and purity. It restores God's moral and ethical character in us and establishes His truth that counteracts the lies, deceit, and falsehoods of Satan.

The command for believers to be transformed by the renewing of the mind is saliently stated in Romans 12:1–2:

Therefore, brothers, by the mercies of God, I urge you to present your bodies as a living sacrifice, holy and pleasing to God; this is your spiritual worship. Do not be conformed to this age, but be *transformed* by the renewing of your mind, so that you may discern what is the good, pleasing, and perfect will of God (emphasis added).

The conclusion is this: these verses warn the believer about the pressures brought to bear on the Christian by the world. "The world" is that system of unbelieving mankind that is directed and animated behind the scenes by Satan and is enmeshed in the carnal desires of man's sinful nature and deceived, faulty ways of thinking (Ephesians 2:2–3). The world is rife with godless values and appeals to our baser instincts. It squeezes and pressures the believer to give in and to conform to its behavior and thinking. The world presents a persistent, insistent, and powerful pressure to conform.

The only way a believer can overcome this pressure and find victory in living his life according to God's will is through the continual renewing of his mind. The thought-life of the believer must be continually redirected and refocused on the Lord and His truths. The disciple must be built up in his faith, fortified by the Holy Spirit, to be strong and steadfast.

This is why Romans 12:1 challenges us to present our body as a living sacrifice to do the will of God in order to please and glorify Him. This is the basis for renewing the mind. The renewal of the mind, however, is facilitated as the believer immerses himself in the Word of God, in daily yielding to the leading of the Holy Spirit, in personal study and meditation, in hearing the Word taught or preached, in fellowship with other believers as they share spiritual truth with one another, in music that expresses the Word, and in prayer as the believer draws on the resources of spiritual strength and power provided by the Lord.

Living the Christian Virtues

Living out Christian virtues under the influence of the Holy Spirit is an essential element of Christian conduct (Galatians 5:22–23; Colossians 3:12; 2 Peter 1:5–7). Galatians 5:22-23a enumerates those virtues:

> But the fruit of the Spirit is love, joy, peace, patience, kindness, goodness, faith, gentleness, self-control.

Before he tells us about this passage regarding the fruit of the Spirit, Paul informs us about the works of the flesh (vs. 19–21). He mentions that those are sexual immorality, moral impurity, promiscuity, idolatry, sorcery, hatreds, strife, jealousy, outbursts of anger, selfish ambitions, dissensions, factions, envy, drunkenness, carousing, or anything similar. This describes the character and behavior that is typical of the unsaved. Unfortunately for the believer, there can, at times, be a strong propensity toward these behaviors that were a part of the old self and continue to lurk around.

In contrast to "the works of the flesh," the apostle then mentions "the fruit of the Spirit." Fruit is something that is produced. This fruit is the result of a spiritually healthy life. To grow fruit requires growth of the tree or plant to the point of being able to bear fruit and time to develop. A good tree produces good fruit. So it is with the Christian. The spiritual life of a healthy believer bears fruit due to the sanctifying work of the Holy Spirit in the believer's life.

Love is the first characteristic of the fruit of the Spirit on this list because all of the other characteristics are probably products of love. The disciple who loves God and loves others will put the Lord and others first, and therefore he will experience deep *joy*. This joy is an inner sense of rich fulfillment and happiness. That quality of agape or supernatural love also produces *peace*. Peace in Scripture denotes a sense of well-being, wholeness, and spiritual health. It is an inner tranquility that results from a person being at total inner rest. At times, it can be almost like a surreal experience of pleasure.

When my wife and I flew to Papua New Guinea to spend time with our daughter and son-in-law and their family who have been missionaries there since 2001, we landed on a grass runway at the town of Namatanai on the island of New Ireland. Our son-in-law, Aaron, was running a little late to meet us and take us to their home in the tribal village. Diana and I gathered our things and walked the short distance to the terminal, a building that, at best, looked like a small roadside fruit stand. Some native people were sitting on rough wooden benches out front, and although they did not know English, they graciously offered my wife and me a bench to sit on. We sat under the shade of the canopy but could still feel the heat as we watched heat waves drift across the runway and watched the gentle breeze softly move the fields of tall grass nearby. Feeling the light breeze off the ocean caressing us and hearing the sounds of a few large insects a little distance from us, we sat under the blue sky marked only with a few floating white clouds. A sweet serenity settled over us and seemed to sink into the innermost recesses of our being. The peace of God was with us, and there was no fear, no worry, and no care. It was as if time were suspended as we felt the peace of God wash over us and the joy of the Lord filling our hearts. We sat there quietly drinking in every moment. That feeling could have lasted a lifetime without a split-second of boredom. It felt like heaven itself! That is a perfect picture of what the fruit of peace is like as it is produced in the believer's life by the Holy Spirit.

Love also produces longsuffering, goodness, and meekness. *Longsuffering* refers to patience and understanding when dealing with other people. *Goodness* is character that is morally good and spontaneously generous. *Meekness* is a submissive spirit that does not demand its way or its rights and is not easily provoked, but is disposed to acquiesce to the needs and desires of others. Meekness does not imply weakness, however. The image is similar to that of an ox pulling a plow. He does so meekly, but with great power.

Faithfulness and *self-control* are qualities that also flow from love. Love causes us to speak the truth and to be faithful in our dealings with others. It also demands that we have self-control in our lives in order to treat others well and to set a good example for them.

These virtues are only made possible as fruit in the disciple's life when the disciple is genuinely surrendered to the Holy Spirit. The Holy Spirit is not the one who serves us to make this possible. We are His servants! To surrender is to do His will and to be used by Him to touch the lives of others. When we think of how we are to act toward the Holy Spirit, we should always picture a highway YIELD sign. That is to be our answer to Him in whatever He directs.

Family Relationships

Another vitally important area of Christian conduct is developing and maintaining proper family relationships (Ephesians 5:22, 25 & 6:1; Colossians 3:18–21; 1 Peter 3:1–7).

Good family relationships are another feature of Christian conduct that is emphasized numerous times in the New Testament epistles. Good family relationships are an important part of the believer's spiritual life, bearing testimony that glorifies God before the world. Since God is a relational being, relationships are highly important to Him. Family relationships will be healthy and good as the Christian consistently yields control of his life to the Holy Spirit and the fruit of the Spirit becomes a part of his character. In their book *Formula for Family Unity*, Dr. Walter Fremont and his wife, Trudy, strongly emphasize that good character is a very significant factor in maintaining good family relationships. It is one of four keys to a successful marriage: commitment, character, caring, and communication. I have used these principles successfully in leading *The Keys to a Successful Marriage Seminar"* with numerous groups of married and engaged couples.

The essential nature of the husband-wife relationship is described in Ephesians 5:22–33. The basic principle is mutual submission, which is found in verse 22. The husband is submissive because he is required to be submissive to Christ and to be like Christ, – a selfless, sacrificial, servant-leader for his wife and children. Like Jesus was submissive to the Father, the earthly husband is to be submissive to the Lord Jesus (1 Corinthians 11:3). The wife is to be obediently submissive to her husband (1 Corinthians 11:3; Ephesians 5:22–24). It is for this reason that the husband, like Christ, chooses to love his wife so much that he willingly gives up his rights and prerogatives to meet her needs. Quite rare is the woman who would not follow the leadership of a man who loves her unconditionally and serves her needs sacrificially.

The woman is also motivated by love and submission. The verse does not say she must love her husband, although she probably will as he shows sacrificial love for her. Titus 2:4 states that the older, mature women are to teach the younger women how to love their husbands (Greek: with natural, familial affection). Ephesians 5:22 says that she must be submissively obedient in following his leadership. Her submission is first to the Lord (1 Peter 3:5–6). Her submission to the Lord is because of her trusting Him with her life and with all of her circumstances. This trust enables her to be submissive to her husband so that he will be able to sense the Lord's conviction and to hear Him speaking to him. As she is submissive, she does not covertly try to change her husband. Rather, she trusts the Lord to change him, or at the very least to work things out circumstantially for her well-being. The wife, in her love and submissiveness to the Lord, will also be submissive to her husband. She will be a good follower and will respect and support him as her leader.

Ultimately, as the husband and wife both fulfill their roles in submission to the Lord, their relationship becomes a partnership, with mutual love and respect, as Peter mentions in his passage on the marriage relationship. The unity that is developed over time and through many joys and trials will prove to be highly beneficial spiritually in their development as well as richly fulfilling in their lives. It will lay the foundation for their children to be loving and submissive to the Lord and to have a pattern of how to develop their own healthy marriage relationships.

Relationships in the Church

Practicing right relationships in the local church is monumentally important when it comes to Christian conduct (1 Timothy 3:15; Romans 12:9–10; Ephesians 4:1–3; Philippians 2:1–4; Colossians 3:12–16; James 3:13–18).

It is sad to realize that many churches and pastors have experienced painful divisions caused by pride and self-will. This pride and self-will are sometimes between the people of the church and sometimes includes the pastor. When this occurs, rather than the unity that comes through humility and submission, there will be division and destruction. The New Testament epistles address this issue again and again.

The apostle Paul declares in 1 Timothy 3:15 that we should all learn how we ought to properly conduct ourselves in the church, the local assembly. He emphasizes that we should conduct ourselves accordingly because the church is the pillar and foundation of the truth. In effect he is saying that the effectiveness of the church's witness, testimony, and success in its mission is dependent on the way believers conduct themselves in their covenant relationship with one another. He may also be indicating that the church's future viability can be at stake due to the long-term effects of division and in-fighting, making unity vitally important to the church's spiritual health and future longevity. Sadly, some churches have gone through cycles of in-fighting and division. Those churches suffer spiritual and numerical decline, and die slowly over a long period of time, leaving spiritually wrecked lives in their wake.

In Romans 12:9–10, Paul specifically urges believers to love one another and to show family affection to one another. He tells them to outdo one another in showing honor to each other. He admonishes them to be in agreement with one another, and not to be proud. They are exhorted to do everything possible to live at peace with one another and to be forgiving.

Paul spent more time in Ephesus than in any other single place doing ministry. As he writes to the church he founded there, he calls on them "to walk worthy of their calling, with all humility and gentleness, with patience, accepting one another in love, diligently keeping the unity of the Spirit with the peace that binds us." Behind this call for unity he presses the great truths and convictions of our faith: "one body and one Spirit, one hope; one Lord, one faith, one baptism, one God and Father of all." How blatantly disrespectful to God, how irreverent and detestable it is, when because of selfishness and pride, believers rip churches apart and cause division within the body!

Writing to a church that Paul had the most intimate fellowship with, the church at Philippi, he tenderly requests:

> Fulfill my joy by thinking the same way, having the same love, sharing the same feelings, focusing on one goal (i.e. contextually: advancing the gospel). Do nothing out of rivalry or conceit, but in humility consider others as more important than yourselves.

And on what basis does he make this appeal? On one that is most incredible and amazing! Philippians 2:5–8 gives us what is called the "kenosis," the self-emptying of Christ. He was in the form of God but took upon Himself the form of a slave! From commanding millions upon millions of angels, He became a lowly slave to serve the Father, and in serving the Father, to serve mankind. Paul tells us all to have this same attitude and mindset that Jesus had. Too many irreverently ignore this truth and selfishly demand their way, their comfort and convenience in terms of their wants and interests. They regard these things as more important than the needs of others, as more important than the advancement of the gospel and more important than the glory of God. When believers in the church do that, the very sacrifice of our Savior is ignored and devalued. When that happens, there is a failure to reverence and to emulate the love and sacrifice of Jesus Christ.

In Colossians 3, the apostle calls for believers to put on "heartfelt compassion, kindness, humility, gentleness, and patience, accepting one another and forgiving one another if anyone has a complaint against another. Just as the Lord has forgiven you, so also you must forgive." Then he says, "Above all, put on love – the perfect bond of unity."

James, the half-brother of Jesus and pastor of the church of Jerusalem, does a masterful job of painting a picture of the dynamics of relationships in the church for us. In James 3:13–18 he speaks of "wisdom's gentleness." He then says that "bitter envy and selfish ambition" will cause a believer to brag and to lie in defiance of the truth. Furthermore he declares that this kind of wisdom is not from God but is earthly, sensual, and demonic! He then states that where "envy and selfish ambition" exist that there is disorder and evil of every kind. This is a sad reality in some churches.

Finally, with eloquence, James describes heavenly wisdom, describing it as "pure, peace-loving, gentle, compliant, full of mercy and good fruits, and without favoritism and hypocrisy." He finishes by observing: "And the fruit of righteousness is sown in peace by those who make peace" (James 3:18).

The truths found in the passages above stand as God's standard for the conduct of His people. He will certainly judge His people based on their conduct. Far too much division and destruction have occurred because Christian people have been selfish rather than submissive to church leaders, to the church body, and to God Himself. Submission before the Lord and seeking His mind and will result in a unity of spirit and purpose that transcends all differences of opinion and all desires.

Christian Testimony

Living a Christian testimony before unbelievers is critically important when it comes to integrity and witness (Matthew 5:16; Ephesians 2:10; Colossians 4:5–6; 1 Peter 2:12, 18). Every individual Christian has a high and holy calling, "the upward call of God in Christ Jesus," according to Philippians 3:13–14. In Matthew 5:16, Jesus told us, "You are the light of the world!" Because of this, we have a grave responsibility to shine the light of Christ from our lives and into a sin-darkened world. Our personal testimony before the world is a serious matter. Jesus tells us our lives are to bring glory and honor to God.

In Ephesians 2:10, Paul explains to us that we are God's workmanship, God's creation, His masterpiece. The idea is that He has designed and created us with a purpose in mind. He elaborates by saying that we are created for good works, and that God has prepared these good works so that we should do them as we live our lives. How profound! Imagine it. God designed us for a specific purpose and had in mind exactly how He planned for us to function so we would accomplish that purpose. Not only did Jesus mention "good works" in Matthew 5:16, but now Paul addresses them as well. Good works encompass a broad range of actions arising from the Spirit-empowered fruits of salvation. These include all kinds and varieties of good words and actions, from evangelism to feeding the hungry, to encouraging the downtrodden, to caring for the sick. If Jesus did it as a part of His life, there is a good bet that it is also expected from us, His people. And it all establishes an outward testimony to those who watch our lives.

Respect for Government

Manifesting a submissive attitude toward governing authorities is also very important in terms of testimony and witness (Romans 13:1–7; Titus 3:1; 1 Peter 2:13–14). The Christian standard is to be submissive and obedient to government and governmental authorities. In some circumstances, when the government is evil, this can be very difficult to do. However, the basis for our submission and obedience is that all authority is God-ordained, according to Romans 13:1–7. To rebel against any authority is to be in rebellion against God.

There is a caveat, however. Since God is the highest authority of all, if an earthly authority commands that we do anything that is in direct violation of God's command, then we have both the right and the responsibility to respectfully refuse to obey the earthly authority. We should be careful that our refusal to obey does not display a rebellious spirit. It is always appropriate to assure the authority of our desire to be obedient and to make a respectful appeal to be released from the government's demand that is contrary to God's command.

Civil disobedience should be our last resort, and believers must realize that their obedience to God rather than to human authority may result in suffering. There are clear instances of civil disobedience in Scripture like Exodus 1:17; Daniel 3:16–18; Daniel 6:7, 10; and Acts 4:19. Civil disobedience should be exercised judiciously and reservedly. It must be exercised only when to obey the government would explicitly disobey God. As a last resort, civil disobedience must be exercised to remain faithful to God. And civil disobedience must always be peaceful resistance.

Noticeable in the Word of God in both Jesus and Paul is the restraint they each demonstrated in refusing to project themselves into the politics of the day. This is not to say that Christians should not be involved in politics, but that the cause of the gospel and politics should not be wedded to the church or to the cause of Christ. The mission for Jesus and Paul required that they remain distant from the fray of political issues of their day. Having said that, the principle of being salt should be lived out by Christians in the government and culture on a personal and individual basis.

It is also appropriate to respectfully remonstrate when the government infringes on religious freedom or attempts to tear down standards of morality. However, in terms of politics and partisanship, we should realize that God probably does not care much about our petty political issues. However, He does care enormously for the souls of people. Disputes over politics can do great harm when attempting to reach people with the eternally crucial message of Christ's salvation for us. We would do well to remember that God can use the worst political problems to serve His will, and since He will at times use them for good purposes, we should avoid being frustrated and politically rancorous.

Maintaining a Vigilant Attitude

Maintaining a watchful or vigilant attitude and responsible actions in the face of spiritual warfare is crucial to spiritual success (Ephesians 6:10–18; 1 Peter 5:8). An important part of Christian conduct is to work at being vigilant and discerning. The idea of being vigilant is to be alert and cautious. Believers are admonished to realize that they are in a spiritual war with an enemy that is powerful and cunning. It is therefore imperative that each believer, like a soldier, be alert and on-guard all the time.

The Greek word for vigilance or watchfulness is used in a number of passages and shows that the believer's vigilance is important in many respects. First, believers should be vigilant in regard to false teachers and false teaching.

> I know that after my departure savage wolves will come
> in among you, not sparing the flock; and from among
> your own selves men will arise, speaking perverse things,

to draw away the disciples after them. Therefore *be on the alert*, remembering that night and day for a period of three years I did not cease to admonish each one with tears (Acts 20:29–31; NASB ; emphasis added).

Paul recognized the inevitability of false teachers and knew that their teachings would be destructive to individuals and to churches. In 2 Peter 2:1, Peter warns that false teachers will secretly or stealthily bring in "destructive heresies, even denying the Master who bought them." Typically, false teaching is difficult to detect early on because it is an aberration of the truth. That is, it contains enough truth to sound credible. It is usually not a blatant in-the-face denial of the truth or a sharp departure from the Word of God in most cases. Instead, it begins by using the Scriptures in a way that twists them to mean something other than their true meaning.

For these reasons, believers are warned to beware and to be vigilant with regard to doctrine. Keen alertness is required to detect these destructive heresies. Many true believers will also be sucked in, deceived, and led astray. Ultimately, many of the false teachers will be recognized as apostates, those who have departed from the true Christian faith. As John says, "They came out from among us but they were not of us" (1 John 2:19). John means that they were never truly saved or true believers in Christ although at first they appeared to be. In time, their demonically inspired doctrines would lead them to deny orthodox truth or the genuine Christian faith.

The problem of false teachers and false doctrines will increase by the unleashing of waves of demonically inspired doctrines in the latter days. Paul warns:

Now the Spirit explicitly says that in the latter times some will depart from the faith, paying attention to deceitful spirits and the teachings of demons (1 Timothy 4:1).

Vigilance, alertness, discernment, and watchfulness involve staying strong and firm in the faith. 1 Corinthians 16:13 admonishes us: *"Be on the alert*, stand firm in the faith, act like men, be strong" (NASB; emphasis added). It also involves vigilance regarding opposition by Satan as we are warned by 1 Peter 5:8: "Be of sober spirit, *be on the alert.* Your adversary, the devil, prowls around like a roaring lion, seeking someone to devour" (NASB; emphasis added).

Furthermore, vigilance must be an attitude included in our prayer life. This is what Colossians 4:2 instructs: "Devote yourselves to prayer, *keeping alert* in it with an attitude of thanksgiving" (NASB; emphasis added).

Being alert is a part of keen anticipation of Christ's coming! Matthew 24:42 challenges us: "Therefore *be on the alert*, for you do not know which day your Lord is coming" (NASB; emphasis added). (See also Matthew 24:43 & 25:13; 1 Thessalonians 5:6; and Revelation 16:15.)

We are strongly admonished by Christ Himself to be vigilant, alert, and watchful in assessing the spiritual condition of our local church. In Revelation 3:2, Jesus commands: "*Be watchful*, and strengthen the things which remain, that are ready to die, for I have not found your works perfect before God" (NKJV; emphasis added).

Spiritual discernment, alertness, and awareness are to characterize the Christian's conduct in regard to all of life. Vigilance and discernment protect the believer and the church from false teaching, from allowing sin to make inroads, and from subtle spiritual decline.

Are you a vigilant disciple? Should you be strengthening your own vigilance, alertness, and discernment? How do you do it? We increase vigilance and discernment by meditating on the Word of God, by soul-searching prayer, and by learning to evaluate every doctrine and to discern every spirit, as to whether they are from God or from other sources.

One of the quickest ways to spot false teaching is to examine what the teaching is regarding Christ, His death and His resurrection. If Jesus Christ and His death and resurrection aren't supreme and preeminent in the group's teaching, then the teaching is most likely heretical and they may possibly be a cult. The book of Colossians is a case in point of judging teaching by how it treats Christ and His redemptive work. Another vital principle to use is to determine if a teaching is consistently taught in the Bible. A particular teaching must be clearly consistent in the Word of God or it should be questioned and not accepted until further investigation can confirm its truthfulness. God never contradicts Himself. If a doctrine based on one Scripture is clearly in conflict with another that is quite clear, the teaching is not from God.

If there is no genuine Christian character and conduct, then there is no authentic Christianity. So, at this moment, will you commit yourself or reaffirm your commitment to pursue the development of Christian character in your life and to faithfully put into practice the principles of Christian conduct?

Chapter 6

The Defense of Authentic Christianity

The Godless, Secular Worldview vs. the Christian Worldview

Worldviews

Secular Humanism – the Godless Worldview

The Christian Worldview

Introduction to Worldviews

Dr. David Jeremiah wrote a bombshell of a book, *I Thought I'd Never See the Day! – Culture at the Crossroads*. His book defines and describes the seismic shift that has occurred in the character and culture of our nation. The chapter titles give us the overview of this seismic shift. I thought I'd never see the day:

- When Atheists Would Be Angry
- When Christians Wouldn't Know They Were in a War
- When Jesus Would Be So Profaned
- When Marriage Would Be Obsolete
- When Morality Would Be in a Free Fall
- When the Bible Would Be Marginalized
- When the Church Would Be Irrelevant
- When a Muslim State Could Intimidate the World
- When America Would Turn Her Back on Israel
- When Changing Your Mind Could Save Your Life

One quick and basic illustration from his book will give us some perspective. "In 1982, the ninety-seventh United States Congress, by joint resolution, authorized President Ronald Reagan to proclaim 1983 the 'Year of the Bible.' The resolution passed and became Public Law 97-280. Fast-forward to May 2009, when a group of sixteen members of Congress introduced a bill to designate 2010 another 'Year of the Bible.' OneNewsNow of American Family News Network conducted a poll asking this question: 'What are the chances Congress would approve a bill designating 2010 as the 'Year of the Bible?' Of the 7,681 respondents, 86 percent said the probability was 'slim to none.' They were correct - Congress did not pass the measure. In only twenty-seven years American leaders moved from official affirmation of the Bible to refusing to affirm it. And most Americans probably didn't notice."

The monumental question is this: How did we get from where we were as a nation to where we are today in relation to our beliefs, character and culture? This shift came as a result of an educational shift from a biblical worldview to a secular, godless worldview. That educational shift has occurred by means of public education, various kinds of literature, Supreme Court decisions, television and other kinds of media, and cultural pressures to conform to the politically correct mantra. To understand the seismic shift, we must have a clarion understanding of the Judeo-Christian worldview that prevailed in our nation for almost two hundred years and the new secular, godless worldview that has supplanted the Judeo-Christian worldview in our nation's psyche.

According to *Focus on the Family Magazine* July / August 2004, a recent nationwide survey completed by the Barna Research Group determined that only four percent (4%) of Americans have a "biblical" worldview. When George Barna looked at "born again" believers in America, the results were a dismal nine percent (9%)!

What Is a Worldview?

A worldview is a framework from which we view reality and make sense of life and the world. "It's any ideology, philosophy, theology, movement or religion that provides an overarching approach to understanding God, the world and man's relations to God and the world" says David Noebel, author of *Understanding the Times*.

There are seven basic questions that are usually the components of a worldview:

1. What is prime reality – what is really real?
2. What is the nature of external reality, that is, the world around us?
3. What is a human being?
4. What happens to a person at death?
5. Why is it possible to know anything at all?
6. How do we know what is right and wrong?
7. What is the meaning of human history?

Whether conscious of it or not, every person has some kind of worldview. A personal worldview is a combination of all you believe to be true. What you believe becomes the driving force behind every emotion, decision, and action. Therefore, it affects your thoughts and actions in all areas of life: philosophy, science, theology, anthropology, economics, law, politics, art, and social mores.

In 1982 the state of Massachusetts began charging some parents who were sending their children to Christian schools with violating the truancy laws of the state. A group of pastors planned to meet before the Massachusetts Joint House-Senate Education Committee in Boston. They organized a series of speeches on pertinent subjects and assigned several of us to speak on specific related topics. I was asked to address the rationale for Christian education in terms of how it differed philosophically and theologically from public education. Someone suggested that research at Bridgewater State College at Bridgewater, Massachusetts, might prove helpful in preparation. Bridgewater State was founded by Horace Mann, the father of public education, and it was the first teachers' college in the United States. It has continued to be a leading college in the state for educating teachers. Mann successfully promoted the idea of public education in the 1930s and founded Bridgewater State College, now Bridgewater State University, in 1840. In their library I discovered two volumes that presented the opposing worldviews with clarity. The experience of presenting my findings to the state legislators was gratifying. Whether they agreed with us or not, they gave us a fair and respectful hearing. They were gracious in their demeanor and dealings with us. As a result of the hearing and a large rally of over five thousand people in support of Christian education at Framingham, Massachusetts, the state relented and desisted from prosecuting parents.

A part of the information I discovered at Bridgewater State College was from two excellent books on the subject of the philosophy of education. The finest of my findings are explained below.

What Are the Two Basic Worldviews?

In *The Philosophy of Education*, edited by Hobert W. Burns, professor at Syracuse University, and Charles J. Brauner, professor at Purdue University, two contrasting, competing worldviews are outlined demonstrating their distinct differences. The two worldviews are synoptic summaries of beliefs and assumptions that form around such concepts as:

- The origin, nature, and destiny of the universe;
- The origin, nature, and purpose of man;
- The origin, nature, and limits of knowledge; and
- The origin and nature of values.

The following uses the pattern and some of the details of Burns and Brauner, but is significantly revised in wording to more correctly represent each worldview in today's language.

The Judeo-Christian Worldview

The Origin, Nature, and Destiny of the World

- The universe was created by God ex-nihilo, or out of nothing.
- Matter receives its energy and purpose from God and is directed by Him toward that purpose.
- Nature and the universe are under the permanent control and guidance of God.

The Origin, Nature, and Purpose of Man

- Man is both a physical and a spiritual being.
- Man is a special creation of God.
- The ultimate destiny of man is either restorative or retributive.

The Origin, Nature, and Limits of Knowledge

- Man is a rational being and rationality makes knowledge possible.
- Truth is absolute since it is an extension of God's being and of His creation.
- A correct apprehension of truth can only be achieved by spiritual understanding.

The Origin and Nature of Values

- Moral standards are derived from the character of God and are therefore absolute, unchangeable, and eternal.
- Values are eternal.

The Contemporary Atheistic Secular Worldview

The Origin, Nature, and Destiny of the Universe

- The universe is simply matter, and matter has always existed.
- The universe is all we can know.
- The universe and matter are in a state of flux or change.
- The universe yields only problematic knowledge, never certainty.
- Organization within the universe is all by chance.
- Existence can only be attributable to that which is quantitatively measureable.

The Origin, Nature, and Purpose of Man

- Man is a cosmic accident.
- Man is an animal evolved from the lower animals.
- Man has no fundamental purpose, and therefore man is unimportant and life is meaningless.
- The only purpose man has is that purpose that he sets for himself.

The Origin, Nature, and Limits of Knowledge

- Knowledge is purely a chemical function in man's brain.
- All knowledge is relevant and not empirical.

The Origin and Nature of Value

- Values are grounded in materials and sensory pleasures.
- There are no standards of value – value is relative to the individual.

The foregoing is sufficient to illustrate the concept and the differences of these two primary worldviews. Although many other worldviews exist in the United States, these two major worldviews are predominant. Unfortunately, the concepts of the secular humanist worldview permeate most of the education and media in the United States. It is well past time that Christians face this reality and determine what we can and should do to counteract it.

If we are to have any success in pushing back against the avalanche of godless propaganda that comes at us through media, humanistic education and pop culture, then all Christians must endeavor to educate themselves with substantive knowledge of the Bible, theology, and apologetics (the reasoned defense of the Christian faith). The present climate of spiritual darkness and blindness cries out for Christians who are knowledgeable enough and bold enough to intelligently articulate what Christianity really is and how it dramatically and dynamically differs from the unsatisfying, empty worldviews and lifestyles of our culture.

Christians must begin to make the best choices they possibly can in selecting education for their children, taking into careful consideration the worldview that dominates the educational system into which they are choosing to place their child. When children are subjected to a daily diet of anti-Christian worldview in their education, then strong counter measures must be taken to assure that they understand the differences in worldviews and are taught specific content regarding those differences.

Pastors must challenge their people to study and grow. We should provide our people with excellent resources for discipleship, study, and spiritual development. We should educate our people regarding worldviews. We must firm up the foundations of the faith by preaching messages that ground our people in the knowledge of those foundations.

The most strategically important and critical action that must be taken and is essential to rebuilding a Christian worldview in our culture, is for Christian leaders, pastors, and apologists to develop a national strategy to teach and instill a biblical worldview in people, starting with Christian people. A graded curriculum should be developed that can be used in after-school programs for students attending public schools, for home-school students, for students in Christian schools, for all students in Christian colleges, and for use in evangelizing those who have not yet believed in Christ and the Bible. Key to the success of this teaching is the preparatory work of teaching the parents of these students about worldviews and involving them in the process of teaching their children the Christian foundations that will develop a Christian worldview in their children. The secular humanists have had and have employed a national strategy since the 1930s as will be explained below. Their strategy has succeeded in practically demolishing the underpinnings of our Christian culture in America. Meanwhile Christian leaders have done little to nothing to effectively counter the propaganda and brainwashing of the secular humanists. A new, national movement supported by a broad spectrum of Christian denominations and all who are recognized on a national scale as Christian leaders, must be supported and promoted vigorously.

All noble attempts in the political arena, through media and publications of great volumes on apologetics, in spite of the good they have accomplished, have nevertheless failed to stem the tide of godless, secular humanism that bombards all Americans constantly via education, the media, and pop-culture. The only hope we have to restore our nation is to rebuild the spiritual and moral foundations from the ground up. And that is also the only hope we have to preserve Christianity in our nation.

As Psalm 11:3 states:

> If the foundations are destroyed, what can the righteous do?

The context and Hebrew grammar of this verse is referring to the moral and spiritual foundations that are the support structures of a culture or society.

Firming Up the Foundations of Faith –
Establishing a Christian Worldview

God's Creation – Faith in the Existence of God
God's Word – Faith That God Has Spoken
God's Law – Faith in Moral Absolutes
God's Purposes – Faith in the Gospel (Redemption
of Mankind and the Universe)

These four fundamental foundations have been eroded by religious modernism, secular humanism, post-modernism, and numerous other philosophies and religious ideologies. They must be defended and propagated on a national scale in order to restore a Christian worldview in the culture. A cosmic war is raging in the United States today as God's kingdom of truth and righteousness is clashing with Satan's kingdom of falsehood and unrighteousness. Will you be a committed soldier of Jesus Christ to stand in the gap and make up a protective wall in this day of spiritual war?

The Impact of the Humanist Manifestos on Worldviews

Humanist Manifesto I was written in 1933 by John Dewey, "the father of progressive education" in America and was signed by thirty-four liberal humanists in the United States. John Dewey was an avowed atheist who wrote: "There is no God and there is no soul. There is no room for fixed, natural law or moral absolutes" (*Humanist Manifesto I*). He was the first president of the American Humanist Association. Many of its signers, like him, were leaders in the fields of education, government, and the Unitarian clergy.

Humanist Manifesto II, the 1973 update of the previous document, was originally signed by one-hundred-sixty, but eventually by more than two-hundred of society's leaders. It superseded the original *Humanist Manifesto*, proclaiming itself a "positive declaration for times of uncertainty." The following statements from the manifestos affirm their beliefs and reveal the basic tenants of godless, secular humanism.

Atheism

"Religious humanists regard the universe as self-existing and not created . . . We find insufficient evidence for belief in the existence of a supernatural; it is either meaningless or irrelevant to the question of the survival and fulfillment of the human race. As nontheists, we begin with humans, not God, nature not deity. Nature may indeed be broader and deeper than we now know; any new discoveries, however, will but enlarge our knowledge of the natural . . . But we can discover no divine purpose or providence for the human species. While there is much that we do not know, humans are responsible for what we are or will become. No deity will save us; we must save ourselves."

Evolution

"Humanism believes that man is part of nature and that he has emerged as the result of a continuous process . . . Holding an organic view of life, humanists find that the traditional dualism of mind and body must be rejected . . . Humanism recognizes that man's religious culture and civilization, as clearly depicted by anthropology and history, are the product of a gradual development due to his interaction with his natural environment and with his social heritage. The individual born into a particular culture is largely molded to that culture . . . science affirms that the human species is an emergence from natural evolutionary forces. As far as we know, the total personality is a function of the biological organism transacting in a social and cultural context. There is no credible evidence that life survives the death of the body. We continue to exist in our progeny and in the way that our lives have influenced others in our culture."

Amorality

"We affirm that moral values derive their source from human experience. Ethics is autonomous and situational, needing no theological or ideological sanction. Ethics stems from human need and interest. To deny this distorts the whole basis of life. In the area of sexuality, we believe that intolerant attitudes, often cultivated by orthodox religious and puritanical cultures, unduly repress sexual conduct. The right to birth control, abortion, and divorce should be recognized. While we do not approve of exploitive, denigrating forms of sexual expression, neither do we wish to prohibit, by law or social sanction, sexual behavior between consenting adults. The many varieties of sexual exploration should not in themselves be considered 'evil.' Without countenancing mindless permissiveness or unbridled promiscuity, a civilized society should be a tolerant one. Short of harming others or compelling them to do likewise, individuals should be permitted to express their sexual proclivities and pursue their life-styles as they desire."

The current situation in education in the United States comes into clear focus as we consider some facts as stated in *The Rebirth of America.* "Modern progressive education was introduced and spread across this country. The great architect of that new movement was John Dewey at Columbia Teachers College . . . Many people when they think of progressive education think of some sort of methodology of teaching which may be somewhat different. But they fail to see that beneath the methodology is something vastly more important and that is the ideology, or if you will, the theology that underlies the modern progressive educational movement." This source then accurately and correctly identifies the heart of this new theology: "an educational system where, instead of having God at the center, we would have man." It then correctly notes "'humanism gradually became the dominant ideology of the American public school system" (p. 122).

It is no wonder that Dr. W. P. Shofstall, the state Superintendent of Schools in Arizona, said in 1973: "The atheists have, for all practical purposes, taken over public education in this country" (*The Rebirth of America;* p. 123). Martin Luther, the great reformer, declared: "I am much afraid that schools will prove to be great gates of hell unless they diligently labor in explaining the Holy Scriptures, engraving them in the hearts of youth. Every institution in which men are not increasingly occupied with the Word of God must become corrupt."

How incredibly sad the status of public education is in America today. Abraham Lincoln said: "The philosophy of the classroom is the philosophy of government in the next generation" (Quotation referenced by Dr. Paul A Kienel, Executive Director of the Association of Christian Schools International, *Christian School Comment,* Volume 13, No. 3). The foundations our nation was built on have been eroded to the extent that they have been virtually destroyed.

The Christian Worldview

A Universe Charged with the Grandeur of God

The following material on the Christian Worldview is almost completely taken from Focus on the Family's *Truth Project®*, produced by Focus on the Family and is used by permission.

In the Western world, up to the end of the seventeenth century, the theistic worldview was clearly dominant. If battles were fought, the lines were drawn within the circle of theism. Being born in the Western world now guarantees nothing. Worldviews have proliferated.

Below are some of the primary tenants of the Christian worldview:

God is infinite and personal (Triune), transcendent and immanent, omniscient, sovereign and good.

God is infinite.

This means that He is beyond scope, beyond measure, as far as we are concerned. No other being in the universe can challenge Him in His nature. All else is secondary. He has no twin but is alone the be-all and the end-all of existence.

God is personal.

This means God is not mere force or energy or existent "substance." God is HE; that is, God has personality. Personality requires two basic characteristics: a) self-reflection, and b) self-determination.

God is transcendent.

This means God is beyond us and our world and separate from the world as the Creator is to be distinguished from His creation.

God is immanent.

This means God is with us in our world. He is present and involved with earth and mankind.

God is omniscient.

This means that God is all-knowing. He is the Alpha and the Omega and knows the beginning from the end.

God is sovereign.

This is really a further ramification of God's infiniteness, but it expresses more fully His concern to rule, to pay attention, as it were, to all the actions of His universe. It expresses the fact that nothing is beyond God's ultimate interest, control and authority.

God is good.

This is the prime statement about God's character. From it flows all others. Goodness is the essence of His character. God's goodness is expressed in two ways, through holiness and through love. God's goodness means then, first, that there is an absolute standard of righteousness and, second, that there is hope for humanity.

God created the cosmos ex nihilio (out of nothing) to operate with a uniformity of natural causes in an open system.

God created the cosmos ex nihilio (out of nothing).

God is "He who is," and thus He is the source of all else. No material universe existed, and no physical matter existed before God created it. God spoke it into existence.

God created the cosmos as a uniformity of natural causes in an open system.

The cosmos was not created to be chaotic. The universe is orderly. The nature of God's universe and God's character are, thus, closely related. The system is open, and that means it is not programmed. God is constantly involved in the unfolding pattern of the ongoing operation of the universe. And so are we as human beings!

Human beings are created in the image of God and thus possess personality, self-transcendence, intelligence, morality, gregariousness and creativity.

The key phrase here is "the image of God." That people are made in the image of God means they are like God. "We are like God" puts the emphasis where it belongs – on the primacy of God.

We are personal because God is personal. So we participate in part in a transcendence over our environment. In short, people have personality and are capable of transcending the cosmos in which they are placed in the sense that they can know something of that cosmos and can act significantly to change the course of both human and cosmic events. Personality is the chief thing about us as human beings, as, I think it is fair to say, it is the chief thing about God who is infinite both in His personality and in His being.

How does God fulfill our ultimate longing? He does so in many ways: by being the perfect fit for our very nature; by satisfying our longing for interpersonal relationship; by being in His omniscience the end of our search for knowledge; by being in His infinite Being the refuge from all fear; by being in His holiness the righteous ground of our quest for justice; by being in His infinite love the cause of our hope for salvation; by being in His infinite creativity both the source of our creative imagination and the ultimate beauty we seek to reflect as we ourselves create.

In Christian theism human beings are indeed dignified. Human dignity is derived from God. But though it is derived, people do possess it, even though it is a gift. So human dignity has two sides. As human beings we are dignified, but we are not to be proud of it, for it is a dignity borne as a reflection of the Ultimately Dignified. Yet it is a reflection. So then people who are theists see themselves as a sort of midpoint – above the rest of creation. This is then the ideal balanced human status. It was in failing to remain in that balance that our troubles arose.

Human beings can know both the world around them and God Himself because God has built into them the capacity to do so and because He takes an active role in communicating with them.

The foundation of human knowledge is the character of God as

Creator. We are made in His image. As He is the all-knowing knower of all things, so we can be the sometimes-knowing knowers of some things. The Word is eternal, an aspect of God Himself. From the meaning of the Greek word for "Word," "logos," we understand that Christ was and is logicality, intelligence, rationality, and meaning in the fullest and infinite sense because He was and is the revelation of God.

Out of this intelligence the world, the universe, came to be. And therefore, because of this source the universe has structure, order, and meaning.

God Himself is forever so beyond us that we cannot have anything approaching total comprehension of Him. God wants us to know Him, and He takes the initiative in this transfer of knowledge. This initiative is called revelation. God reveals, or discloses, Himself to us in two basic ways: a) by general revelation, and b) by special revelation. In general revelation, God speaks through the created order of the universe. Special revelation is God's disclosure of Himself in extra-natural ways: a bush that burns, the Ten Commandments, the inspired Scriptures, and climactically in His Son. The main point for us is that theism declares that God can and has clearly communicated with us.

Human beings were created good, but through the Fall the image of God became defaced, though not so ruined as not to be capable of restoration; through the work of Christ God redeemed humanity and began the process of restoring people to goodness, though any given person may choose to reject that redemption. Human "history" can be subsumed under four words – creation, fall, redemption, glorification.

Because God by His character set the standards of righteousness, human goodness consisted in being what God wanted people to be – beings made in the image of God and acting out that nature in their daily life.

Human beings were created with the capacity for self-determination. God gave them the freedom to remain or not to remain in the close relationship of image (man) to original (God).

People of all eras have attempted to set themselves up as autonomous beings, arbiters of their own way of life. The result of this act of rebellion was death.

Our self-transcendence was impaired by the alienation we experienced in relation to God. Human intelligence also was impaired. Morally, we became less able to discern good and evil. Socially, we began to exploit other people. Creatively, our imagination became separated from reality. We have become alienated from God, from others, from nature and even from ourselves. This is the essence of fallen humanity.

But humanity is redeemable and has been redeemed. That God has provided a way back for us does not mean we play no role.

Redeemed humanity is humanity on the way to the restoration of the defaced image of God – in other words, substantial healing in every area – personality, self-transcendence, intelligence, morality, social capacity, and creativity.

Glorified humanity is humanity totally healed and at peace with God, and individuals at peace with others and themselves.

For each person death is either the gate to life with God and His people or the gate to eternal separation from the only thing that will ultimately fulfill human aspirations.

Do I disappear – personal extinction? Do I hibernate and return in a different form – reincarnation? Do I continue in a transformed existence in heaven or hell? Christian theism clearly teaches the last of these. Those, who respond to God's offer of salvation populate the plains of eternity as glorious creatures of God – completed, fulfilled, but not sated, engaged in the ever-enjoyable communion with God and of the saints.

Ethics is transcendent and is based on the character of God as good (holy and loving).

God is the source of the moral world as well as the physical world. God is the good and expresses this in the laws and moral principles He has revealed in Scripture.

Made in God's image we are essentially moral beings, and thus we cannot refuse to bring moral categories to bear on our actions. Theism, however, teaches that not only is there a moral universe but there is an absolute standard by which all moral judgments are measured. God Himself – His character of goodness (holiness and love) – is the standard. Christians and Jews hold that God has revealed His standard in the various laws and principles expressed in the Bible.

The fullest embodiment of the good, however, is Jesus Christ. He is the complete man, humanity as God would have it to be.

History is linear, a meaningful sequence of events leading to the fulfillment of God's purposes for humanity.

Several basic turning points in the course of history are singled out for special attention by biblical writers. These turning points include the creation, the Fall, the revelation of God to the Hebrews (which includes the calling of Abraham from Ur to Canaan, the exodus from Egypt, the giving of the law, the witness of the prophets), the incarnation, the life of Jesus, the crucifixion and resurrection, Pentecost with the coming of the Holy Spirit, the spread of the good news via the church, the second coming of Christ and the judgment.

Looked at in this way, history itself is a form of revelation. The most important aspect of the theistic concept of history is that history has meaning because God – the Logos (meaning itself) – is behind all events.

Christian theism is primarily dependent on its concept of God, for theism holds that everything stems from Him.

So the greatness of God is the central tenet of Christian theism. That there are "God adumbrations in many daily forms" signal to us that God is not just in His heaven but with us – sustaining us, loving us and caring for us. Fully cognizant Christian theists, therefore, do not just believe and proclaim their view as true. Their first act is toward God – a response of love, obedience and praise to the Lord of the Universe – their Maker, Sustainer, and, through Jesus Christ, Redeemer and Friend.

(This ends the material taken from The Truth Project)

To illustrate the impact of the Christian worldview, I will use the origin of man or humanity. Man is created in the image of God, according to the first chapter of Genesis and the book of James. Inherent in being made in the image of God are three principles.

First, there is the principle of *the value of human life*, each and every human life. This principle in its practical application means that human life should be tenaciously protected and preserved, from the womb until death (Psalm 139). This means that abortion and any form of violence that terminates human life, or that physically mutilates or degrades human life, is evil and morally repugnant. That includes abortion and euthanasia. The Bible does allow for capital punishment (Genesis 9:6 et. al.) and for the protection of life and property (see the laws of God in Exodus and Deuteronomy).

A second principle is *the dignity of human life*. Because we are made in the image of God, every human should conduct their lives with a certain amount of dignity that lives up to who we are in the image of God. And every human being should be given the respect due to the dignity that God has endowed them with regardless of race, ethnicity, ability, intelligence, physical appearance, religion, or moral behavior. Showing respect to people who believe in a false religion or who live a lifestyle that is immoral does not imply agreement with their religious views or their immoral lifestyle, but still respects them as being made in the image of God. How we treat our fellow humans on a day-to-day basis, in business, in social settings, regarding their rights, in ethical behaviors, all apply to this principle.

There is a third and important principle that follows. *The purpose of human life* is directly reflected in humans being made in the image of God. The purpose of human life is to properly display the image of God and by doing so, to render glory to God. Because humans are fallen and sinful, the original image of God has been marred in us. That image can be restored through redemption. By redeeming us, our lives are redeemed and restored to the unmarred image of God. This begins with saving faith in the redemptive work of Jesus Christ, continues as a pattern of growth toward the full image of God (Ephesians 2:10 & 4:13, 24; Colossians 2:9-10), and is finalized and finished in the eternal state (Philippians 3:21; 1 John 3:2; Jude 24-25).

If you want to explore many of the practical results of the Christian worldview, you may want to read *What If Jesus Had Never Been Born*, by D. James Kennedy. It is an eye-opening read.

Does God Exist?

Evolution vs. Christianity

Evolution's Assault on Christianity

Spokespersons for Public Broadcasting System's *Evolution* series asserted that "all known scientific evidence supports Darwinian evolution" as does "virtually every reputable scientist in the world." Shortly thereafter more than one hundred scientists wrote *"A Scientific Dissent from Darwinism."* They stated: "We are skeptical of claims for the ability of random mutation and natural selection to account for the complexity of life. Careful examination of the evidence for Darwinian theory should be encouraged." Then their names were listed. The following are a few examples: Henry F. Schaefer, Nobel Nominee, Director of Center for Computational Quantum Chemistry, the University of Georgia; Fred Sigworth, Professor of Cellular & Molecular Physiology, Yale Graduate School; Stephen C. Meyer, Ph.D. Philosophy of Science, Cambridge University; and Jed Mascosko, Postdoc. Researcher Molecular Biology, University of California at Berkeley. The rest of the individuals named were equally impressive.

What do some scientists who are themselves "believers" in evolution say? Professor Louis T. More, one of the most vocal evolutionists, stated: "The more one studies paleontology (the fossil record), the more certain one becomes that evolution is based on faith alone." Or take Professor D. M. S. Watson, a famous evolutionist who made the remarkable observation that evolution itself is a theory universally accepted "not because it has been observed to occur or can be proved by logically coherent evidence to be true, but because the only alternative – special creation – is clearly incredible." British evolutionist Sir Arthur Keith says, "Evolution is unproved and unprovable. We believe it because the only alternative is special creation which is unthinkable."

The famous scientist Sir Ambrose Fleming completely rejects the theory of evolution as does Harvard scientist Louis Agassiz, probably one of the greatest scientists America has produced. Sir Cecil Wakeley,

K.B.E., C.B., LL.D., M.CH., Doctor of Science, F.R.C.S., past president of Royal College of Surgeons of Great Britain, said: "Scripture is quite definite that God created the world, and I for one believe that to be a fact, not fiction. There is no evidence, scientific or otherwise, to support the theory of evolution."

Professor Enoch, zoologist at the University of Madras said: "The facts of paleontology seem to support creation and the flood rather than evolution. For instance, all the major groups of invertebrates appear suddenly in the first fossiliferous strata, the Cambrian strata, of the earth with their distinct specializations indicating that they were all created almost at the same time." Professor Enoch was the leading scientist in France, author of an eighteen-volume encyclopedia on zoology, whose knowledge of zoology, according to the evolutionist Theodosius Dobzhansky, is absolutely encyclopedic. He came out with an attack only a few years ago that reputedly demolished evolution on every front.

The theory of evolution has at least two major problems: (1) The missing links are still missing! Michael Denton in *Evolution – a Theory in Crisis*, states: "The universal experience of paleontology . . . (is that) while the rocks have continually yielded new and exciting and even bizarre forms of life . . . what they have never yielded is any of Darwin's myriads of transitional forms." (2) In his *Origin of the Species*, Charles Darwin said: "If it could be demonstrated that any complex organism existed which could not possibly have been formed by numerous, successive, slight medications, my theory would absolutely break down." Biochemist Michael Behe, professor of biochemistry at Lehigh University, who was himself an atheist, was challenged by Michael Denton's book, *Evolution – a Theory in Crisis*. He decided to investigate the evidence for evolution for himself. He knew that if evolution was going to work, it had to succeed at the microscopic level of amino acids, proteins, and DNA. And the cell is Behe's world - an incredible, intricate Lilliputian world where a typical cell takes ten million atoms to build. Following his own personal investigation, Behe came to reject evolution and wrote a book titled *Darwin's Black Box*, a highly technical work, demonstrating reasons that evolution cannot be true.

The theory of evolution has powerful implications beyond science. If the universe has eternally existed, then a materialistic, atheistic, survival of the fittest philosophy is inevitable. And what has that produced? In Germany it produced Nazism and the holocaust. It produced Marx's theory of dialectic materialism, which spawned Communism and the mass murder of one hundred million people or more! It has supported abortion that has taken the lives of millions of innocent unborn children in the United States alone. And teen suicide and much of the murder and mayhem in our society is a result of teaching that there is no God because we are all cosmic accidents with no purpose. We humans are, according to evolution, only the highest form of animal.

Finally, Professor David Allbrook, Professor of Anatomy at the University of Western Australia, says that evolution is "a time-honored scientific tenet of faith." You may choose to "believe" in evolution, but remember, that it is a matter of faith, for evolution is only a theory and not a scientific fact.

Intelligent Design

A Reasonable Scientific Theory as an Alternative to Evolution

Lee Strobel, a former atheist, holds a Master of Studies in Law degree from Yale Law School and was an award-winning editor for the *Chicago Tribune.* He became a Christian after using his journalistic investigative skills and his legal skills regarding the laws of evidence to discover whether the Gospels were trustworthy or not. As a result of his research he came to faith in God and Christ. Strobel then wrote the book, *The Case for Christ.* Among a number of brilliant books he has written is also one titled *The Case for a Creator.* In that book he examines the fascinating evidences that compelled him to believe that there had to be an intelligent designer behind the universe. Strobel states: "My road to atheism was paved by science . . . but, ironically, so was my later journey to God."

"Critics of the theory of intelligent design often assert that it is simply a re-packaged version of creationism," states Jonathan Witt, Ph.D., Senior Fellow, Discovery Institute. In his article *The Origin of Intelligent Design: A brief history of the scientific theory of intelligent design*, he says that the idea of intelligent design reaches back to Socrates and Plato, and the term "intelligent design" as an alternative to blind evolution was employed as early as 1897 by Oxford scholar F.C.S. Schiller in an essay. Opponents of the theory of intelligent design often insist that it emerged as a conspiracy to circumvent the 1987 Supreme Court decision, Edwards vs. Aguillard; however, the theory of intelligent design predates that decision by many years. In *By Design,* journalist Larry Witham traces the immediate roots of the intelligent design movement in biology to the 1950s and 1960s and the movement itself to the 1970s. Biochemists were unraveling the secrets of DNA and discovering that it was part of an elaborate information processing system that included nanotechnology of unparalleled sophistication.

Later biochemist Michael Behe took the findings regarding DNA to their natural conclusion with his insights into what he called "irreducible complexity." Behe's signal work was based on the previous work of Michael Polanyi, who in 1967 argued that "machines are irreducible to physics and chemistry," and that "mechanistic structures of living beings appear to be likewise irreducible." Mathematician William Dembski would find Polanyi's work so influential that he would name Baylor University's Michael Polanyi Center after him.

Polanyi's work also influenced the seminal 1984 book *The Mystery of Life's Origin* by Charles Thaxton, Ph.D., Physical Chemistry, Iowa State University, Walter Bradley, Ph.D., Materials Science, University of Texas, Austin, and Roger Olsen, Ph.D., Geochemistry, Colorado School of Mines. Those authors argued that matter and energy can accomplish only so much by themselves, and that some things can only "be accomplished through what Michael Polanyi has called 'a profoundly informative intervention.'"

Seven Evidences for Intelligent Design

The Evidence of the Fine Tuning of the Universe

The evidence for intelligent design pervades all of the scientific disciplines including astronomy. In 1973, a meeting of the world's most eminent astronomers and physicists in Poland to commemorate the 500th birthday of the father of modern astronomy, Nicolaus Copernicus, took place. Of the dozens of lectures that would be presented during the festivities, only one would be remembered decades later. Its author, Brandon Carter, was a well-established astrophysicist and cosmologist from Cambridge University. His paper was *Large Number Coincidences and the Anthropic Principle in Cosmology.*

In essence the anthropic principle came down to the observation that all the myriad laws of physics were fine-tuned from the very beginning of the universe so that it appeared to be designed for the emergence of human life. It turns out that many mysterious values and relationships in physics could be explained by one overriding fact: Such values had been necessary for the creation of life. The physicist Robert Dicke was the first to draw attention to this relationship. Scientist John Wheeler, one of the most prestigious practitioners of cosmology, became interested in the idea in the 1960s. Then at Wheeler's urging, Brandon Carter presented the observation in full-blown form at the Copernican festivities. Furthermore, no matter what alternative scenario you tried to cook up, the most minuscule changes in the fundamental constants completely eliminate the possibility of life. Francis Bacon (1561-1626) observed: "A little science estranges a man from God; a little more brings him back."

In the *National Catholic Bioethics Quarterly*, Autumn 2003, William Harris and John Calvert authored an article titled *Intelligent Design – The Scientific Alternative to Evolution.* They state: "The central claim of ID (intelligent design) theory is that design is empirically detectable."

Many astrophysicists and cosmologists have recognized for years that the universe appears to be "fine-tuned." This refers to the existence of very precise and intricately balanced mathematical constants underlying physical laws. The force of gravity, the mass of the electron, the charge of the proton, etc. are specific, real values. Were they even slightly different from what they are, not only would life not exist, nothing of any significance would exist! The Living Seas Exhibit at Walt Disney World's EPCOT describes Earth as "a small sphere of just the right size that lies just the right distance from its mother star." If Earth were slightly closer to the sun, all its water would boil away and life would be impossible. If

Earth were slightly farther away from the sun, all its water would freeze and the terrestrial landscape would be nothing but barren deserts.

"Would anything in our universe change if the gravitational constant was a little stronger or a little weaker? That calculation was done in the 1970s by John Barrow and Frank Tipler, and the answer was astounding. If we take any of the fifteen physical constants and tweak them a tiny little bit, the whole thing doesn't work anymore" (*A Place for Truth;* pgs. 80-81).

In *A Place for Truth,* it says: "Back in the early 1980s, physicists were writing books promoting atheism, saying, 'God doesn't exist because physics explains everything.' One of the more famous was Paul Davies's book *God and the New Physics* published in 1983. Just one year after he wrote it, he published another book, *Superforce,* in which he asserted that 'the laws of physics themselves are so exquisitely and elegantly crafted that that by itself demands a need for a divine creator.' Three years after *Superforce,* Davies published a book called *Cosmic Blueprint,* in which he described the latest design evidence observed in the universe in the solar system. He detailed various characteristics of the universe that must be exquisitely fine-tuned in order for any conceivable form of life to exist. And he concludes his book saying that the evidence for design has become so 'overwhelming' there must be Someone behind it all to explain why it's all here."

The Evidence of Appearance of Design in Living Systems

There are numerous scientific evidences supporting the theory of intelligent design. One of those is "apparent design." This simply means that there is an impressive appearance of design in living systems. The complex creativity is convincing that a designer or engineer created many similar yet various designs that are both aesthetically interesting and functionally efficient.

The Evidence of Irreducible Complexity

"Irreducible complexity" is additional evidence. Law and luck explanations of life's origins are rendered less likely in light of

241

observations relating to the nature of cellular complexity. Lee Strobel in *The Case for a Creator* points out one example, bacterial flagellum. A flagellum is on the order of a couple of microns. A micron is about 1/20,000th of an inch. Most of the length of the bacterial flagellum is the propeller. The motor itself would be maybe 1/100,000ths of an inch. Yet the propeller can spin at ten thousand revolutions per minute! Even the notoriously high-revving Honda S2000 has a redline of only nine thousand revolutions per minute! In spite of all of our technology, we cannot even begin to create something like this. People who see a drawing of it say that it looks like something from NASA.

One simple fact regarding the D.N.A. of human beings supports the concept of irreducible complexity in an astonishing way. Scientists now know that three billion pairs of chemicals make up the DNA of human beings, according to CNN Headline News, Wednesday, November 24, 1999. Talk about complexity of information!

Consider a few simple illustrations of intelligent design. Say, human cells – what do we learn from them? The human brain is made up of thirty billion cells, and the body is made up of a trillion cells; yet at any given moment, in the life of any one cell, thousands of events are taking place! Just one molecule of hemoglobin, the blood-clotting agent is amazing in design. One molecule is made up of 3,032 atoms of carbon, 4,812 atoms of hydrogen, 780 atoms of nitrogen, 4 atoms of iron, 880 atoms of oxygen, and 12 atoms of sulfur – a total of 9,520 atoms, each of which has to be hooked up to the other atoms in a precise and proper way. How would you like to figure out a precise formula and arrangement like that?

The Evidence of Biological Information

A fourth scientific evidence for intelligent design is "biological information." Living systems are characterized by the presence of vast amounts of information, (e.g. DNA). There is no known law of physics or chemistry or process that can produce information that has a semantic characteristic; complexity, yes, but not information.

Francis S. Collins, the esteemed Director of the Human Genome

Project, states that the human genome adds up to 3.1 billion letters. He says that if we decided we were going to read the human genome tonight, we would probably regret it after we got started because we would be reading seven days a week, twenty-four hours a day, for thirty-one years. The inimitable amount and complexity of genetic information of a single human cell is awe-inspiring!

The Evidence of Similarities in Biological Systems

One piece of scientific evidence that supports intelligent design is "similarities in biological and human-made systems." While evolutionists use arguments from similarities to support the theory of evolution, similarity can just as easily point to a common designer. One example is the Morse Code's conceptual similarity to the genetic code. In fact, the genetic code was discovered by using man-made coding systems. While evolution would explain these similarities as evolved by need for function, in conflict in some cases is that some organs of animals are a match genetically while having absolutely no similarity of function. How does a person who believes in an intelligent creator view these similarities? We see the same infinitely intelligent mind using patterns and models to make a vast array of animals and plants, making unique and interesting changes and modifications as He creates them.

The Evidence of Complex Design and Ineffable Beauty

Consider the designs below. Do you know what they are? Do you know who designed them?

The exquisite designs above are only a few examples of snowflakes similar to those photographed by Alwyn Bentley of Vermont. He was the first person to successfully photograph snow crystals, which are commonly known as snowflakes. Bentley photographed his first snowflake on January 15, 1885. He would capture more than 5,000 images of crystals in his lifetime describing them as "tiny miracles of beauty" and as "ice flowers." Google "Alwyn Bentley snowflakes" and see dozens of his amazing photographs. Bentley photographed several thousand of them, and no two were alike. Amazingly, they all have six points or sides.

In *Ravished by Beauty,* it is observed that the famous and classic theologian John Calvin began his *Institutes* with the importance of God as the creator. In *Ravished by Beauty* we read: "In the first book of his *Institutes*, Calvin joined the beauty of a stunning cosmos with the mystery of God's inner life as Holy Trinity. As he understood it, the transcendent Creator of all things is at heart a sharing of persons bound together in inexplicable delight, reaching out in love to a world meant for relationship. To what end does 'God by the power of his Word and Spirit create heaven and earth out of nothing?' asks Calvin. Why is there such 'unlimited abundance, variety, and beauty of all things?' So that we might 'take pious delight in the works of God open and manifest in this most beautiful theater,' he answers. The Trinity's joy is made complete in a creation that sings in response" (*Ravished by Beauty*; p. 62).

In *Archives of Origins,* the brilliant scientist Albert Einstein states:

> My religion consists of a humble admiration of the illimitable superior spirit who reveals himself in the slightest details we are able to perceive with our frail and feeble minds. Everyone who is seriously involved in the pursuit of science becomes convinced that a spirit is manifest in the laws of the universe – a spirit vastly superior to that of man. The scientist is possessed by the sense of universal causation . . . his religious feeling takes the form of a rapturous amazement at the harmony of natural law, which reveals an intelligence of such superiority that, compared with it, all the systematic thinking and acting of human beings is an utterly insignificant reflection.

The Evidence of Human Personality,
Reason, Morality, and Spirituality

A world of material matter, of evolution and organization by chance, has some difficult questions to answer. Can chemical causes explain the origin of human personality? Man is a sentient being possessed of self-consciousness, rich personality, abstract reasoning, and innate moral and spiritual consciousness. Is the chance development of matter able to explain these phenomena? It certainly would not seem so. As Leander Keyser expresses it in *The Philosophy of Christianity*:

> Could the personal have evolved from the non-personal
> by means of resident forces? Remember our axiom:
> Every effect must have an adequate cause.

J. P. Moreland, an eminent apologist, has written two impressive volumes regarding man's soul and consciousness, *The Evidence of the Soul and Consciousness of Man,* and *The Soul: How We Know It's Real and Why It Matters.*

The magazine *Y-Origins* Volume 1, p. 85, makes this profound statement: "What process in natural selection could have led to human consciousness? Oxford zoologist Richard Dawkins admits that nothing in naturalistic evolution accounts for it. 'Why this should have happened is to me, the most profound mystery facing modern biology'" (Richard Dawkins; *The Selfish Gene*; Oxford University Press; 1989; p.59). While some naturalists like Dawkins remain atheists, others are reconsidering their positions in light of new discoveries.

An Associated Press article dated December 9, 2004, relates how one of the world's leading atheists was so struck by the evidence for design that he renounced the atheism he had taught for over half a century. "At age eighty one, after decades of insisting belief is a mistake, Oxford Professor Anthony Flew has concluded that some sort of intelligence or first cause must have created the universe. 'A super-intelligence is the only good explanation for the origin of life and the complexity of nature, Flew said in a telephone interview from England.'"

There are several highly impressive videos by Illustra Media that remarkably demonstrate intelligent design that I highly recommend: *Living Waters – Intelligent Design in the Oceans of the Earth*, *Metamorphosis – The Beauty and Design of Butterflies*, and *Flight*. Beautifully and professionally produced, these videos present astounding information in support of intelligent design. They can be ordered from some on-line retail outlets.

Those who do not believe in an infinitely intelligent designer must answer some compelling questions. From where does the complex design and the ineffable beauty of the earth and the universe originate? Don't such beauty, majesty and design require the imagination and intelligence of an artist of great creative genius? And where did the complexity of human personality come from? And how did human beings get a rich variety of temperament, skills, mental acumen, personality traits, individual tastes, and passions and drives? Furthermore, where did man's abstract thinking ability, his creativity, his spirituality and moral consciousness originate?

The conclusion seems clear. The evidence that the universe and our Earth are designed for the purpose of sustaining life, including human life, is compelling and overwhelming. In relation to intelligent design's scientific evidences, some of us, and especially Christians, recognize in the universe around us an infinitely wise and powerful Creator.

Having learned all that we have learned, there is only one appropriate response. That response is to worship the amazing, awesome Creator, our God! Therefore, after one more brief point and the hymn that immediately follows it, we will consider what it means to worship in the next chapter.

St. Francis of Assisi expressed the joy and thrill of recognizing and praising the Almighty for His wonderful works in creation. Read the marvelous words of his great hymn *All Creatures of Our God and King*.

All Creatures of Our God and King

All creatures of our God and King, Lift
up your voice and with us sing
Alleluia! Alleluia!
Thou burning sun with golden beam, Thou
silver moon with softer gleam,
O praise Him, O praise Him! Alleluia! Alleluia! Alleluia!

Thou rushing wind that art so strong, Ye
clouds that sail in heav'n along,
O praise Him! Alleluia!
Thou rising morn, in praise rejoice, Ye lights of evening, find a voice,
O praise Him, O praise Him! Alleluia! Alleluia! Alleluia!

Let all things their Creator bless, And worship Him in humbleness,
O praise Him! Alleluia!
Praise, praise the Father, praise the Son, and
praise the Spirit, three in one,
O praise Him, O praise Him! Alleluia! Alleluia! Alleluia!

Chapter 7

The Development of Authentic Christianity

Three Essentials in Creating a Culture of Authentic Christianity

While the foregoing chapters cover virtually all that concerns authentic Christianity, there are three areas of ministry that are essential to creating an atmosphere of authentic Christianity. Those are authentic worship, authentic preaching, and authentic mission.

Authentic Worship

Have we ever paused to ask ourselves this strategic question: "What is the purpose of our church services?" Why are we really doing what we are doing when we meet together? Are we designing our services for the purpose of attracting large crowds? Are we planning our services for the purpose of making people feel good? Are we creating our services for the purpose of entertaining?

Another crucial question is "Why do we attend church services?" Do we attend to perform a weekly obligation so we will feel that we have fulfilled our responsibility to God? Do we attend because we feel it is expected of us by our family and friends? Why do we attend, really?

But an hour is coming, and now is, when the true worshipers will worship the Father in spirit and truth; for such people the Father seeks to be His worshipers. God is spirit, and those who worship Him must worship in spirit and truth. (John 4:23-24 NASB).

The overarching purpose of the church is to worship the God of all creation. The primary activity for all of eternity will be thrilling, ecstatic worship. While that does not necessarily mean that is all we will do in eternity, it will be primary to be sure. Shouldn't our goal and focus, therefore, be on worshiping God here and now? Shouldn't our goal for our church services be to focus on and to foster genuine worship? And since that should be our goal, then what is genuine worship?

The Definition and Description of Authentic Worship

Newsweek, May 7, 2001, had an article titled *"Faith Is More Than a Feeling."* The article stated: "Now scientists are telling us that one half of the brain, or a portion thereof, is wired for religious experiences . . . programmed . . . to find pleasure in escaping the confines of self."

St. Augustine said: "Thou hast made us for Thyself, O Lord, and our hearts are restless till they find rest in Thee." There is a vacuum inside each of us that can only be filled and satisfied with God. Man is an ethno-centric being. We are incurably religious because our Creator has made us that way. Even those around us who claim to be against all religious expression hold within themselves beliefs that are religious in their nature. The fact that people have found alternative ways to have spiritual experience is evidence of the vacuum within man that yearns for religious fulfillment.

But what, we may ask, is real worship. Is it just a feeling? Is it merely sentimentality? Whatever it is, the Psalmist expressed the pure pleasure of worship when he declared,

Better a day in Your courts than a thousand anywhere else. I would rather be at the door of the house of my God than to live in the tents of wicked people (Psalm 84:10).

Imagine that! One day worshiping God in His presence is better than a thousand days anywhere else doing anything else!

Perhaps the best way to define and describe worship can be found in the statement of William Temple, the late Archbishop of Canterbury (1942–1944). He said:

> Worship is the submission of all our nature to God.
> It is the quickening of conscience by His holiness;
> The nourishment of mind with His truth;
> The purifying of imagination by His beauty;
> The opening of the heart to His love;
> The surrender of will to His purpose –
> And all of this gathered up in adoration, the most selfless emotion of which our nature is capable and therefore the chief remedy for that self-centeredness which is our original sin and the source of all actual sin.

This is such a rich definition and description that we should pause to think about it. Let's look together at each of the statements to more fully grasp its meaning. In each of these we will consider an individual in the Bible who personified each particular principle.

The Submission of All Our Nature to God

Jacob at the Jabbok River is our example of complete submission to God (Genesis chapter 32). As Jacob wrestled with God, he became a broken man who was ultimately clinging to God and trusting God to bless him. Jacob came to the end of himself. He realized that God alone was sovereignly in control of all of the circumstances of his life. And then in a moment of crisis he realized that God was his only hope, the only one who could help him. So he finally surrendered himself completely to God. He quit scheming and plotting - attempting to do it all on his own, and in surrender of everything, he left it all in God's hands. All too often, that is the point many of us have to arrive at before we are able to submit fully. Jacob's nature was changed as he was no longer a conniver, cunningly directing his own life. He became a prince, full of grace and patience, fruits of his submission to God.

Submission requires brokenness. Our will must be broken. We can't submit to God unless we fully turn loose of ourselves and our own will. We must come before God with a broken and contrite heart (Psalm 34:18 and 51:17). God delights in any person who is broken and submissive to Him. And this is where real, authentic worship starts.

The primary word for worship in the Old Testament means, "to be brought low in humility; to be abased; to have one's arrogance knocked out of him." One of the main words for worship in the New Testament is proskuneo (προσκυνεω). It means "to prostrate oneself; to give reverence to; to bow before; thereby showing our adoration and submission."

When was the last time you knelt before God in earnest prayer? Today, there is a reluctance to assume an attitude of complete submission before almighty God. Many people miss the experience of the ecstasy of worship because they are unwilling to surrender themselves in adoration and love to God.

The Quickening of Conscience by His Holiness

There is no more poignant moment in the Old Testament than when Isaiah was in the Temple grieving and worshipping after the legendary king Uzziah had died. The LORD appeared to him and the train of the Almighty's robe filled the entire Temple. God's glory and majesty overwhelmed Isaiah as he heard angelic beings, Seraphim, crying out:

> Holy, holy, holy is the LORD God of Hosts! The whole
> earth is full of His glory (Isaiah 6:3 NASB).

Isaiah's conscience was quickened, brought to life, by the holy presence of God, and he cried out:

> Woe is me, for I am ruined, because I am a man of unclean lips and live among a people of unclean lips; for my eyes have seen the King, the LORD of hosts (Isaiah 6:5 NASB).

True worship brings us into the presence of a holy God. We come face to face with Him and realize how infinitely pure and holy He is and how impure, polluted, sinful, and imperfect we are. Peter experienced this when he saw the miracle of the overwhelming catch of fish. He came to shore, knelt before Jesus and said, "Depart from me, O Lord, for I am a sinful man." The poor sinner in the Temple when seeing the sacrifice on the altar beat on his chest and cried out, "God! Be merciful (Greek: propitious) to me, *the* sinner" (emphasis added based on the Greek New Testament).

To worship is to be gripped by God's holiness in such a way as to be humiliated and humbled by our own sinfulness and unworthiness. It is to feel ourselves at the mercy of God and unworthy of the grace of God.

The Nourishment of the Mind with His Truth

All we need to do to discover a perfect example of this truth is to watch the apostle Paul. He had a fertile mind to receive God's revelation. He had been educated in Old Testament law by none other than Gamaliel, the most prestigious professor of the law of Moses in his day.

It was Paul who enlarged on the principles and concepts of the gospel in the book of Romans including the doctrines of justification, sanctification and glorification. He was the one who was used to reveal the monumental truths about the Church in Ephesians, and the treasures resident in the person of Christ in Colossians. Paul was the apostle God used to expound the rich implications of the kenosis or self-emptying of Christ in Philippians. And the Lord used Paul to expand on the doctrine of Christ's coming in 1st and 2nd Thessalonians.

Paul's mind was disciplined and imaginative, and the Holy Spirit used this to engage Paul not only in writing much of the New Testament, but also to draw him into worship. His exclamations of praise burst forth in many of his epistles. One example is Romans 11:33–36. Verse 33 says: "Oh, the depth of the riches both of the wisdom and knowledge of God! How unsearchable His judgments and untraceable His ways!" And then in his opening of the letter to the Ephesians: "Blessed be the God and Father of our Lord Jesus Christ, who has blessed us with every spiritual blessing in the heavens in Christ" (Ephesians 1:3). After explaining the wonderful truth about the Church, Paul exclaims: "For this reason I bow my knees to the Father of our Lord Jesus Christ, from whom the whole family in heaven and earth is named" (Ephesians 3:14–15 NKJV).

The Purifying of the Imagination by His Beauty

If there was one person who stands out as appreciating and adoring the beauty of the LORD it is David. This truth is celebrated throughout the Psalms. In Psalm 27:4, for example, he opens his heart:

> I have asked one thing of the LORD; it is what I desire:
> to dwell in the house of the LORD all the days of my
> life, gazing on the beauty of the LORD and seeking
> Him in His Temple.

That God loves beauty is clear from instructions concerning formal worship given to us in the Old Testament. Priestly garments are to be beautiful (Exodus 28:2, 40). The Temple is to be garnished for beauty (2 Chronicles 3:6). Temple singers are instructed to praise God's beauty of holiness (2 Chronicles 20:21).

The angelic seraphim cried in the Temple, "Holy, holy, holy is the LORD God of hosts: the whole earth is full of His glory" (KJV). All of creation displays and announces the glory and beauty of God. Flowers and trees; plains and prairies; forests and hills; mountains and valleys; lakes and seas; the sun, moon, and stars — all proclaim His glory, majesty, and beauty! The very finest of human artistry, whether it is music, poetry, sculpture, artistic painting, architecture or decorating, is a reflection of the creativity of man as made in the image of God, and of God's delight in beauty.

Beauty is an integral part of God's being and of His creation. Believers are admonished to think and meditate on things of beauty because they are revelations of God's beauty (Philippians 4:8). Since beauty is an expression of God's being, we are to enjoy and celebrate that beauty continually. This is the heart of true worship.

The Opening of the Heart to His Love

One particular individual stands above all others in appreciating and opening his heart to God's love. That person was the apostle John. At the Last Supper, he leaned on Jesus with unabashed love and affection. This and other instances clearly demonstrate how open he was to God's love. God's love enthralled him, and he wrote extensively about it. It is for this reason that he is often called "the Apostle of love."

Unlike Peter who always had something to say about everything, we never hear John speaking in any of the Gospels. John's mind must have been continually engaged in thinking about the meaning of all Jesus was saying and doing. And what seems to have captivated his mind and imagination the most was God's love. John's Gospel and his letters proclaim the love of God again and again. God's love was the compelling motif of his writings.

> For God so loved the world, that He have His only begotten Son, that whoever believes in Him shall not perish, but have eternal life (John 3:16 NASB).

The heart of true worship is a love relationship with God. Worship expresses itself in extolling God's love for us and in exclaiming our love for Him. There cannot be true worship apart from this exchange of love. The first of the Ten Commandments says that we are to have no other gods before Him (in His presence). He is jealous of our love. God is to have first place in our hearts and lives, and there is not to be any room given to any other god in our lives. Jesus declared that the first and greatest commandment is to "love the Lord your God with all your heart, with all your soul, and with all your mind."

Where did Jesus get this from? Jesus is quoting Deuteronomy 6:5. However, the book of Deuteronomy, the book most quoted by Jesus, is filled with instructions for us to love God. (See Deuteronomy 10:12; 11:1, 13, 22; 13:3; and 30:6, 16, 20.) It is interesting that every time God chose to discipline Israel as His people in the Old Testament, it was because they had lost their love for Him and loved other gods. God wants our love above all else.

The Surrender of Our Will for His Purpose

The life of Moses is an amazing illustration of a life continually surrendered to do God's will and to be on mission for Him. Moses's first experience of worship at this deep level was at the burning bush (Exodus 3). His life was consumed in doing the will of God and fulfilling his life's mission God had for him.

Moses gave up the throne of the world empire of his day, Egypt. He forsook the riches, luxuries, pleasures, power and prestige that could have been his for the taking. In exchange he accepted struggle, disrepute, poverty, hardships, and monumental challenges in order to fulfill God's destiny for his life.

It is no different for you and me. We must choose between the acceptance and praise of the world or following Christ and the shame and reproach that comes with that commitment. We must choose our own destiny or surrender to the will of God for our lives. Worship is genuine surrender in that moment of time.

The Adoration of God

We should ask ourselves whether our personal worship of God is genuine and authentic. Am I keenly aware of God's holiness and sensitive in my conscience to my sinfulness and unworthiness? Is my mind being continually nourished with God's truth? Does the beauty of God captivate my mind so that impure, carnal visuals and music become unappealing and repulsive? Is my heart continually exercised by God's love for me and my love for Him? Is my heart filled with a desire to use my life to fulfill God's purposes and to glorify Him? And do I enjoy just contemplating and adoring God for who He is and for all that He is?

We should also evaluate our corporate worship services to make sure that they are encouraging and fostering true worship. Are our worship services God-focused — focused on the Father, Son, and Holy Spirit; and redemption-focused? Is this the emphasis in our music? Is it the emphasis of our preaching? Is it the emphasis of most everything we do in our services?

The Elements of Authentic Worship

In Volume I of *History of the Christian Church,* Phillip Schaff lists six elements of worship practiced by the apostolic church:

1. The preaching of the gospel
2. The reading of portions of the Old Testament with practical exposition and application (They did not yet have the New Testament)
3. Prayer
4. The Song
5. Confession of faith
6. The administration of the sacraments (baptism & the Eucharist or Lord's Supper)

Schaff states that our confession of faith permeates all the other aspects of worship. The teaching of the Word was first of all teaching from the Old Testament, the only Scripture they had at the time. Obviously however, "the apostles' doctrine," or teachings that later became the New Testament, were also included in the teaching and received special attention and emphasis (Acts 2:42). The following are all elements of Christians confessing their faith: the teaching and affirmation of the teachings of the New Testament regarding Jesus Christ (Romans 10:9-13), baptism, the Lord's Supper, singing, and prayer.

The four elements of authentic worship should therefore be:

1. The Proclamation and Teaching of the Word — especially the New Testament
2. Prayer
3. Singing
4. Observance of the Ordinances of Baptism and the Lord's Supper (or Eucharist)

Preaching as an Important Element of Worship

Dr. Donald Whitney observes, "Reverently and responsively listening to God's Word preached is one of the highest forms of honoring and worshiping God." J. I. Packer, author and theologian, states: "Congregations never honor God more than by reverently listening to His Word with a full purpose of praising and obeying Him once they see what He has done and what He is doing, and what they are called to do." Martin Luther wrote: "The highest worship of God is the preaching of the Word." Preaching will be addressed more fully in this chapter as the second essential of developing a culture of authentic Christianity.

Singing as an Important Element of Worship

> Let the message about the Messiah dwell richly among you, teaching and admonishing one another in all wisdom, and singing psalms, hymns, and spiritual songs, with gratitude in your hearts to God (Colossians 3:16).

Singing and music must be important to God. After all, the largest book of the entire Bible is a hymnal or songbook! It's the book of Psalms. And this hymnal we call Psalms is located at the very center and heart of the Bible.

In 1 Chronicles 15 David brought the Ark of the Covenant, representing the presence of God, to Jerusalem. David instructed the leaders of the Levites to prepare a choir and an orchestra for the event.

Instruments included harps, lyres, trumpets, ram's horns, and cymbals. There was singing and music in celebration of the Lord. In 1 Chronicles 25 a lengthy list of names is given of those Levites who were to serve as singers and instrumentalists. Apparently there was an oratorio-sized choir of several hundred singers and a very large orchestra, requiring all the planning and preparations they would today.

During the dedication of the Temple in 2 Chronicles 5 it states that the musicians were dressed in fine linen and of them one hundred and twenty priests were blowing trumpets (v. 12), and then in verse 13 it says:

> The trumpeters and singers joined together to praise and thank the LORD with one voice. They raised their voices, accompanied by trumpets, cymbals, and musical instruments, in praise to the LORD.

In addition to the one hundred and twenty trumpeters, there were also many other instrumentalists, and still more singers. Music was a big deal in celebrating the arrival of an artifact that represented the presence of God. Should it be any less important to make the fullest and best use of music to celebrate God today?

Jesus and His disciples sang hymns during the Passover meal, the Last Supper, as was the custom of all the Jews. Those hymns found in Psalm 113 through Psalm 118 were praises to God and are called the Hallel.

Several New Testament passages are believed by biblical scholars to have been hymns sung by the early church. These include: Ephesians 5:14; Philippians 2:5–11, 1 Timothy 1:15 and 3:16; 2 Timothy 2:11–13; Hebrews 2:9; and 1 Peter 3:10–12. After instructing believers in Ephesians 5:18 to be filled with the Holy Spirit, Paul reveals to us in the very next verse that one of the results of this will be "speaking to one another in psalms, hymns, and spiritual songs, singing and making music to the Lord in your heart."

Last but not least, we are told about music in heaven praising Christ and giving glory to God. We find this in Revelation 5:8–10.

Why Are We to Sing?

The first reason we are to sing is that the redeemed have a song in their heart that compels expression in praise. We can't help it! It is the way God has wired us. Revelation 5:9 says, "And they sang a new song, saying, 'Worthy are You to take the book and to break its seals; for You were slain, and purchased for God with Your blood men from every tribe and tongue and people and nation.'" Later Revelation 14:3 declares: "And they sang a new song before the throne and before the four living creatures and the elders; and no one could learn the song except the one hundred and forty-four thousand who had been purchased from the earth."

Another reason for worshiping in singing is that the Lord has commanded it. He calls on us, and indeed on all of His creation, to offer Him praise in song. God created us as emotional beings, beings made in His image. It is this seat of our emotions that cries out for us to express our joy musically. It connects us with Him heart to heart.

Ten times in Scripture we are called on to give praise to the Lord in song. One such example is:

> Sing a new song to the LORD; sing to the LORD, all the earth. Sing to the LORD, praise His name; proclaim His salvation from day to day (Psalm 96:1–2).

Other examples that exclaim God's desire that we worship Him in singing are Psalm 100:1–2 and 1 Chronicles 16:23.

Singing also benefits us as it builds up our spirit and our faith. The truths we experience through the act of giving praise to the Lord bring refreshment and encouragement to our hearts. Singing also reinforces biblical truths in our hearts and minds (Colossians 3:16–17). This truth brings us to the answer of our next question.

What Are We to Sing?

Throughout the Bible the recurring theme about singing is that it should praise and extol God by declaring His attributes and His works. Examples of this are numerous:

> The Song of Moses & Israel (Exodus 15)
> The vast majority of the psalms in the book of Psalms
> The Magnificat of Mary (Luke 1:46–55)
> The singing of Paul & Silas in prison (Acts 16:25)
> The greatest solo to be sung in the future (Hebrews 2:12)

The other main theme of our singing should be Jesus Christ and His work of redemption. This, once again, is the "new song" of redemption, the celebration of Christ's work of redemption.

Even pagans cited by historians made mention of the Christians who sang about their Christ when they gathered on Sundays for their worship. John Calvin remarked: "Singing has great power and vigor to move and inflame men's hearts." Calvin also pictured the church as the "orchestra" in the theater of God's glory. "When we sing, we pray twice," Augustine said.

Many of the high-church style hymns are richly replete with biblical doctrine. They emphasize both extolling God and praising Jesus Christ and His redeeming work. There are also many plainer hymns that are filled with good biblical and doctrinal content. Differing from these gems are many traditional hymns found in our hymnals that are weak and anemic in their doctrinal content. Frankly, some of them sound old, stale, clunky, and musically outdated. In spite of this, many church members cling to them because they have sung them all of their lives.

When we think about much of the newer, contemporary Christian music, we also see a mixed situation. The contemporary chorus movement began with songs aimed at extolling God, and some do so very commendably. Others express love and devotion to the Lord in words of passionate testimony. There are some that do in fact give us rich doctrinal lyrics. Ideally, these should be utilized along with the best of the better traditional hymns for their doctrinal content to enable worship to be genuine "worship in truth" (John 4:24). The words of the better traditional hymns should sometimes be wedded to new, fresh music. Unfortunately, there are also a significant number of contemporary songs that are doctrinally shallow and too repetitive in their texts. Others lack a clear, beautiful, easy-to-follow melody.

The primary principle in terms of music selection is that our first consideration should be the lyrics' expression of deep worshipful truths regarding God, Christ, and redemption. With that in mind, there is certainly room for a variety of styles and genres to be utilized.

How Are We to Sing?

First, we are to sing *to the Lord* (Psalm 96:1; cf. Ephesians 5:19). Singing as an act of worship coming from the heart is to be directed to the Lord. We are singing and giving testimony before Him. Our hearts open to Him and our praise, adoration, love, gratitude and submission pour out to Him.

With this in mind, it is obvious that our singing should always be full of passion: How could it be otherwise if gratitude, joy, and praise are truly filling our heart and thrilling us? If they are, we should be spontaneously breaking out in praise and song! Our singing is a celebration of who God is and what He has done for us. Sadly, in the modern American church, this is often missing. Listen and you only hear people going through the motions. Think of Whoopi Goldberg in the movie "Sister Act" as she sings "I Will Follow Him." When we sing to our Lord, everyone around us should know just how wonderful it is to know Him and experience Him. It should be the spontaneous expression of the joy of our hearts overflowing in praise!

> Hallelujah! Praise God in His sanctuary. Praise Him in His mighty heavens. Praise Him for His powerful acts; praise Him for His abundant greatness. Praise Him with trumpet blast; praise Him with harp and lyre.

Praise Him with tambourine and dance; praise Him with flute and strings. Praise Him with resounding cymbals. Let everything that breathes praise the LORD. Hallelujah! (Psalm 150)

The Focus of Authentic Worship

Robert Letham in his book on *The Holy Trinity* declares: "God-centered worship (can worship be anything else?) by definition must give center stage to what is distinctive of Christianity, the high-water mark of God's self-revelation in the Bible" (p. 407). He emphasizes the need for worshiping God in His triune being – Father, Son, and Holy Spirit. With regard to music, he then says: "Examine any hymnbook or chorus book you can find, and search for compositions that are clearly Trinitarian. You won't find many!" (p. 407) (For a list of songs that speak of the Trinity, see Appendix B and search also for contemporary songs that include all members of the Trinity.)

Worship services should be planned to exalt God for who He is, to magnify His Son Jesus Christ, to open hearts so they can hear the Holy Spirit, and to proclaim the good news of the saving power of the cross - the redemptive sacrifice of Christ. In exalting God for who He is, there should be emphasis not only on His divine attributes, but also on His triune being. The Father is to be worshiped. The Son is to be worshiped. And the Holy Spirit is to be worshiped. And God as the triune God is to be worshiped!

There is one more practice that should be considered in regard to worship services. I know many may disagree with what is about to be said, but please hear it out and prayerfully consider it. In perhaps a sincere effort to gain rapport with people, worship leaders may decide to dress down. Ragged jeans and the sloppy look may make them look relevant to the spectators in the crowd, but are they the spectator we should be pleasing? Isn't the one and only real spectator of our worship the Lord? Isn't He the most important one observing our worship? Shouldn't the way we dress say that we are coming into the presence of One who is worthy of our respect?

Worship is the ultimate issue, and one that faces each one of us in our individual lives. What is your worship like? Is loving God and adoring Him at the very center of your life and at the core of your being? Do you relish times of personal and private worship, of worship expressed in your daily work and service because you perform that out of love for God and Christ? Do you yearn for every opportunity to be gathered with God's people to worship Him corporately?

Authentic Preaching

Preaching the Gospel and the Word of God

Can you imagine what this world would be like without preaching? What if Jesus had never preached? What if Peter had never preached those great sermons recorded in the book of Acts? What if the apostle Paul had never preached? And what if heroic preachers like Martin Luther, George Whitefield, John Wesley, Charles Haddon Spurgeon, D. L. Moody, Charles Finney, Billy Sunday, Bob Jones, George W. Truett, R. G. Lee, Billy Graham. D. James Kennedy, and many other great and notable preachers had never preached the gospel resulting in millions upon millions trusting Christ as their savior? Multiply that millions times more as faithful, unknown pastors have preached in pulpits across the world and throughout the centuries and have been the instrument of millions coming to Christ. Most of us can testify that preaching is what brought the crucified Savior and risen Lord to our attention so that we might understand the gospel and believe. And what resulted? Our lives were transformed and we have an eternal hope!

The world would be a place of even greater darkness, destitution, and depravity than it is if it were not for the life-transforming power of preaching! The gospel is still "the power of God for salvation," and the principle still rings true, "And how will they hear without a preacher" (Romans 10:14)?

There are dozens of references to the preaching of Jesus and His apostles found in the four Gospels. And from Acts through the epistles of the New Testament preaching is mentioned more than seventy times. The Scriptures speak of men being sent to preach (Romans 10:15 and 1 Corinthians 1:17), being appointed as a preacher (1 Timothy 2:7), and the power of salvation being unleashed by preaching (1 Corinthians 1:18, 21). And a solemn and fearful warning is given to those who are called to preach but refuse or fail to do so (1 Corinthians 9:16).

We all need to be aware of the biblical concept of preaching since we are either on the proclaiming end or the receiving end of God's message proclaimed. An understanding of God's view and our responsibility in the matter of preaching will make our experience of preaching far more beneficial to us spiritually and practically. So, let's consider some important principles about preaching.

The Appointment of Preaching

> For since in the wisdom of God the world through its wisdom did not come to know God, God was well-pleased through the foolishness of the message preached to save those who believe (1 Corinthians 1:21).

Donald Whitney declares in his book, *Spiritual Disciplines of the Church,* the following about preaching: "God was pleased to ordain preaching. He has determined that He would reveal Himself to people through His Word by means of preaching. Preaching in the broad sense means the proclamation of God's truth by any and every legitimate means. But the word translated preaching in 1 Corinthians 1:21 means more than that! The Greek word, *kerruso,* is the word the New Testament uses to refer to what we normally think of as pulpit preaching." Preaching in this sense involves proclaiming God's revelation, the Scriptures, to a group of people by someone who speaks from a position of gravity and authority as a spokesman for God. The authority of God's Word results in grave responsibility for those who hear it and makes them responsible before God to obey it. When God speaks to us and we ignore or reject what He has said, we do so to our own temporal and eternal peril.

This word *kerruso* is the word used for a herald for a king announcing the message on behalf of the king. It is the king's message. His subjects who hear his message are well aware of its authority and of their responsibility to submit themselves to it.

While the detailed contents and substance of the following is my own writing, I want to acknowledge with gratitude Dr. Donald Whitney's permission to use main topics in the outline that are his ideas from his book, *Spiritual Disciplines Within the Church: Participating Fully in the Body of Christ.* Those include the following four biblical facts about preaching and the alliterated major topics such as "The Authority of Preaching," "The Accountability of Preaching," etc. I highly recommend Dr. Whitney's two books about the spiritual disciplines.

Consider the following four biblical facts about preaching:

1. Jesus Preached!
   Matthew comments: From that time Jesus began to preach and say, "Repent, for the kingdom of heaven is at hand"(Matthew 4:17). Then Luke remarks: "But He said to them, 'I must preach the kingdom of God to the other cities also, for I was sent for this purpose.' So He kept on preaching in the synagogues of Judea" (Luke 4:43–44).

2. Jesus Sent the Apostles Out to Preach
   Matthew tells us that Jesus declared: "And as you go, preach, saying, 'The kingdom of heaven is at hand'" (Matthew 10:7). Peter reported of Jesus: "And He ordered us to preach to the people, and solemnly to testify that this is the One who has been appointed by God as Judge of the living and the dead" (Acts 10:42).

3. Preaching Was Paul's Method
   Galatians 1:23 reports: "but only, they kept hearing, 'He who once persecuted us is now preaching the faith which he once tried to destroy.'" And when Paul

265

described God's call and purpose for his life: "For this I was appointed a preacher and an apostle (I am telling the truth, I am not lying) as a teacher of the Gentiles in faith and truth" (1 Timothy 2:7). He also stated: "For Christ did not send me to baptize, but to preach the gospel" (1 Corinthians 1:17).

In commenting on this matter of preaching, Don Whitney continues: "Preaching was and is the method explicitly appointed by God. God's ordained method, preaching, is always relevant because it is timeless, transcultural, and simple. It doesn't require equipment, money, organizations, or buildings."

4. Preaching Is God's Method of People Being Saved!
1 Corinthians 1:21 declares this truth: "God was well-pleased through the foolishness of the message preached to save those who believe."

The Authority of Preaching

The content of true biblical preaching is the message of God. Preaching is speaking forth the revelation of God — His Word, His message!

The Old Testament prophets were speaking forth the revelation of God. They were declaring His Word and His message. Their cry was, "Thus says the Lord!" In contemporary English they were saying, "This is what God declares to you!" There is a strong similarity of function and position between the Old Testament prophets and today's Bible preacher. This similarity is found in two statements by the apostle Paul.

In 2 Timothy 3:16, we read:

All Scripture is inspired by God and profitable for teaching, for reproof, for correction, for training in righteousness; so that *the man of God* may be adequate, equipped for every good work (emphasis added).

"The man of God" is a technical term used seventy-six times in the Old Testament for various individuals who were Old Testament prophets. The similarity between the prophet of the Old Testament and the preacher of today is that they both speak the revelation or message of God to the people. The Old Testament prophets received special revelation and then spoke it, and sometimes when directed by the Spirit, they also wrote it down as Scripture. Today's preacher declares the revelation of God or message of God by accurately preaching the Scriptures, God's Word, the Holy Bible.

Another New Testament reference that uses the term "man of God" is found in 1 Timothy 6:11 as Paul admonishes the young pastor, his protégé, Timothy:

But flee from these things, you *man of God*, and pursue righteousness, godliness, faith, love, perseverance and gentleness (emphasis added).

Returning to 2 Timothy 3:16-17 we observe that Paul was encouraging Timothy by explaining to him the inspiration and authority of the Holy Scriptures and their practical, powerful usefulness. He was urging Timothy to proclaim the Scriptures with confidence and boldness knowing that the Scriptures are profitable and will be effective in transforming people's lives. We know in this passage that Paul is talking to Timothy about preaching because he immediately gives a solemn charge to Timothy urging him to "preach the Word" (2 Timothy 4:2 NKJV).

The preacher is not to preach his opinions, psychology, or ideas from books. He is commanded by God to "preach the Word." The preacher is not to decide how to please his people according to what they want to hear, and then craft a sermon or sermon series using some proof-texts to support his ideas. He is one who is charged to preach the Word of God. Each preacher will be individually judged according to God's standard by the Lord Jesus Christ for whether he has been faithful to that calling and sacred responsibility. It is a matter of greatest gravity. The responsibility of the preacher is greater than any other human responsibility because it has to do with the eternal destiny of souls and eternal rewards and results in the lives of the people who hear the message.

Whether preaching is expositional, textual, or topical, preaching must be an explanation and application of the Word of God. It should be practical and applicable. It should be warm and devotional, speaking to people's hearts. It should be convicting and convincing. And it should always call for decision and commitment. With this in mind, it must be God's message to man. It should be what God is saying to every individual through His Word. It should compel reverence for God and submission to Him and His Word.

The authority of preaching is not the preacher's authority. It is the authority of the Word of God. It is God speaking as the preacher faithfully and accurately proclaims the Word of God. When the preacher proclaims it faithfully and accurately, God's Word spoken by the preacher is one of absolute authority. Just as the herald announces the king's message or edict, so the biblical preacher announces the message of the King!

One of the most remarkable accounts of the Old Testament portraying the preaching of God's Word is found in Nehemiah 8:1–6:

> All the people gathered together at the square in front of the Water Gate. They asked Ezra the scribe to bring the book of the law of Moses that the LORD had given Israel. On the first day of the seventh month, Ezra the priest brought the law before the assembly of men, women, and all who could listen with understanding. While he was facing the square in front of the Water Gate, he read out of it from daybreak until noon before the men, the women, and those who could understand. All the people listened attentively to the book of the law. Ezra the scribe stood on a high wooden platform

made for this purpose. . . . Ezra opened the book in full view of all the people, since he was elevated above everyone. As he opened it, all the people stood up. Ezra praised the LORD, the great God, and with their hands uplifted all the people said, "Amen, Amen!" Then they bowed down and worshiped the LORD with their faces to the ground.

Several things about this remarkable account are noteworthy. First of all, the people were hungry to hear the Word of God. They were eager to hear it. Then observe their reverence for the Word as they stood up to listen to it read. The attentiveness of the people was extraordinary as they drank it in from daybreak until noon. What did the preacher do? He gave praise to God because of His Word, His law! And having heard the Word of God, the people gave the LORD praise and worshiped Him with joy and rejoicing (See also Jeremiah 20:9).

This story is a poignant and picturesque portrayal of preaching from God's point of view. How richly blessed our churches and our world would be if all of the dynamics of this picture became reality in our worship services.

The Accountability of Preaching

The Accountability of the Preacher

The Bible makes clear the awesome accountability of the preacher. It declares that the preacher will stand before God in eternity to give a personal account of his preaching. What a grave responsibility! Listen to this solemn, weighty charge in 2 Timothy 4:1–2: "I solemnly charge you in the presence of God and of Christ Jesus, who is to judge the living and the dead, and by His appearing and His kingdom: preach the word; be ready in season and out of season; reprove, rebuke, exhort, with great patience and instruction."

The Accountability of the People

When people hear the word God has spoken, then accountability for what is done in response by those who have heard it follows. The most graphic description of this accountability is found in Hebrews 4:12–13: "For the word of God is living and effective and sharper than any two-edged sword, penetrating as far as to divide soul, spirit, joints, and marrow; it is a judge of the ideas and thoughts of the heart. No creature is hidden from Him, but all things are naked and exposed to the eyes of Him to whom we must give an account."

In view of this accountability, Hebrews 13:7, 17 admonishes: "Remember those who led you, who spoke the word of God to you; and considering the result of their conduct, imitate their faith. Obey your leaders and submit to them, for they keep watch over your souls as those who will give an account. Let them do this with joy and not with grief, for this would be unprofitable for you."

The sense of eternal judgment when adequately discerned is sobering and appalling. As Scripture states in view of judgment, "It is a fearful thing to fall into the hands of the living God." God will hold His people, each of us, accountable for whether we follow and obey His Word that has been preached to us.

The Applications of Preaching

The gospel must be at the center of our preaching. It is the heart and soul of Christian truth and should be the heart of the Christian message. John C. Ryland aptly stated: "No sermon is of any value, or likely to be useful, which has not the three R's in it; *ruin* by the fall, *redemption* by Christ and *regeneration* by the Holy Spirit."

Unfortunately gospel preaching as the heart and soul of preaching is not the norm in American churches today. That is why some Christian leaders are sounding the alarm about the absence of the gospel in preaching today.

In *The Gagging of God*, D. A. Carson writes: "We must herald, again and again, the rudiments of the historic gospel. The primary content is the historic gospel . . . While many evangelicals today think of the 'gospel' as the 'simple gospel' — something that can be articulated in three, four, five, or six memorable points to be shared during personal evangelism — a study of the 'gospel' word-group in the New Testament shows that what is at stake is more commonly what might be called the 'comprehensive gospel' . . . All of our preaching and teaching must revolve around the great, central truths of the gospel."

Dr. Lewis Sperry Chafer, co-founder of Dallas Theological Seminary and author of an eight-volume *Systematic Theology*, stated that seventy-five percent of all preaching should be gospel preaching. This is not, of course, that most preaching should be the ABC's of salvation or the simple gospel. The gospel itself is wonderfully comprehensive and has many ramifications and implications. Again, Dr. Don Whitney declares: "The centerpiece of the message preached by the church should be Jesus Christ and His Cross. That's not to say that all sermons should only be about Jesus and His crucifixion. But it does mean that the life and work of Christ is the main message that the church should preach."

Unfortunately, much preaching, even in many evangelical churches, tends to follow a philosophy of preaching what people want to hear in order to draw crowds. Harry Emerson Fosdick was one the leading originators of this kind of preaching. In his book, *A History of Fundamentalism in America*, Dr. George W. Dollar, no direct relation to this author, said of Fosdick: "While at Montclair he decided against expository preaching, for he believed congregations were not interested in the meaning of texts; his sermons became more and more like lectures on problem-solving techniques and attitudes. Their themes were items of personal and current interest, and he drew from the accumulated wisdom of the past, within the Bible and outside, for his answers. In this way he offered solutions to the common problems of disillusionment, defeat, and despair. He used modern psychology, which he valued as an ally." Unfortunately, the influence of Harry Emerson Fosdick's preaching philosophy and methods filtered down and were adopted by many pastors in succeeding generations including today's!

In sharp contrast to preaching to people's felt needs, there is God-centered preaching. Rather than focusing on humans and our needs, the focus of God-centered preaching is God, the multi-faceted glories of His being and the awesome wonders of His works. John Piper's book, *The Supremacy of God in Preaching*, explains and illustrates the exaltation of God in proper preaching. Making God supreme in our preaching can be imaginative and thrilling. Getting people to glimpse His glory feeds the souls of the saints and brings the unconverted into contact with His infinite holiness and astounding grace. The greatest need all humans have is God Himself! God alone is the fountain that quenches every human thirst. He alone can satisfy the hungry heart. Preaching that focuses people's attention on God is transformative as described in 2 Corinthians 3:18:

> We all, with unveiled faces, are looking as in a mirror
> at the glory of the Lord and are being transformed into
> the same image from glory to glory.

Also missing from nearly all contemporary preaching today is the doctrine of hell. This neglect is a radical contradistinction to the preaching of Jesus Christ who Himself spoke vividly of hell in almost all of His recorded sermons. Jesus talked more about hell than He did about heaven. Hell is a revelation of the infinite justice of God in response to the terrible sinfulness, rebellion, depravity, and stubborn unbelief of mankind. And because hell highlights God's infinite justice, it provides a bold relief for the wondrous love and mercy of God that saves men from that eternal punishment that comes from that holy and inflexible justice. Therefore, without hell, there can be no proper appreciation for the wondrous outpouring of God's grace in the incredible sacrifice of His Son. It is the understanding of this "Amazing Grace" that is bestowed through Christ to all who believe in Him as their Lord and Savior that causes those true believers to rejoice, dance and sing! It is being assured in the experience of our heart, that in spite of our sin and deserving of the justice of hell, God has lavished His love on us in His Son as He hung between heaven and earth bleeding and dying on the cross!

Let's be plain about this. It is the desire for popularity and success that influences most preachers today to shy away from preaching on hell. They are afraid that it will cost them their crowd. They will personally answer to almighty God in the day of the judgment of their works. They are watchmen on the wall who have failed to sound the alarm and to warn people of coming judgment. They have no real compassion for lost people. Why did Jesus preach so much about hell? It's because He did not want anyone to go there! He was not desirous that anyone would perish (2 Peter 3:9). Let us herald with boldness and brokenness the need for sinners to escape eternal separation from God in hell by repenting and believing the glorious gospel of God's love, mercy, and grace in Christ and His blood.

On Sunday, December 10, 2017, on his radio program the wonderful apologist Ravi Zacharias observed that without a recognition and belief in eternal destiny, heaven or hell, everything loses its depth of meaning. Only when there is belief in eternal destiny does life take on profound significance. Only then do we rightly comprehend God.

When choosing a local church to join, one of the primary criteria should be the preaching of the Word. The proclamation of God's Word is the foundation of the spiritual structure of a church and is the fountain of all spiritual blessing, of life and health. In actuality, the faithful, powerful, compassionate, and fearless preaching of God's Word should be our first and foremost consideration in deciding on a church home.

Paul in his last letter, Second Timothy, was passing the torch to a new and younger generation of preachers. He chose to express his dying passion to a faithful young pastor he had mentored. He bequeathed to Timothy the mantle of defending the truth of the gospel. As he relinquished his responsibility, he made it clear to Timothy that he was entrusting the gospel's defense and proclamation to him. Paul had finished his race, but the race was a relay race, so he passed the torch to Timothy to run the next leg of the race. And Timothy passed the torch on to the next generation, and now the torch has been passed to today's God-called preachers. Now it is our responsibility to defend and proclaim the gospel and to ensure that it is passed on to the next generation of preachers so that they, in turn, can pass it on to those after them.

Two strong admonitions and challenges are issued to Timothy in the last chapter of Paul's last letter. "Timothy, preach the Word!" he exclaims. He warns him that the day will come when many will not want the truth and will not tolerate it. Instead, they will gather to themselves teachers who will give them soothing messages. Many people in churches today have itching ears. As pastors speak soothing words it sounds comforting to their listeners' ears. It is like the soothing feeling of scratching your ears when they itch. We can see the truth of this declaration today. We live in a day when many people do not want to hear the truth. They want to hear preachers preach soothing messages – messages that make them feel good.

Paul's second admonition was: "Do the work of an evangelist!" Certainly, this declares the important place of the gospel in the preaching of the Word.

We must return to the faithful proclamation of God's Word if we are to rebuild an authentic Christian culture in our churches. It will not be popular, and it will not be easy. Faithful proclamation of God's Word will doubtless soon result in real persecution. Even now, some people will reject the truth and walk away from it and from the preacher just as they did when Christ preached the hard truth (John 6:60–67). But at the end of the day, faithful preaching of God's Word will produce genuine, eternal fruit and will bring us acquittal when we stand before the judgment seat of Christ to give an account of our stewardship of the preaching ministry entrusted to us.

You may want to read a marvelous poem below by the prince of preachers, Charles Haddon Spurgeon. It is a poem that has special meaning for preachers.

Immanuel

By Charles Haddon Spurgeon
Spurgeon has been called the Prince of Preachers

When once I mourned a load of sin,
When conscience felt a wound within,
When all my works were thrown away,
When on my knees I knelt to pray,
Then, blissful hour, remembered well,
I learnt Thy love, Immanuel!

When storms of sorrow toss my soul,
When waves of care around me roll,
When comforts sink, when joys shall flee,
When hopeless gulfs shall gape for me,
One word the tempest's rage shall quell,
That word, Thy name, Immanuel.

When for the truth I suffer shame,
When foes pour scandal on Thy name,
When cruel taunts and jeers abound,
When "bulls of Bashan" gird me round,
Secure within my tower I'll dwell,
That tower, Thy grace Immanuel.

When hell, enraged, lifts up her roar,
When Satan stops my path before,
When friends rejoice and wait my end,
When legion'd hosts their arrows send,
Fear not, my soul, but hurl at hell
Thy battle cry, Immanuel.

When down the hill of life I go,
When o'er my feet death's waters flow,
When in the deep'ning flood I sink,

When friends stand weeping on the brink,
I'll mingle with my last farewell
Thy lovely name, Immanuel.

When tears are banished from mine eyes,
When fairer worlds than these are nigh,
When heaven shall fill my ravished sight,
When I shall bathe in sweet delight,
One joy all joys shall far excel,
To see Thy face, Immanuel.

Authentic Mission

Making Disciples at Home and Around the World

The Great Commission is given with various emphases in five different passages of Scripture: Matthew 28:18-20; Mark 16:15; Luke 24:46-49; John 20:21-23; and Acts 1:8. In these passages there exists what I call *The Seven Laws of the Great Commission*. The Seven Laws are as follows:

1. We are authorized by the One with sovereign authority (Matthew 28:18).
2. We are commissioned by Christ himself (John 20:21).
3. We are given a challenging vision – to reach the entire world (Mark 16:15).
4. We have a great, powerful, life-changing message (Luke 24:46-47; Romans 1:16).
5. We have a demanding task – to make disciples (Matthew 28:19).
6. We have the promise of Christ's presence with us in our mission (Matthew 28:20).
7. We have the promise that the Holy Spirit will empower us in our witness (Acts 1:8).

The field is the world. And the fields are white, meaning they are ripe and ready for harvest. But the laborers are few! Churches must be challenged and mobilized to evangelize the lost and to make disciples on many levels. In Acts 1:8 the command of Jesus was for His disciples to be witnesses in Jerusalem, Judea, Samaria and to the remotest parts of the earth. Christ's command requires our churches to have a vision that is local, regional, national, and universal in scope. It requires us to strive to engage in doing the work of making disciples on all of those levels.

Making disciples begins with "baptizing them." Evangelism, bringing people to faith in Christ, and baptism, leading them to confess their faith in Christ as they also commit themselves to be His disciple, is the beginning phase of making disciples. So it begins with evangelism, the witness of the gospel as Jesus commanded in Acts 1:8, and is declared and initiated by baptism as a public witness and commitment.

What does it mean to be witnesses for Jesus Christ? This word and concept is applied specifically and formally to the twelve apostles in the book of Acts numerous times (Acts 1:8, 22; 2:32; 3:15; 5:32; 10:39, 41; 13:31; 22:15, 20; & 26:16). Obviously the apostles are no longer alive, and so it has become the responsibility of all Christians to bear witness of Christ and His saving power.

So, what is required to be a witness for Jesus Christ today? First, you must have a personal experience and conviction of the truth of Christ and His saving power. You cannot witness unless you have something to witness about – something you know with certainty by personal experience. In order to be an effective witness you must also know the Scriptures adequately. Peter and the other apostles used the Old Testament Scriptures about the Messiah, Jesus, in regard to His divine appointment, ministry, death and resurrection. We too must know the Scriptures well enough to be able to use them to show those we witness to the authority of God's Word in regard to Jesus Christ and His salvation.

In order to be a witness for Christ, and this may sound bit bizarre to us, you must open your mouth with something important to say. That is exactly what both Jesus and Peter did. It is found in the peculiar phrase "Philip opened his mouth (Acts 8:35) or "Opening his mouth, Peter said." This statement that sounds peculiar to us is a euphemism from that time or era meaning that someone was speaking something of great importance. Too often Christians have been heard saying, "I will let my life be a witness." Guess what? That is not possible. You have to open your mouth in order to testify. People will never learn about Christ unless you tell them about Him. Romans 10:17 states it perfectly:

So faith comes from what is heard, and what is heard comes through the message about Christ.

We must meet the lost on their turf, where they are. Most will never darken the door of a church to hear the message of the gospel. The Great Commission literally says, "As you are going, make disciples of all ethnic groups." It is wherever we go and wherever there are people who need to hear the message. It means telling our neighbors, friends, relatives, co-workers, and people we meet everywhere we go. It means starting Bible studies in apartments, jails, prisons, work-places, with our neighbors and anywhere and everywhere it is possible. We must get the gospel outside of the four walls of the church!

Last, but by no means least, we must rely entirely on the guidance and empowering of the Holy Spirit. He will guide us in what to say and He will empower our witness about Christ. Pray for His guidance and power.

The command of Christ is to "make disciples." In America the problem has been that we have done some significant although shallow evangelism, but failed to make disciples. Dallas Willard speaks to that by stating: "The 'Great Omission' has been that the Church has been making 'Christians' or converts rather than making disciples – and there is a difference!" Furthermore he observes, "The word *disciple* occurs 269 times in the New Testament. *Christian* is found only three times and was first introduced to refer precisely to disciples of Jesus" (Dallas Willard in *The Great Omission*).

As we look at the early church, the church made disciples in two ways. First, the church taught and developed disciples out of those who were already saved on the Day of Pentecost under Peter's preaching.

This was done as the authentic spiritual disciplines of the church were carried out with supreme devotion:

1. Teaching the New Testament doctrines and deportment;
2. Fellowship;
3. Corporate Prayer; and
4. Observance of the Lord's Supper.

The pulpit ministry is not the only venue that should provide teaching. We should also teach in venues such as Sunday School, small groups, children's clubs, etc. Refer back to the chapter on the authentic spiritual disciplines of the church. The chapter on *The Dynamic of Essential Christianity: Discipleship – The Lost Secret of Authentic Christianity* will also provide some specific ideas in regard to disciple-making. It is vitally important to realize that making and training disciples is not optional. It is a specific command from our Lord and Master, Jesus Christ.

A second part of the strategy of the apostolic church was to send out evangelists like Phillip and missionaries like Paul and Barnabas for the purpose of evangelizing, discipling individuals and establishing churches. Paul in particular illustrates a carefully planned strategy to spread the gospel although he also demonstrates flexibility in following the Spirit's leadership. Both a planned strategy and flexibility to follow the Spirit's leading are needed in our missionary efforts.

In order to fulfill the Great Commission, it is necessary to take the gospel to the ends of the earth reaching all ethnic groups on the face of the globe. Thus, foreign missions are a great and important part of the strategy for fulfilling our Lord's command. At the same time, we must realize that the largest unreached people group is always the next generation. For this outreach, many more faithful and dedicated national missionaries are needed. Foreign missionaries eventually go home. National missionaries go on preaching and teaching.

My son-in-law and daughter, Aaron and Lori Luse, have served as missionaries with New Tribes Mission, now Ethnos 360, in Papua New Guinea since 2001. They have had the privilege and joy of reaching a primitive tribe of precious people on a large tropical island, New Ireland. In his book of fascinating stories with devotional applications, *Tales from the Tribe*, Aaron gives the following statistics: "Today, out of the 6,900 languages of the world, only 636 have a complete Bible, and over 1,700 don't even have a single verse of Scripture written in their language.[1] While the English speakers of the world have approximately 900 different translations of the Bible, there are still millions of people who have none.[2]" ([1]Wycliffe Global Alliance, *Resources: Scripture Access Statistics*, 2017; August 25, 2017; [2]American Bible Society. *Record: Bible Q &A*. December 2, 2009) There is obviously an enormous amount of work to be done to reach the world with the gospel and to make disciples of all ethnic groups!

Our churches must cast a challenging vision for their members so that the spiritual lost condition and needs of countless millions of souls around the world grips our hearts. The love of God for the world must compel us to develop strategies for getting the gospel to people who have no knowledge of it. We must come to have God's love and passion for all people in our hearts. Christ said this was the second greatest commandment . . . "love your neighbor as yourself." If we have that love, we will certainly want them to have the opportunity to hear the message of life and to know Christ. We will want their lives to be blessed by the wonderful grace of God and for them to experience eternity worshipping and glorifying the Savior with us.

The hymn, *O Zion, Haste*, poignantly expresses the vision of making disciples world-wide:

O Zion, Haste
Mary Ann Thompson

O Zion, haste, thy mission high fulfilling:
To tell to all the world that God is Light;
That He who made all nations is not willing
One soul should perish, lost in shades of night.

Behold, how many thousands still are lying
Bound in their darksome prison-house of sin,
With none to tell them of the Savior's dying,
Or of the life He died for them to win.

Proclaim to every people, tongue and nation
That God in Whom they live and move is love;
Tell how He stooped to save His lost creation,
And died on earth that man might live above.

Give of thy sons to bear the message glorious;
Give of thy wealth to speed them on their way;
Pour out thy soul for them in prayer victorious –
And all thou spendest Jesus will repay!

Chorus
Publish glad tidings, tidings of peace:
Tidings of Jesus, redemption and release.

About the Author

Calvin Eugene Dollar, Jr. is a graduate of Bob Jones University and has completed some post-graduate studies. He has served in pastoral ministry for more than forty five years serving churches in Georgia, West Virginia, Massachusetts, Iowa, Kansas, and Oklahoma.

He has fellowshipped and worked closely with conservative, evangelical pastors of other denominations including Assembly of God, Baptist, Christian, Lutheran, Methodist, Nazarene, and Presbyterian, all strong believers in the gospel and in the essential doctrines of the Christian faith.

Calvin has served on local and state boards of three denominations and on a national board for one of them. He has been director and speaker for several daily radio ministries and co-founded a college ministry, serving as president of its board. In addition he was sponsoring pastor in the founding a mission church for Native Americans and was the lead pastor in founding a large and successful ministry to junior and senior high school students attending public schools.

As the requested representative of groups of pastors, Calvin has addressed state legislative committees in several states. He was also at the forefront of leadership for the Christian school movement in Massachusetts, taught in two Christian schools, and served on the board of trustees of a Bible college and seminary.

Calvin and his wife, Diana, were married in 1970 and have four children and many grandchildren.

Bibliography

A Christian Manifesto; Francis A. Schaeffer; Crossway Books

A Different Gospel- Updated Edition; D. R. McConnell; Hendrickson Publishers

A History of Fundamentalism in America; George W. Dollar; Bob Jones University Press

A Place for Truth – Highlights from the Veritas Forum; Edited by Dallas Willard; IVP (Inter Varsity Press) Books

A Novel Approach: The Significance of Story in Interpreting and Communicating Reality; Michael Matthews; Tellwell Talent Publishers

A Quest for Vitality in Religion; Findley B. Edge; Broadman Press; 1963

A Righteousness of God for Unrighteous Men; E. J. Forrester; George H. Doran Co.; Copyright 1926 by the Sunday School Board of the Southern Baptist Convention

Albert Barnes' New Testament Commentary; Albert Barnes; "Power Bible" CD

American Apostasy: The Triumph of Other Gospels; editor, Richard John Neuhaus; Article: "Different Gospels: The Social Sources of Apostasy;" Peter L. Berger; Eerdmans Publishing Co.

An Exposition on Prayer: Igniting the Fuel to Flame Our Communication with God; 4 Volumes; James Rosscup; AMG Publishers

And the Place Was Shaken: How To Lead a Powerful Prayermeeting; John Franklin; Broadman & Holman Publishers

Apostolic Preaching and Its Development; C. H. Dodd

Ashamed of the Gospel: When the Church Becomes Like the World; John MacArthur; Crossway Books / Good News Publishers

Authentic Christianity by Ray C. Stedman

Baker Encyclopedia of Apologetics; Norman Geisler; Baker Book House

Baptism in the New Testament; G. R. Beaseley-Murray; Eerdmans Publishing Co.

Biblical Intolerance; D. M. Lloyd-Jones; Banner of Truth

Can a Man Live Without God? Ravi Zacharias; Word Publishing; 1994

Can I Trust the Bible; Howard Vos; Moody Press; 1963

Choosing Your Faith; Mark Mittelberg; Willow Creek Resources

Christian Apologetics; Norman Geisler; Baker Book House

Christian Evidences: Fulfilled Bible Prophecy; Alexander Keith; Klock & Klock Christian Publishers, Inc.; 1984

Christian Theology; Millard J. Erickson; Baker Book House

Christianity and Liberalism; J. Gresham Machen; Eerdmans Publishing Co.

Christianity Through the Centuries; Earl E. Cairns; Zondervan Publishing Co.

Christianity and World Religions: The Challenge of Pluralism; Sir Norman Anderson; Inter-Varsity Press

Christianity in Crisis; Hank Hannegraff; Harvest House Publishers

Commentary to the Epistle to the Romans; Martin Luther; Zondervan Publishing House

Darwin's Black Box – The Biochemical Challenge to Evolution; Michael Behe; Simon & Schuster

Darwin on Trial; Phillip E. Johnson; Washington: Regnery Gateway

Darwinism Under the Microscope: How Recent Scientific Evidence Points to Divine Design; James P. Gills & Tom Woodward; Charisma House Publishers

De Trinitate; St. Augustine of Hippo

Developing Your Secret Closet of Prayer: Principles for Intimacy with God; Richard A. Burr; Christian Publications; Camp Hill, PA

Didache ("The Teaching" – Manual of the Church in the late Apostolic era)

Dismantling Evolution; Ralph O. Muncaster; Harvest House Publishers

Doctrine That Dances – Bringing Doctrinal Preaching and Teaching to Life; Robert Smith, Jr.; B & H Academic (B&H = Broadman & Holman)

Easter Enigma – Are the Resurrection Accounts in Conflict? John Wenham

Evangelical Dictionary of Theology; Walter A. Elwell, Editor; Baker Book House

Evangelicals Now: "Who Is a Christian?" Iain Murray; April 1989

Evolution: A Theory in Crisis; Michael Denton; Bethesda: Adler & Adler

Except Ye Repent; Harry A. Ironside; Baker Book House

Faith Alone; R. C. Sproul; Baker Book House

Fresh Faith; Jim Cymbala; Zondervan Publishing House

Fresh Wind, Fresh Fire; Jim Cymbala; Zondervan Publishing House

Fundamentals of the Faith; Edited by Carl F. H. Henry; Zondervan Publishing House

God – The Evidence – The Reconciliation of Faith and Reason in a Postsecular World; Patrick Glynn; Forum – an Imprint of Prima Publishing; 1977

God's Not Dead – Evidence for God in an Age of Uncertainty; Rice Broocks; W Publishing Group – Thomas Nelson Publishers

Gripped by the Greatness of God; James MacDonald; Moody Publishers

History of the Christian Church; 8 Volumes; Phillip Schaff; Eerdmans Publishing Co.

Holman Christian Standard Bible; Broadman & Holman Publishers; Nashville, TN

Human Destiny; Sir Robert Anderson; London: Pickering & Inglish; 1913

I Never Thought I'd See the Day! – Culture at the Crossroads; David Jeremiah; Faith Words – New York, Boston, Nashville; © 2011

I Will Build My Church; Alfred Kuen; Moody Press

Illustrations for Preaching & Teaching – from Leadership Journal; Craig Brian Larson, Editor; Baker Book House; ©1993

Jesus Christ Among Other Gods; Ravi Zacharias; Word Publishing Group

Kingdom Triangle; J. P. Morgan; Zondervan Publishing Co.

Know Why You Believe; Paul Little; Inter-Varsity Press; 1988

Let the Nations Be Glad – The Supremacy of God in Missions; John Piper; Baker Academic

Life Essentials; Tony Evans; Moody Press

Many Infallible Proofs; Henry M. Morris; Master Books; 1974

Medicine in the Bible and the Talmud; Fred Rosner; KTAV Publishing House, Inc.; 1995

Mere Christianity; C. S. Lewis; Simon & Schuster Publishers

More Than a Carpenter; Josh McDowell

Multiply – Disciples Making Disciples; Francis Chan; David C. Cook Publishing Co.

New American Standard Bible – Updated Edition; Foundation Publications of the Lockman Foundation

New King James Version, Thomas Nelson Publishers

New International Version, Zondervan Publishing Co.

None of These Diseases; S. I. McMillen; Fleming H. Revell; 1984

Not a Fan – Becoming a Completely Committed Follower of Jesus; Kyle Idleman; Zondervan Publishing Co.

Not All Roads Lead to Heaven – Sharing an Exclusive Jesus in an Inclusive World; Baker Book House

Notes on the Miracles of Our Lord; Richard Trench; Fleming H. Revell Co.

Philosophy of Education: Essays and Commentaries; Edited by Hobert W. Burns and Charles J. Brauner; The Ronald Press Co.; New York

Problems in Education and Philosophy; Charles J. Brauner and Hobert W. Burns; Prentice-Hall Inc. Publishers; Englewood Cliffs, NJ; ©1965

Reasons Skeptics Should Consider Christianity; Josh McDowell & Don Stewart; Campus Crusade for Christ – Here's Life Publishers; 1981

Reckless Faith: When the Church Loses Its Will To Discern; John MacArthur; Crossway Books (A division of Tyndale Publishers)

Repentance: The First Word of the Gospel; Richard Owen Roberts; Crossway Books

Resurrection; Hank Hanegraaff; Thomas Nelson Publishing Co.

Science Speaks; Peter W. Stoner; Moody Books; 1963

Scientific Creationism; Henry M. Morris; Master Books; 1985

Second Peter & Jude – MacArthur Commentary; John MacArthur; Moody Press

Spiritual Disciplines for the Christian Life; Donald S Whitney; NavPress

Spiritual Disciplines Within the Church: Participating Fully in the Body of Christ; Donald S. Whitney; Moody Publishers

Spiritual Leadership – Moving People on to God's Agenda; Henry & Richard Blackaby; Broadman & Holman Publishers

Systematic Theology; Augustus Strong; Judson Press

Systematic Theology – 8 Volumes; Lewis Sperry Chafer; Dallas Seminary Press

Systematic Theology – 4 Volumes; Norman Geisler; Bethany House

Systematic Theology – *An Introduction to Biblical Doctrine*; Wayne Grudem; Inter-Varsity Press / Zondervan Publishing House

Tales from the Tribe – *A Missions-Focused Devotional from the Jungle to Your Home;* Aaron Luse; Author Academy Elite

The Apostolic Preaching of the Cross; Leon Morris; Eerdmans Publishing Co.

The Battle for the Resurrection; Norman L. Geisler; Thomas Nelson Publishers

The Bible and Modern Science; Henry M. Morris; Moody Press; 1968

The Biblical Basis for Modern Science; Henry M. Morris; Baker Book House; 1984

The Blind Watchmaker; London: Longman, 1986

The Case for Biblical Christianity; E. J. Carnell; Eerdmans Publishing Co.

The Case for a Creator; Lee Strobel; Zondervan Publishing Co.

The Case for Christ; Lee Strobel; Zondervan Publishing Co.

The Case for Easter; Lee Strobel; Zondervan Publishing Co.

The Christian Faith in the Modern World; J. Gresham Machen; Wm. B. Eerdmans Publishing Co. Grand Rapids, MI; 1947

The Church in God's Program; Robert Saucy; Moody Press

The Coming Evangelical Crisis – Current Challenges to the Authority of Scripture and the Gospel; John H. Armstrong, General Editor; Moody Press

The Cost of Discipleship; Dietrich Bonhoeffer; Simon & Schuster

The Cross Is Not Enough: Living as Witnesses to the Resurrection; Ross Clifford & Philip Johnson; Baker Books

The Cross of Christ; John R. W. Stott; Intervarsity Press

The Cruelty of Heresy: An Affirmation of Christian Orthodoxy; C. FitzSimons Allison; London: SPCK

The Dawn of World Redemption; Erich Sauer; The Posternoster Press

The Defense of the Gospel in the New Testament; F. F. Bruce; Eerdmans

The Divine Conspiracy; Dallas Willard; HarperOne

The Epistle to the Romans; Charles Hodge; Banner of Truth Trust

The Epistle to the Romans; John Murray; The New International Commentary on the New Testament; Eerdmans Publishing Co.

The Evidence of the Soul and Consciousness of Man; J. P. Moreland;

The Existence and Attributes of God; Stephen Charnock; Baker Book House

The Forgotten Trinity – Recovering the Heart of Christian Belief; James R. White; Bethany House Publishers

The Fundamentals; 4 Volumes; Edited by R. A. Torrey, A. C. Dixon, and others; Baker Book House

The Gagging of God – Christianity Confronts Pluralism; D. A. Carson; Zondervan Publishing

The Historical Reliability of the Gospels; Craig Blomberg; Leicester: Inter-Varsity Press; 1987

The History of Creeds: Creeds of Christendom, with a History and Critical notes; Volume II. Harper & Brothers. 1877

The Holiness of God; R. C. Sproul; Tyndale House Publishers

The Holy Spirit; John Walvoord; Zondervan Publishing House

The Holy Trinity – In Scripture, History, Theology, and Worship; Robert Letham; P & R Publishing; Phillipsburg, NJ

The Inspiration and Authority of the Bible; B. B. Warfield; Presbyterian & Reformed Publishing Co.

The Jesus You Can't Ignore – What You Must Learn from the Bold Confrontations of Christ; John MacArthur; Thomas Nelson Publishers

The Knowledge of the Holy; A. W. Tozer; Harper Collins

The Language of God: A Scientist Presents Evidence for Belief; Francis S. Collins; Free Press

The Life and Epistles of St. Paul; W. J. Conybeare & J. S. Howson; Eerdmans Publishing Co.

The Life and Times of Jesus the Messiah; Alfred Edersheim

The Life of Jesus Christ; James Stalker; Fleming Revell Co.

The Mind of Paul; William Barclay;

The New Evidence That Demands a Verdict; Josh McDowell; Thomas Nelson Publishers

The New Testament Documents – Are They Reliable? F. F. Bruce; Inter Varsity Press

The Origin of Paul's Religion; J. Gresham Machen; Eerdmans Publishing Co.

The Passion of Jesus Christ; John Piper; Crossway

The Person and Work of Christ; B. B. Warfield; Presbyterian and Reformed Publishing Co.

The Philosophy of Christianity; Leander S. Keyser; Lutheran Literary Board; Burlington, IA; ©1928.

The Philosophy of Education – Essays and Commentaries; Editors: Hobert W. Burns and Charles J. Brauner; Ronald Press Co.; New York; ©1962.

The Privileged Planet; Guillermo Gonzalez & Jay Wesley Richards; Regnery Publishing

The Promise of Trinitarian Theology; Colin E. Gunton; T & T Clark Publishers

The Quest for Character; John MacArthur; J. Countryman, a division of Thomas Nelson Publishers

The Rebirth of America; The Arthur S. DeMoss Foundation; Copyright 1986

The Resurrection of Jesus – A Jewish Perspective; Pinchas Lapide; Augsburg Publishing House

The Scandal of the Evangelical Mind; Mark A. Noll; Wm B. Eerdmans Publishers

The Savior and the Scriptures – A Case for Scriptural Inerrancy; Robert P. Lightner; Baker Book House; 1966

The Signature of God; Grant R. Jeffrey; Frontier Research Publications; 1996

The Soul: How We Know It's Real and Why It Matters; J. P. Moreland; Moody Publishers

The Supremacy of God in Preaching; John Piper;

The Trinity; Bickersteth; Kregel Publications

The True Image: The Origin and Destiny of Man in Christ; Phillip Edgcumbe Hughes; Eerdmans Publishing Co.

The Truth Wars – Fighting for Certainty in an Age of Deception; John MacArthur; Thomas Nelson Publishers

The Worship Hymnal; Lifeway; Nashville, TN

Theological Dictionary of the New Testament (Abridged in One Volume) by Geoffrey W. Bromiley and edited by Gerhard Kittel and Gerhard Friedrich

Theological Dictionary of the New Testament; 4 Volumes; Edited by Colin Brown; Regency / Zondervan Publishing Co.

True Discipleship – The Art of Following Jesus; John Koessler; Moody Publishers

What Christians Believe – A Biblical & Historical Summary; Alan F. Johnson and Robert E. Webber; Zondervan Publishing House; Grand Rapids, MI

What If Jesus Had Never Been Born; D. James Kennedy & Jerry Newcombe; Thomas Nelson Publishers

What If the Bible Had Never Been Written; D. James Kennedy & Jerry Newcombe; Thomas Nelson Publishers

When the Crosses Are Gone: Restoring Security to a World Gone Mad; Dr. Michael Youssef

When Skeptics Ask; Geisler / Brooks; Victor Books

Vital Apologetic Issues; Edited by Roy Zuck; Kregel Publications

Why Baptism? Bruce L. Shelley; IVP Books

Why I Believe; D. James Kennedy; Word Publishing; 1980

Why We Love the Church; Kevin DeYoung & Ted Kluck; Moody Publishers

Y-Origins Magazine; Volume 1; Campus Crusade for Christ & Bright Media Foundation; See internet for more information

Y'shua: The Jewish Way to Say Jesus; Moishe Rosen; Moody Press

Appendix A

Discipleship Resources

Christianity – A Follower's Guide; Pete Briscoe, Editor; Broadman & Holman Publishers

Christ's Call to Discipleship; James Montgomery Boice; Moody Press

Discipleship Essentials; Gary Ogden; Inter-Varsity Press

Disciplines of a Godly Man; R. Kent Hughes; Crossway Books: Good News Publishers

Experiencing God: How to Live the Full Adventure of Knowing and Doing the Will of God; Henry T. Blackaby & Claude V. King; Broadman & Holman Publishers

Leadership Essentials; Gary Ogden; Inter-Varsity Press

Life Essentials; Tony Evans; Moody Publishers

Multiply: Disciples Making Disciples; Francis Chan & Mark Beuring; David C. Cook Publishing Co.

Not a Fan: Becoming a Completely Committed Follower of Jesus; Kyle Idleman

Spiritual Disciplines for the Christian Life; Donald S. Witney; Navpress

Spiritual Leadership; Henry & Richard Blackaby; Broadman & Holman Publishers

The Disciple-Making Church; Bill Hull; Fleming H. Revell Co.

The Disciple-Making Pastor; Bill Hull; Fleming H. Revell Co.

The Dynamics of Discipleship Training; Gary W. Kuhne; Zondervan Publishing House

The Explicit Gospel; Matt Chandler with Jared Wilson

The Good News We Almost Forgot – Rediscovering the Gospel in a 16th Century Catechism; Kevin DeYoung; Moody Publishers

The Kingdom-Focused Church; Gene Mims; Broadman & Holman Publishers

The Making of a Disciple; Keith Phillips; Fleming H Revell Co.

The Master's Plan for the Church; John MacArthur; Moody Press

Transformational Church; Ed Stetzer & Thom S. Rainer; B & H Publishing Group

True Discipleship – The Art of Following Jesus; (Book & Companion Guide); John Koessler; Moody Publishers

What Every Christian Should Know About Growing: Basic Steps to Discipleship; LeRoy Eims; Victor Books – Scripture Press Publications

Appendix B

Apologetics Resources

A Christian Manifesto; Francis A. Schaeffer; Crossway Books

A Place for Truth – Highlights from the Veritas Forum; Edited by Dallas Willard; IVP (Inter Varsity Press) Books

Baker Encyclopedia of Apologetics; Norman Geisler; Baker Book House

Can a Man Live Without God? Ravi Zacharias; Word Publishing; 1994

Can I Trust the Bible; Howard Vos; Moody Press; 1963

Christian Apologetics; Norman Geisler; Baker Book House

Christian Evidences: Fulfilled Bible Prophecy; Alexander Keith; Klock & Klock Christian Publishers, Inc.; 1984

Christianity and Liberalism; J. Gresham Machen; Eerdmans Publishing Co.

Christianity and World Religions: The Challenge of Pluralism; Sir Norman Anderson; Inter-Varsity Press

Darwin's Black Box – The Biochemical Challenge to Evolution; Michael Behe; Simon & Schuster

Darwin on Trial; Phillip E. Johnson; Washington: Regnery Gateway

Darwinism Under the Microscope: How Recent Scientific Evidence Points to Divine Design; James P. Gills & Tom Woodward; Charisma House Publishers

Dismantling Evolution; Ralph O. Muncaster; Harvest House Publishers

Easter Enigma – Are the Resurrection Accounts in Conflict? John Wenham

Evolution: A Theory in Crisis; Michael Denton; Bethesda: Adler & Adler

God – The Evidence – The Reconciliation of Faith and Reason in a Postsecular World; Patrick Glynn; Forum – an Imprint of Prima Publishing; 1977

God's Not Dead – Evidence for God in an Age of Uncertainty; Rice Broocks; W Publishing Group – Thomas Nelson Publishers

Jesus Christ Among Other Gods; Ravi Zacharias; Word Publishing Group

Kingdom Triangle; J. P. Morgan; Zondervan Publishing Co.

Many Infallible Proofs; Henry M. Morris; Master Books; 1974

Medicine in the Bible and the Talmud; Fred Rosner; KTAV Publishing House, Inc.; 1995

Mere Christianity; C. S. Lewis; Simon & Schuster Publishers

More Than a Carpenter; Josh McDowell

None of These Diseases; S. I. McMillen; Fleming H. Revell; 1984

Philosophy of Education: Essays and Commentaries; Edited by Hobert W. Burns and Charles J. Brauner; The Ronald Press Co.; New York

Problems in Education and Philosophy; Charles J. Brauner and Hobert W. Burns; Prentice-Hall Inc. Publishers; Englewood Cliffs, NJ; ©1965

Reasons Skeptics Should Consider Christianity; Josh McDowell & Don Stewart; Campus Crusade for Christ – Here's Life Publishers; 1981

Resurrection; Hank Hanegraaff; Thomas Nelson Publishing Co.

Science Speaks; Peter W. Stoner; Moody Books; 1963

Scientific Creationism; Henry M. Morris; Master Books; 1985

The Battle for the Resurrection; Norman L. Geisler; Thomas Nelson Publishers

The Bible and Modern Science; Henry M. Morris; Moody Press; 1968

The Biblical Basis for Modern Science; Henry M. Morris; Baker Book House; 1984

The Blind Watchmaker; London: Longman, 1986

The Case for Biblical Christianity; E. J. Carnell; Eerdmans Publishing Co.

The Case for a Creator; Lee Strobel; Zondervan Publishing Co.

The Case for Christ; Lee Strobel; Zondervan Publishing Co.

The Case for Easter; Lee Strobel; Zondervan Publishing Co.

The Christian Faith in the Modern World; J. Gresham Machen; Wm. B. Eerdmans Publishing Co. Grand Rapids, MI; 1947

The Evidence of the Soul and Consciousness of Man; J. P. Moreland;

The Historical Reliability of the Gospels; Craig Blomberg; Leicester: Inter-Varsity Press; 1987

The Language of God: A Scientist Presents Evidence for Belief; Francis S. Collins; Free Press

The New Evidence That Demands a Verdict; Josh McDowell; Thomas Nelson Publishers

The New Testament Documents – Are They Reliable? F. F. Bruce; Inter Varsity Press

The Origin of Paul's Religion; J. Gresham Machen; Eerdmans Publishing Co.

The Philosophy of Christianity; Leander S. Keyser; Lutheran Literary Board; Burlington, IA; ©1928.

The Philosophy of Education – Essays and Commentaries; Editors: Hobert W. Burns and Charles J. Brauner; Ronald Press Co.; New York; ©1962.

The Privileged Planet; Guillermo Gonzalez & Jay Wesley Richards; Regnery Publishing

The Signature of God; Grant R. Jeffrey; Frontier Research Publications; 1996

The Soul: How We Know It's Real and Why It Matters; J. P. Moreland; Moody Publishers

What If Jesus Had Never Been Born; D. James Kennedy & Jerry Newcombe; Thomas Nelson Publishers

What If the Bible Had Never Been Written; D. James Kennedy & Jerry Newcombe; Thomas Nelson Publishers

When Skeptics Ask; Geisler / Brooks; Victor Books

Vital Apologetic Issues; Edited by Roy Zuck; Kregel Publications

Why I Believe; D. James Kennedy; Word Publishing; 1980

Y-Origins Magazine; Volume 1; Campus Crusade for Christ & Bright Media Foundation; See internet for more information

Appendix C

Songs Teaching the Trinity
or Triune Being of God

The following songs can be found in "The Worship Hymnal" published by Lifeway Worship of Nashville, Tennessee.

All Creatures of Our God and King	# 11
(or use verse 5 which is called *The Keswick Doxology*)	
Because We Believe	# 519
Come, Thou Almighty King	# 336
Doxology (traditional)	# 668
Eternal Father, Strong to Save	# 643
Father, I Adore You	# 566
Glorify Thy Name	# 18
Glory Be To the Father	# 669 & # 670
God, Our Father, We Adore Thee	# 337
Holy, Holy	# 74
Holy, Holy, Holy	# 68
How Great Is Our God	
Shine, Jesus, Shine	# 491
There Is a Redeemer	# 279
Wonderful, Merciful Savior	#162
Worthy of Worship	# 3

Printed in the United States
By Bookmasters